USING COMPUTERS IN THE LAW

LAW OFFICE WITHOUT WALLS

Third Edition

By

Mary Ann Mason, Ph.D, J.D.
Associate Professor, Law and Social Welfare
School of Social Welfare
University of California, Berkeley

Robert Harris, M.A.
Computer Consultant

WEST PUBLISHING CO.
ST. PAUL, MINN., 1994

American Casebook Series and the WP symbol are registered trademarks of West Publishing Co.
Registered in the U.S. Patent and Trademark Office.

COPYRIGHT © 1984, 1988 WEST PUBLISHING CO.
COPYRIGHT © 1993 By WEST PUBLISHING CO.
                        610 Opperman Drive
                        P.O. Box 64526
                        St. Paul, MN 55164–0526
                        1–800–328–9352
Library of Congress Cataloging-in-Publication Data

Mason, Mary Ann.
    Using computers in the law : law office without walls / by Mary
Ann Mason and Robert Harris. — 3rd ed.
        p.   cm.
    Includes index.
    ISBN 0–314–02396–8
    1. Law offices—United States—Automation.   I. Harris, Robert
(Robert F.)   II. Title.
KF320.A9M3   1994
340'.0285—dc20   93–41189
                                                        CIP

ISBN 0–314–02396–8

Mason & Harris, Computers 3rd ACB

INTRODUCTION

Law Office Without Walls was first published under the title Using Computers in the Law with a chapter about law office without walls. Since the introduction of this book, computers have evolved and as a result there is hardly a law office without computers in them. As computers have evolved, so has their use. Initially few law offices had computers, relying instead on dedicated word processors. Later, computers were introduced but were used mostly as fancy word processors and database devices. Increasingly, computers are changing **how** law offices work. However, law firms today have barely tapped the vast potential of the computer. The purpose of this book is to expand your mind to the possible uses of the computer which is already on your desk. The computer is a potential link to each person in your office and to the outside world. You no longer are in an office behind a closed door, but can contact virtually anyone anywhere using your computer, and can obtain an unlimited amount of information from almost anywhere in the world.

The concept "law office without walls" can be seen in three dimensions: 1) communications within the office among lawyers, paralegals, secretaries and other office workers, 2) communications between members of the office and the outside world, i.e. other lawyers, courts, witnesses, experts, and 3) obtaining information from internal and external sources.

Communications within an office used to be a matter of making multiple copies of memos, transcripts and other documents, filing the originals with a filing system, and distributing the copies to the appropriate people. That was the simple part. Once the material was distributed to someone, notes were made and then passed to other parties who were working on the same issues. At that point confusion often occurred since that party may have had a copy of his own with his own notes on it. It then became a rather large task of keeping track of the information as it flowed back and forth between the individuals involved. The more people involved, the more confusing it could become to keep track of the notes and related matter pertaining to the documents. While word processors and databases helped, it was still a manual system dependent on the print outs and the notes they contained. With the increased use of Local Area Networks (LANs) and electronic mail (email) within an office, material can be sent directly to the parties in the office, notes made on the document itself, copies sent back to the sender, and revised work back to a central file server for archiving. Notes and memos can easily be stored and all of this work accomplished without print outs. This not only saves wasted paper (a consideration these days) but avoids confusion. Computers automatically date documents, note when they were modified, and, with the assistance of document comparison programs, indicate changes. Email in an office allows people to contact each other and make replies without the disadvantages of phone tag. Documents can be attached to memos and sent to the office mate entirely in their absence. Filing of the documents and their changes on a file server eliminates much of the wasted time spent trying to retrieve printed documents from a filing cabinet. If a document was located in a filing cabinet it was necessary to "sign it out" which meant someone else had to wait for its return, or a copy had to be made wasting more time and paper. Instead a copy of the file can be made on the computer in seconds. Newer versions of "groupware" software even allow a trail of all the mark-ups recorded by each person. Computer systems actually bring the working parties closer together in an office without them having to be in the same physical space at the same time.

The law library traditionally was a room filled with books that took up a large amount of space and cost a large amount of money. If the law office had heavy use, there might even be more than one copy of the books. Today CD–ROM is becoming increasingly popular as a means of distributing large amounts of information inexpensively. The majority of the cost when buying a law library on disc is not the actual cost of the disc, but rather all the expense in gathering and assembling the information. Most important to the law office is the fact that these devices can be tied into a law office computer network and the entire library of information be made accessible to every member of the office. No longer does one have to wait until someone is finished with a bound volume. More than one person can read the same disc volume at once. Even more significantly, by having the law library on disc, quotation and citation becomes extremely easy-simply copy and paste the required material into a brief. The law library has been reduced to a small computer component on a table, yet that component will let more people use the library at one time than the print library ever did. Most law offices today have access to LEXIS or WESTLAW via modem. Because of the costs involved in using these on line databases for research, usage of these services may be limited. What is to be remembered is that compared to the cost of sending someone to a library to look up information, access to these services directly from the office is quite cost effective. In addition, in a traditional library you may encounter the problem that the material is in use somewhere else in the library or may even have been checked out. With on line databases thousands of people can access the same material at the same time without interference. Material is often updated within hours of a court decision, certainly much faster than any traditional printed publication.

By extension the office network can be accessed from outside the office via modem. Indeed the concept of a physical office where all activities occur is obsolete. Software packages are now available that allow access directly to a user's machine as well as to the network, including the file server and the printers. Working at home it is possible to obtain the files needed, copy them, return the revised files and print them directly, all over the phone lines. Memos can be left with the in house email system for co-workers as well as sending them documents. At the same time mail can be picked up from the office. It is possible to check schedules and reschedule events, all by modem. New high speed modems combined with new software even allows one to control the office computer itself from outside the office. At this level of sophistication the office is no longer a physical location, but merely an extension of where you are. To borrow from the current computer jargon, the office is now a virtual office.

In addition to accessing the office system from home or elsewhere, contact is easier with outside companies, attorneys, or courts. Many courts today accept fax as a means of communication. With the fax modem a computer document can be filed directly without having to print out the document. Documents can also be received directly into the computer via a fax modem. With the appropriate software the document can be transferred to a word processor and worked on. Communication with other law offices using either commercial email services, fax modems or direct call in shortens the turn around when deadlines are crucial. While law offices are not banks or manufacturers, they are often involved with complex business issues that require communication with banks. Accessing banking information over phone lines can be a vital key in business negotiations. Law firms involved in trust management can now reconcile accounts via the modem.

The concept of the law office without walls then is a metaphor for the greater freedom, both physical and mental, which a well-utilized computer system can offer an attorney or legal practitioner. Stretching your imagination to take advantage of the freedom is the aim of this book.

MARY ANN MASON
ROBERT HARRIS

October '93

*

Acknowledgements

We wish to thank the following for their help with graphics material for this book:

Apple Computer
Farallon Computing
T/Maker
Chris Bell of Max Computer systems

*

Friendly User

**There....there...now,
it's all right...let's try it again
Computer**

*

TABLE OF CONTENTS

---

*

USING COMPUTERS IN THE LAW

LAW OFFICE WITHOUT WALLS

Third Edition

*

PART ONE

WHAT DO COMPUTERS DO?

In preparing Law office Without Walls, we are attempting to provide a simple clear discussion of the ways in which computers can be maximized as tools in the legal office. When we refer to computers in the office we are speaking only about Personal Computers (PC). Given the power of PCs today it is very unlikely that any law office except for the largest litigation, would require a larger computer system. In doing so we are addressing two distinct audiences. First, the novice to the use of computers in a legal practice is introduced to the types of tasks which a law office can handle with a computer. In most cases these will be individuals beginning work in the legal profession, or those individuals already involved in a legal practice, but who have not yet computerized.

The second audience and perhaps the largest in numbers, are those who have a computer and are already using it in the legal practice. For those individuals it is our goal to suggest ways in which the computer hardware can be maximized, and the utilization increased. Unlike most other electronic devices in our society, a computer can become more efficient by the addition of new software and other hardware.

We have organized the book into several sections. The first section is introductory and describes ways computers can be used in general terms, the operating system software and hardware and how to make selections. The next section discusses in more detail the types of applications in which computer are used, and the 3rd section is involved with information management and retrieval. In the final section we have included a few case studies of legal practices of different types to illustrate the types of solutions described in the book.

CHAPTER ONE

Twenty Ways to Use Your Computer

The Friendly User

When you drive an automobile you are fortunately not required to know how all parts of the engine or electrical systems work, nor are you required to know how to construct it, or how to repair it. You are simply required to know how to operate it with a certain degree of skill.

If you are the person taking charge of the computerization of your law office you are not required to understand precisely *how* computers work, you also do not have to know how to program a computer, since experienced programmers have spent years developing appropriate programs for your PC which you can purchase and use with no programming knowledge. What you must learn is *what* computers can do for your law practice, and how to operate them for maximum efficiency. You must become a "friendly user" who can communicate what you have learned to others in your office in English rather than computerese.

It is the premise of this book that while virtually all law offices have at least one computer, about 99% are not making full use of what computers can do for their law practice.

Computers are part of the technology which has invaded virtually every law office just as faxes have. A fax is a device used for attorneys to contact each other instantly, for the filing of documents in courts, and to contact clients, banks, other businesses and institutions. The real pressure to have a fax (or any similar technology) lies in the competitive nature of the legal profession today. If most law firms have a fax, then you need one to remain competitive. This projects an image to the client of a law firm that is staying up with the latest technology and therefore is very successful. Can you imagine what would happen if a law firm was wooing a client that was a successful company and the entrepreneur said, "I'll fax you the details in the morning" and all you could say was, "Well, could you mail it to me instead?" Chances are slim of retaining that client when another firm comes along and says to the client that their lawyers can have the information back to the client in a matter of just hours. Likewise the law firm which brings the information to trial on a laptop computer has a distinct edge over the firm which brings mountains of books and papers to court.

When searching for information the computer is capable of providing almost instant answers.

Computers are a particular technology that lawyers need to handle the work load, and to stay current with the competition. However computers are a unique technology. A normal tool such as a fax or a car or a cellular phone does the same job each and every time; you simply turn it on, select a few switches and the equipment does the rest. A computer is entirely different. After you have purchased the hardware, you still need to obtain specialized instructions to operate it. These instructions are not the simple directions normally associated with any device, these instructions are the software programs. Computers are unique in that you can have the same machine for several years, but by either updating your software, purchasing additional software, or using generic software in new ways, the computer can become a completely new tool without having to replace the hardware. In addition new computers are coming out that have increased compatibility and network functions. Over time computers can increase the functionality of every person in the firm by more efficient use of computer technology.

The question then is, "Are the law firms and lawyers using the computer system efficiently? Computers are only as useful as the instructions they are given. Today with the increasing power, availability of software, and enhanced networking, a law firm with a computer system can do many things that change the way work is handled and produced. The original investment in hardware is often realized just from the intended purpose of the original purchase. A firm that installs a personal computer system with a laser printer for word processing, eventually can run all the billing, fax communications, calendar for the office, calendar for the courts, a Rolodex file, ad infinitum.

The vast majority of law offices get stuck on word processing and timekeeping and billing as their first and last computer applications. While these are extremely worthy applications, they are only the beginning of what is possible. To stimulate your imagination, here is a quick overview of the current possible applications of the computer for your law office in plain English. The following chapters will expand the explanations of these applications and offer appropriate advice regarding hardware, software, setting up systems and operating them efficiently. The chapter on Basics will offer an explanation of how computers work, for those who seek a deeper understanding of the technology.

WORD PROCESSING

Given the blizzard of paper that rushes through a law office daily, word processing may be the most used and most useful application of computer technology. Almost all law offices already employ some form of word processing technology. The focus of this book will be on expanding the use of the versatile PC for more than just simple word processing.

The new generation of word processing software for PCs can provide many features which are often overlooked by novices, e.g., combining word processing with other computer functions, such as lightning-like computations and elaborate search and retrievals. The standard abilities to edit, move blocks, create formats, and to store the product permanently or temporarily on the medium upon which it is produced are common to all word processing programs. Sophisticated word processing packages, or combinations of packages, also offer the possibility of merging the text of one file into another, searching for a single term or phrase throughout a document and replacing it with another term or phrase, checking spelling errors, and automatically re-paginating and re-footnoting when changes are made. More recent products will also create indexes, sort, and allow split-screen editing. Some word processing programs have either templates or are themselves developed expressly for the law office, offering such features as pleading paper formats and legal symbols.

Word processing works wonderfully for any document that needs revision, or any document that is repetitive; this describes 99% of the work product of a law office. It is useful for drafting correspondence, memoranda, briefs, and any sort of legal document; it is indispensable for reproducing a previously drafted document, such as a pleading, or a will, and editing only the portions necessary to suit a new client, or a new situation. Word processing functions can also be applied to other applications, such as editing internal management reports, or developing an index of documents to prepare for litigation.

The power and functionality of word processor software for computers today is incredible. Functions such as mail merge and search and replace are now easier and simpler to use as well as more powerful and faster. Software products which enhance and extend the power of word process software is a whole new area. From the simplest new forms and templates that are available to the add on software that increases the function, the proliferation of software has been enormous. Retrieving and archiving of documents created with word processing software is an efficient way to handle the text and documents processed by a law firm. With the addition of Optical Character Recognition (OCR) documents created by others on hard copy can now be word processed and filed.

LITIGATION SUPPORT

The most exciting new application for computers is litigation support. Conventional "wisdom" previously dictated that only litigation matters with 10,000 plus documents were candidates for a computer, and this usually meant a huge mainframe computer located far away from the office. Large law firms are now routinely bringing a computer into the office to handle large cases, and the same computer capability is possible for small law offices using a PC. There is no doubt that a sole practitioner can become just as confused with 172 documents in a personal injury case as the attorneys for AT & T in a 1,000,000 plus anti-trust action. Although a PC might be able to store, search, and retrieve 1,000,-000 documents at the higher end, with hard disk storage it can do very well with 172, or 1720. The ability of the PC to retrieve information by an almost unlimited number of combinations makes it far superior to manual indexing methods.

Currently, there are relatively few attorneys who have made use of PCs to organize documents in preparation for small to medium sized trials, but there is a good deal of interest in this potential application. Packaged software specifically dedicated to this task is now available. It is, however, very easy to use any good data base management software for storing, searching, and retrieving appropriate information, including deposition summaries and interrogatories.

DESKTOP PUBLISHING

A new category of software has come of age in the past few years that is an offshoot of word processing. It is unique to computers and is called Desktop publishing. Desktop publishing combines word processing with graphics and the ability to change the design or format before it is typeset or printed. Previously this was done by graphics and design firms. While the graphics and design firms were generally very skilled organizations well versed in the proper design rules and type style usage, this was often a slow, expensive process and one which did not allow for rapid changes easily. It was not easy for someone to rearrange the materials on short notice, or try out different layouts that may be more esthetically pleasing. With the advent of laser printers and typesetting capabilities, one can easily play the "What If" game by rearranging the elements in a layout without having to take the layout apart and put it together manually. Now a brochure or report could be prepared easily, economically, *in house* allowing for maximum flexibly and ease of revision. A well trained office associate or secretary can produce good looking material easily and affordably. Law firms today often need to advertise their services in a variety of publications or to send to potential clients. The advertising materi- al is easily created with desktop publishing software. As new information about a law firm is input, new ads can be created. With information and technology changing as rapidly as it is these days, a law firm may become involved in a whole new area of practice and need to get the new information publicized. Easy to do when the ads are created in house. A business report format- ted with Desktop publishing software can be changed and updated without having to trash the old format.

GRAPHICS PROGRAMS

Graphics are an essential ingredient in the production of brochures and documents as well as reports. Graphics are useful for presentations. Computer graphics can be extremely useful in preparation of material for courtroom cases in which a representa- tion or enhancement of the evidence makes a convincing argument to a jury. The use of computer graphics in civil court for the purpose of reconstructing auto or airline accidents is fairly common these days. Recently, in a well publicized murder trial in Marin County, the prosecution used a series of graphics to show the jury the disposition of the defendant by the way in which the murder weapon was fired in relation to the way the victim was positioned. The Deputy District Attorney based the graphics on the reconstruc- tion of the crime by the forensic expert in order to show the jury that it was the intent of the defendant to murder the victim.

Graphics can be entered into software programs from various sources to produce excellent pictures or designs at a fraction of what it cost a few years ago. An image can be scanned, created with a mouse or a graphics tablet using a pressure sensitive stylus, or adapted from other artwork already produced. Colors and shapes can be altered easily. Output can be to a page layout program for desktop publishing, directly to a laser or image setter, to 35 mm slides for presentation, to video, or to large screen for overhead projection as in a lecture or demonstration, while directly connected to a computer using presentation software.

In addition to graphics as either a part of a publication or stand alone, graphics may be used with presentation software. Artwork can be incorporated into presentation software and there- by included in the computer screen display or projection, into handouts, and into 35 mm slides for color projection. Statistics can easily be represented in graphic form to illustrate a trend analysis.

Computer graphics today are an essential part of any business. Desktop publishing is the combination of the words and the pictures. The text is usually generated in a word processor. The graphics are generated on the computer or are entered with a scanning device. Scanners today are of very high resolution for very little investment, especially in black and white—what is known as gray scale. The same scanner that is used for OCR can be utilized for the processing of true graphics. Scanning software is now developed that both fully automates the input (cropping, turning picture so it is straight, etc.) and at the same time allows you to process the scan with various tools and filters. In short the entire document can be altered or enhanced. The output of these scanning graphics programs can be transferred to desktop publishing software for layout or transferred to other graphics software.

An extension of graphics software is the category of software called screen dump utilities. It is hard to put this software into any one category as it is applicable to several: word processing, desktop publishing, and graphics. Screen dump utilities allow you to take a "snapshot" of what is on the computer screen and save it as a graphics file. It can then be inserted into a word processor document or a page layout program. In many cases a crude form of this utility is available directly in the operating system as a function key. More sophisticated programs allow you to manipulate what is on the screen before having to save or print the file. The utilities are useful for including a picture of something that is in another software program or a graphic created elsewhere. For instance a graph of yearly expenses in a spousal support suit can be inserted in several different documents: a settlement offer, a trial brief, an accounting statement. In another application, a snapshot can be made of a form that is on a computer and rather than sending it out in printed form, the picture can be sent to another computer or to a fax machine if it is connected to the computer. The graphic from a screen dump can also be printed out and then faxed using a regular fax machine. A part of a form can be captured and sent as a picture across the email to someone. There are many uses of this type of software that make the job a bit easier when familiar with the screen dump utilities.

AUTOMATED SUBSTANTIVE SYSTEMS

Automated substantive systems are the sophisticated offspring of word processing. They will perhaps produce more dramatic changes in law practice than other computer application. An automated substantive system offers a complete package containing all the information necessary to complete a particular legal transaction, such as a divorce or a probate proceeding. Existing commercial systems cover a wide range of sophistication, beginning with a package of simple and specific forms on floppy disks on which variable names or phrases can be merged to an elaborate expert system where documents are created based on experts' thought processes. Some of the simple versions can be used with a dedicated word processor as well as the more powerful PC.

There has been a recent proliferation of software companies which offer automated substantive systems. Matthew Bender has been a leader in this field with a series of form packages for various practice areas such as family law, and personal injury, and insurance, specific only to California and Texas. Other publishers have produced general packages in areas such as family law, personal injury and estate planning which must be modified to individual state law.

But you can easily create document systems yourself which automate the systems you already work with and do not require you to adopt a new system offered by a commercial vendor. This can be done by entering your hard copy forms into word processing software and creating variable merge clauses where names, dates, alternate clauses, or any other variable can be chosen each time a new document is produced. Especially good candidates for this process are legal transactions which require lengthy, but routine paper work, like divorces, trusts, wills, probate proceedings, articles of incorporation, bankruptcy, and real estate closings.

ELECTRONIC SPREADSHEETS

Spreadsheets are a virtually undiscovered treasure trove for law offices. Procedures where computation or financial projections are required, such as tax returns, damage projections in personal injury cases, estate plans, or a five year financial plan for your office can be developed by using an electronic spreadsheet, of which there are many popular and relatively inexpensive varieties to choose from. The expert services once provided by actuaries, economists, and accountants are now available on your desk top computer. A short list of the possible uses of an electronic spreadsheet includes: computing present and future values of pension plans and life insurance policies, computing values of certificates of deposit and other interest bearing securities, with maturity dates, calculating the tax treatment of a real estate purchase over thirty years. The graphics capabilities of most spreadsheets also allows you to create charts, graphs and other visual displays for presentation to clients or juries.

Once you have set up a system on your electronic spreadsheet to project damages in a personal injury case, for instance, you can use that system over and over with other cases; simply plugging in the new facts. Commercial packages of varying degrees of sophistication are also available, particularly in the areas of tax and real estate. Some of these can perform complex computations and organize complicated information into highly individualized finished documents. All procedures which require computation definitely require the power of today's PCs.

With the increased acceptance of spreadsheets have come the publication of special templates and preformatted entry sheets. While spreadsheet programs are merely empty tools waiting to be used, they often have steep learning curves in order to realize their true power. And while it may be easy to create a simple spreadsheet to play the "What If" game with some numbers, it may not be advisable to spend a lot of time creating a template that requires a fair amount of programming time. There are now whole catalogs listing published spreadsheet templates available. Such templates can be purchased very inexpensively—most are in the $50–$100 range, and add functionality to the generic program without learning a new system. Often these templates have been created in a way that makes entry foolproof. As an example of how new software can increase the utilization of the entire system, new spreadsheet templates can be most helpful at a reasonable price.

FINANCIAL MANAGEMENT

Although attorneys pride themselves on the skillful manipulation of the written and spoken word, very few have the luxury of ignoring monetary rewards. With creeping overhead and greater competition, lawyers have become increasingly concerned with the business of running a law office. For that reason, after word processing, computers are most commonly found in the "back room" dealing with timekeeping and billing, and other management concerns. The hope is that computers will provide greater efficiency and therefore greater profits. In addition to timekeeping and billing, computerized financial management can include: general ledger, accounts aging schedules and payroll, as well as various productivity reports.

Law firms have three choices in automating their timekeeping and billing tasks. They can keep all their time manually (on paper) and forward it to a service bureau which runs it through their computer; they can enter their billing information on a terminal in their office which forwards the data by telecommunications to a large computer which processes it, or they can buy a software package to use on their in-house computer.

Performing timekeeping and billing and other financial management chores on the in-house computer is increasingly attractive to law firms. The sophistication of the software has improved greatly, and it is possible to individualize the financial tasks for your practice.

Since the computations required to accomplish timekeeping and billing are not in the same league as those required to send a rocket to Mars, a PC is quite capable of handling the needs of a small law firm, and there is a great deal of packaged software to choose from. For the larger law firm a multi-user computer (minicomputer) may be necessary and the software, which is designed only for that computer system, will be much more expensive. The computer will provide greater efficiency than manual methods, and greater individuality than utilizing an outside computerized client billing service. It can also provide you with a dizzying variety of management reports which can help even the smallest firm keep better track of its time and money. Although it is possible for you to develop your own timekeeping and billing system using a general data base management software package, it is probably safer to delegate this complex task to the commercial vendors who can provide sophisticated software at a reasonable price.

CALENDARS

Next to lightning-like computations, a computer's greatest talent is the storage and retrieval of vast amounts of information at electronic speeds. The larger the computer the more it can store and the faster it can retrieve, but even PCs, have great abilities of storage and retrieval.

Since statutes of limitations that are missed and court appearances that are forgotten are the major cause of malpractice suits, calendaring is a critical aspect of every law practice. A calendar (or docket) may simply track cases in progress with their various deadlines, or it may include the appointments of each attorney as well. Calendaring for fewer than 20 attorneys or paralegals is not a difficult challenge for a PC with a hard disk. The advantage that computerized calendar systems have over manual systems is that the information can be retrieved in more ways than is usually possible with a standardized manual system. For instance the computer will retrieve only the depositions that are scheduled for a given week or month, or only the cases where attorney Brown is the back-up, not the principal attorney. If a case is settled or continued the computer permits almost instantaneous recall of all future activities in that case for editing or deletion.

Computer calendaring systems are one of the fastest growing areas of computer technology. As computer networks grow, as each desk in an office has its own dedicated personal computer on that network, the opportunity to use the computer system for scheduling has likewise increased. Email in an office has dramatically cut down on time and effort spent on trying to communicate by being in the same time space coordinate. Calendars have done the same for people trying to schedule time with each other. With electronic calendars even in the crudest form as a multi-user database, groups of people can be scheduled easily. Dedicated electronic calendars with sophisticated functions have dramatically increased in functionality. Network schedulers are the most widely used groupware programs. A secretary can easily schedule a meeting with a group in one entry. Memos can be included as well as an agenda of the meeting.

Other uses of calendaring systems are:

Court Calendars

Reminder or Tickler files for deadlines

To Do lists

Scheduling of meeting rooms and equipment

While there are many calendar systems available today, some may be more suitable than others. Ideal calendars are those which contain springing dates. That is once you enter the court date, the software automatically figures backward from that date when the deadline is for discovery (e.g., 30 days in California), and the required time necessary for depositions (i.e., if 15 days notification is required, then figuring back this would be 45 days minimum from trial date). Many calendar programs for lawyers will do that provided you enter in the rules for the particular court. The best software companies have an automatic update service that sends you the rules (in software form) necessary to update your calendar as the rules change for your particular court. There are only a few which do this currently and very few which are stand alone programs.

CONFLICT OF INTEREST

Conflict of interest may not seem like a major problem for a small firm, and perhaps it isn't. Rarely does a subsidiary of AT & T request your services while you are simultaneously representing another corporate client against AT & T. Usually the memory of the oldest employee in the office and a quick check of the files (if they are not in deep storage) will suffice. But increasingly, with very large scale litigation, like the current asbestos behemoth, hundreds of attorneys, from the largest firms to the sole practitioner can become involved. Or if you handle personal injury litigation, it is often difficult to keep track of which insurance companies you have represented or opposed. Since it is always better to be safe than sorry, a conflict of interest checks system is a simple matter for a PC, particularly one equipped with large hard disk storage. A New Matter Memo can be expanded to provide useful conflict information, such as AKA's, subsidiaries, opposing counsel, names of individual directors of a corporation, etc. This same computerized New Matter Memo can serve as a useful superindex for all client files, active and closed; instantly producing information such as all the cases your firm has handled in which Darrow was the opposing attorney, or breach of construction contracts was the issue.

At present, stand alone conflict of interest packaged software systems are not available for PCs (though some integrated software does offer this capability in some form as part of the package). However, they can easily be constructed with a database management system, either alone, or in conjunction with a New Matter Memo. The difficulty is that these systems tend to check for conflicts only if the information to be checked is correctly entered. That is most systems will not find a name if it is similar but not exact, often leading to some problems. In addition most of the systems do not allow for importing lists so that all the employees of a firm can be easily added, not just the principals.

COMPUTER ASSISTED TRANSCRIPTION

Another technological breakthrough now offers the *full text* of depositions up to 1800 pages on a single floppy disk which can be searched on your PC. Trial transcripts are now available on disk from many courts. Hours of tedious deposition summaries can be eliminated with this important advance. As an alternative, new technological advances with Optical Character Readers, or scanners, now makes it feasible for you to "read" the paper version of the deposition transcript directly into your computer where you can investigate it with your own search and retrieval software.

IN–HOUSE WORK PRODUCTS INDEX

Most attorneys re-invent the wheel on a far too regular basis. Attorney B may well have already gone through the tedious process of condominium conversion, but unless this fact surfaces in casual conversation, Attorney A in the same firm may have to begin from scratch. Even sole practitioners may have a difficult time recalling their previous work products, and unless they recall the client's name, the memorandum or pleading may be buried forever in deep storage.

A search and retrieval system on a PC can easily handle a super-reference index for hundreds of work products. Not only can the document be recalled by ordinary classifications such as name of client, type of proceeding, etc., but it is possible to search keywords and whole abstracts of text so that you can find a partnership agreement to buy a boat among the thousands of documents your office has produced. This would not have been possible with conventional manual indexes.

In addition to building an index of what is filed on a disk or on back ups in a law office, there can be the tedious task of indexing a brief or document that has been created and a page reference index is needed as well as a table of contents. Every word in a document can be automatically indexed and a page citation list created with new auto indexing software such as On Location or the more powerful MARS system. Unnecessary words can be filtered out ahead of time or edited in a word processor.

LEGAL RESEARCH

Using a modem (the piece of hardware that allows you to transmit and receive information over telephone lines) and an ordinary telephone, your own PC gives you access to more information than you can probably find in the local law library and your community's general library together. Over the past ten years the growth, or one should say explosion of electronic information data bases (information stored on a computer) has been stupendous; some compare the significance of this phenomenon with the invention of the Guttenberg press. What it can mean for you is the almost instant availability of a vast amount of information without leaving your desk.

Most attorneys have had at least some exposure to one of the two major commercial legal data base services: WESTLAW and LEXIS. Both of these services carry the *full text* of all recent case law, federal and state statutory and administrative law, a wide variety of specialty libraries in areas such as tax, labor, energy, securities, bankruptcy, etc., and are increasing their scope daily. In addition from either system you can access very large general information services. In the case of WESTLAW, you can address DIALOG which contains hundreds of information databases. Similarly on LEXIS you can access NEXIS information databases. The information is stored in huge central computers, but the process of search and retrieval is interactive with your PC. This means that you can carry on a dialogue with the central computer, asking questions and re-formulating the question if the response is not suitable. Old researchers must learn some new tricks to become conversant with the central computer, but the results are worth the effort.

Information is unfortunately not as free as the sky above and currently the cost of subscribing to either WESTLAW or LEXIS is considered too steep by most very small law offices. It is possible to share these facilities, as many attorneys share libraries, and some public law libraries and Bar Associations make these electronic services available at reasonable cost. The computerization of information does seem to be relentlessly inevitable, however, and some enthusiasts claim that by the year 2000 print-on-paper publications (as opposed to electronic transmissions) will be as rare as the first books produced by the Guttenberg press.

FACTUAL RESEARCH

Attorneys do not live by law alone, and have constant need for wide-ranging factual information; to pinpoint a corporation's DOW JONES standing, or to determine the rate of increase of violent crime in Nebraska. Using the same PC and modem that was used to interact with WESTLAW, you can contact one of the major data base services, such as Lockheed's DIALOG, NEXIS on LEXIS or BRS, and have the choice of literally hundreds of information data bases, representing all of human knowledge from science, medicine, international affairs, to today's baseball scores. Much of the information offered by these data bases is not full text, so it must be followed through by finding the complete printed publication. The good news is that these services (because they are not full text) are considerably less expensive than the legal data base services.

LEGISLATIVE TRACKING

Trying to track a pending bill through the state legislature or the activities of your local politician or of a Congressional committee was previously a hopeless task without the services of a hired hand at the capitol. Electronic tracking services on both the state and federal levels make democratically public these previously obscure activities. Again, the PC, modem, and the telephone connected to one of the legislative tracking services bring this information to your desk.

COURTHOUSE TRACKING

Using your desktop computer to access the calendar at the courthouse or to check the status of a given case is now a reality in some counties. Most state and federal courts use computers to update case files, generate notices, calendar and share information.

The technology which would allow lawyers to files their complaints from their office via a modem, thereby eliminating a hard (paper) copy exists today, but may not be widely used for many years.

ELECTRONIC MAIL

There are two basic types of email (electronic mail) in wide use today: in house systems on the Local Area Network (LAN), and those that are outside services such as ABA/net, or Compuserve Information Services, one of the largest services with some 3/4 of a million users.

In house systems run on the LAN your computers are attached to. If you have more than one computer in an office, email can be a blessing. In addition to sending messages and memos to each other, files can be transferred to another machine and reminders can be sent. Files and messages can be stored in the computer and dealt with according to priorities assigned to documents. Messages can be printed for further use, archived for reference, and responses made to inquiries without having to contact the person if schedules do not coincide. A word process document can be transferred from a paralegal to a secretary easily. Memos can be sent to groups of people regarding an upcoming meeting.

Email services on a LAN can be linked via modem to email services at other offices. These are called email bridges. Several offices can be connected with bridges. The system automatically calls the other system and transfers the messages in both directions. Moments later the mail is routing to the computer on your desktop and a reminder flashes on the screen announcing mail arrival. In addition local email on a LAN can be connected to outside services. Email services such as Compuserve, MCI Mail, America On Line, Genie, etc. offer many mail services to the user; primarily they allow text to be sent to other users, or in some cases via gateways, to other services.

In addition to files, email services often link with telex and fax machines. For example MCI mail has send and receive telex as an option. For many years an attorney, Henry Ford, in a small corporate law firm communicated with a biotech firm in Singapore by telex as it was the cheapest way to communicate. Most email services also permit the sending of text to any fax machine. Since Henry had a flat rate of $10 per month with MCI for all domestic messages, the costs were minimal when faxing long distance inside the US. The only drawback is Henry could not receive any faxes. For most work, sending text is sufficient. Especially sending overdue notices—who needs a pretty form for that! Since MCI Mail is a flat rate per month for preferred service, and it has an 800 phone number Henry can send a fax for less money to someone than if he used a fax machine (especially long distance—since phone charges on a fax machine add up!)

FAX MODEM/MODEM

As technology increasingly infiltrates our daily lives as well as our work environment, the desire to link the various technologies together increases proportionately. Slowly computers are becoming more integrated with other technologies as the demand and equipment increases. One area of integration is the use of the fax modem or combination modem/fax modem. Electronic mail is generally the preferred route of communication wherever possible because it allows for a document or computer file to be sent to another office or client in the most convenient and cost effective manner. The recipient receives the document and can work on the actual document and likewise return it. To do this requires that the hardware and software be compatible and that both parties subscribe to the same email service. While an increasing number of people do this and there are increasing gateways between the email services, this is still only available to a small segment of the population. Most often the other party has a fax. Traditionally a document would be printed out of a computer and then faxed to the other party. Now fax modems take the transcription step out of the loop. Using a fax modem with a computer is as simple as printing a document to the modem software and sending to a party in an address book. If you are purchasing a modem today for email, consider one that has the fax option built in. In either case fax modems are very inexpensive and are an excellent value for your computer system.

Fred Grant is an attorney in a large law firm specializing in contract law. Fred has a fax modem attached to his laptop computer. He faxes a copy of a contract to a client. While traveling Fred can receive the revised contract from a client by fax directly into his computer. He can then make the necessary changes and additions to the original document stored on his laptop and fax the changes back to the client immediately. With the addition of OCR software, a contract received by fax modem can even be translated directly to a word processing document.

SCANNER/OPTICAL CHARACTER RECOGNITION (OCR)

Optical Character Recognition has been in use for several years. For the most part, it was only worth while at a very large scale because only very expensive systems worked as efficiently as a good typist. Recently the situation has changed dramatically. There are two essential pieces which perform the task of turning characters on a printed page into a word process document. The hardware is a desktop scanner. Prices on the scanner hardware today have fallen to well below $1000 and have optional sheet feeders. The second part is that software for PCs have become so good they produce hardly any errors. Error rates are now above 99% for most text—or about 2 mistakes on a page.

Modem manufacturers are now shipping fax modems which include OCR software. With this new technology, you can now receive a fax from someone and the software will convert this into a word process document that you can edit or use in your word processor software, thus further eliminating paper use.

EXPERT DOCUMENT GENERATION SYSTEMS

Expert systems for document generation help to acquire and organize the knowledge needed to produce a legal document such as a will or contract. Again based on the knowledge gleaned from experts, the computer will "interview" the client to determine their particular needs. In simple situations the system could select and arrange routine pieces of text like building blocks. In more complicated scenarios, like complex contracts, the system could suggest various plans to the user and alert the user to possible pitfalls.

The substantive areas of the law where automated systems are likely to be the most useful are those with a number of set forms and some required computations. This definitely includes all areas of tax practice, trusts and estate planning, probate, divorce, real estate sales and bankruptcy.

The legal and ethical implications of fully automated systems are already being addressed. A brand-new secretary, with no legal training can type in the answers to the interview questions posed by the computer and press the print button which generates the document or series of documents at the conclusions of the interview. This raises the possibility of computer malpractice and attorney dispensability. However, fully automated document preparation systems do not really provide sophisticated legal analysis or give advice. They simply provide the most efficient method of dealing with routine legal transactions.

AD INFINITUM

There are a number of future legally related applications in the brewing stages for your PC, and unlimited possibilities for those in the thinking stages. Software packages that will allegedly predict judge or jury behavior are in the tinkering stages. PC based computer assisted instruction for many substantive law school courses, such as evidence, civil procedure, and torts is already here and being distributed by the Minnesota based Center for Computer based Legal Instruction. Continuing Education of the Bar courses on floppies are now available.

The ABA maintains a Technology Clearinghouse for disseminating information about the use of technology in the legal profession. The clearinghouse is located in Chicago and can be reached at (312) 988–5465, or at email ABA/net: TECH.HOTLINE. The Technology Clearinghouse also schedules visits at the ABA Legal Technology Resource Center. The ABA LawTech Center is set up for legal professionals to test office automation systems without any bias or pressure. State of the art legal software, hardware, peripherals, and on-line services are accessible for the inexperienced to the most sophisticated users. The LawTech Center has direct access to vendors of legal technology for additional support. On display is a wide variety of hardware and software for the legal office.

The Technology Clearinghouse maintains guidelines for the certification of legal software. These guidelines and information about software that meets these guidelines is available. Also available from the Technology Hotline are books and directories for computer systems. Among these are:

Locate (Yr–Yr). An annual directory of software vendors

ABA Software reviews

Collections of articles on solutions for the law office, several basic texts and guides.

Apple computer has announced that by the end of 1992 a new device called a Personal Digital Assistant will be available from consumer electronics vendors. These devices are hand held miniature computers which allow either pen input or voice input. The devices will be capable of recognizing a full range of vocabulary independent of accent or inflection. Once entered the data can be transferred to a workstation or personal computer via wireless transmission. Options for these devices will include CD ROM drives which will allow storage of large amounts of data. CD ROMs are generally used for the updates of large commercial databases, for example Medline.

Quicktime is a multimedia standardized format released by Apple Dec. 1991. The format includes high data compression so that it may be used by both audio and video sources without requiring enormous amounts of disk space. IBM thought so much of it they formed a new company Kaleida with Apple to create multimedia presentations which run on several computer operating systems (when software programs operate on several operating systems this is known as *cross platform*). The software allows for sound, graphics, animation, audio, to be played back on a computer in combination with each other. The documents created can be pasted into other pieces of software such as word processors etc. A person could have a resumé which incorporates a video which is engaged by clicking the cursor. Audio from a speech can be compressed and sent on disk. Presentations can be enhanced with animation. As the technology increases in the digital world, the need to interface this world with the computer increases as well so the information can be organized and disseminated. A video can be edited and enhanced to demonstrate a specific point. These are now tools which are available for a few hundred dollars that previously required an investment of hundreds of thousands. Such systems would be excellent for use in trial presentations, and in corporate presentations. Since this is newly emerging technology, it is difficult to say how it will be incorporated by attorneys.

[G19613]

CHAPTER TWO

The Virtual Office

The fact that computers, unlike typewriters, can communicate with others of their species, provides a radical new dimension to the concept of the law office. Within the office PCs can be linked together to transfer information and to share common data bases or a central high speed printer. Larger computer systems can easily share software as well.

But the most dramatic change is that the information that is the primary product of a law practice is no longer restricted to the physical space of the law office or the law library. It is technologically possible for the attorneys, the paralegals and even the secretaries to perform the majority of their tasks at home or on the road.

Imagine the following scenario. You are sitting in your pajamas on a chaise lounge on the back deck. On your lap is a portable laptop with a built-in modem connected to your telephone line which allows you to communicate with computers anywhere in the world. You are writing a trial brief at home to avoid the noise and pressures of the office. With the aid of the modem built into your laptop computer, you can access appropriate information from your office's electronic files, and with the same modem contact LEXIS in Dayton, Ohio to obtain all relevant case law. You can also contact DIALOG or NEXIS to obtain technical information or facts regarding a similar suit which appeared in the New York Times. When the final draft of the trial brief is completed you can electronically relay it to your office for printing and filing, and relay another electronic copy to your client through MCI Mail. When you have efficiently completed that task you can access the ABA/net and take advantage of their on-line Official Airline Guide to plan your trip to Hawaii.

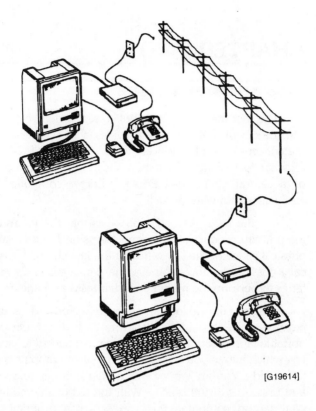

[G19614]

Not only are computers removing the physical barriers between people and places, they are reducing the dependency on paper print out. Messages can be sent back and forth between people without the need for a printout, the material can be edited and checked, and the final print out is all that may be required. With the use of local area networks and electronic mail, documents can even be printed remotely. An attorney on the road who has reworked the final document can now print it at his home office, or with the use of a fax modem, use the fax machine in a hotel lobby as a printing device.

TELECOMMUNICATING

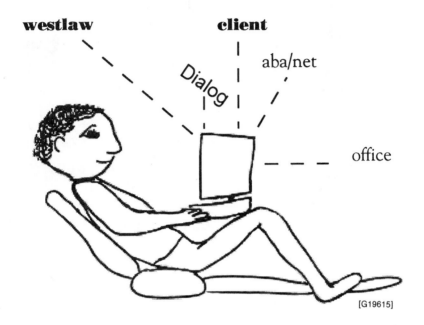

[G19615]

ELECTRONIC HOMEWORK

For some attorneys and paralegals, freedom from files, the library and the secretary may drastically change personal work-styles. Working at home could become the preferred and efficient alternative. Computerization would definitely cut down the need for secretarial support so that a small law office could become an even smaller office, serving as a central information center and possibly a place to meet clients. With the increasing computer sophistication of clients and the courts it may soon be possible to electronically relay that document to client or court without going through the interim time and labor-consuming step of producing a hard (paper) copy and sending it through the mails.

Using a microcomputer makes information retrieval easier

[G19616]

ELECTRONIC MAIL

Why use electronic mail when we have telephones, telex, faxes, and speedy mail services? Any new convenience, like the automobile and the typewriter, are initially greeted by this kind of skepticism, and electronic mail has been slow to catch on among lawyers. There are at least two good reasons to begin using electronic mail: you can leave messages on an electronic switchboard, thereby avoiding telephone tag, and you can send documents faster than with any other form of communications—either directly to the recipient or to a central computer service where they are stored. This all can be done without printing out hard copy.

The American Bar Association has already set up an electronic communications network, ABA/net, which serves as an electronic post office and conference center. A subscribing attorney in San Francisco can almost instantaneously send a brief to the "mailbox" of an attorney in New York who retrieves it, edits it, and returns it before lunch. Shorter messages, which might normally be sent by telephone can be left for later retrieval, presumably avoiding a few rounds of the lawyer's favorite game, "telephone tag". The service will also provide a data base (AMBAR) of all the information, articles, etc., produced by the American Bar Association and American Bar Foundation. It also carries the UPI newswire, and other general service data bases, such as the extraordinarily popular OAG, or Official Airline Guide.

Electronic mail has become a big business and there are several large commercial networks that offer services beyond the ABA/net. The current contenders are: America OnLine, Prodigy, Genie, CompuServe, and MCI Mail. All provide electronic mailboxes, and most offer a variety of express hard copy deliveries to the outside world. MCI's hand-delivered four hour mail can go to 18 cities in less than four hours. Overnight courier delivery reaches over hundreds of thousands of communities worldwide with MCI.

Even if the recipient does not have a computer, electronic mail makes it possible for a Los Angeles attorney to mail a document to a client in New York in two hours. This means if you have a pleading that must be filed that day, or a document which needs immediate delivery, but the client, or attorney has not joined the computer age and does not possess an electronic mailbox, you can telecommunicate your document to the nearest center to its destination. There it is printed out and hand-delivered. MCI will even reproduce your letterhead for a modest fee. You can also send TELEX messages through either MCI or Compuserve, etc.

The current problem with attorneys using electronic mail is that both the sender and receiver must have PCs, modems and communications software. Compatibility is also sometimes a problem. Modems and software are not big investments, but they are not first on many lawyers' priority list. Here are some suggestions to getting going with electronic mail:

1. Become a subscriber to the ABA/net. This inexpensive service, offered by the American Bar Association, allows you to leave messages for other attorneys and provides other valuable services, like the Official Airline Guide and a data base of American Bar Association Journal and American Bar Foundation information. Encourage everyone in your local Bar Association to become members as well so you will have someone to exchange electronic mail with.

2. Purchase a portable computer with a modem and try sending documents directly to your office from home. Take it on a trip and send documents or notes to the central ABA/net computer to be picked up later by your office or you. (You can send them any time, day or night.)

Electronic mail has grown in both use and sophistication in the past few years. Not only are there more services available which have email, but the gateways between them are more accessible. Of course the real issue with electronic mail is often not which system you are on, but how to find out someone's address on the mail system. If I am a member of Compuserve Information Service, I can easily send mail via Internet to someone who is on Internet or a service connected to it. I cannot however easily look up their address as I only have access to the members of Compu-serve. I must first contact that person and obtain his email address (sometimes that takes a bit of doing to decipher as well) and then I am free to send him mail. Many corporations who have their own internal mail system are linked via automatic gateways to the email systems such as Internet.

When a large law firm has a significant number of PCs running on a network, in house email systems are an efficient way of sending memos, announcements or any kind of document, from one computer terminal to another. In the simplest form a memo is sent out over the local area network from one computer to another or to a group of computers. The messages are then received usually with some notification display on the terminal. You may then respond, delete, or store the message for future reference. You may also send any document or program file with the enclosed message as well. If you are working on a spreadsheet and need someone to verify some of the data, then simply sending the spread sheet to the other party is easily accomplished with an email system. Most email systems for in house work allow for conferencing as well. Several people can be hooked up at the same time and view or write to the conference window. Information is shown about who is on the conference and then you are free to write notes to each other.

Local email systems can be used to hook up or bridge several offices in other buildings. These options will allow for accumulat-ing the email until a certain time or number of messages, and then one system automatically dials the other mail system and mail is exchanged. Following the exchange, the mail is sent out over the network to the addressee as it would locally. The system can also be set up so urgent mail is sent out immediately. Most of the local email systems have connections for the outside services. For example it is possible for me to create local mail on my computer, send it over the email on the local area network, to the mail server which has a modem attached. The server then calls Compuserve and the mail is sent to an addressee on Compuserve automatically.

Most major on-line services that feature the email systems also have gateways to fax systems. This is still limited to sending text only faxes and you may not yet receive faxes with this type of system. However it may be quite convenient (you are alone in a hotel room, etc. and need to send a fax and have a modem available to you). In addition it can be quite cost effective. If you join MCI Mail you can request a preferred status account. This option allows you to send virtually unlimited mail messages per month for the flat rate of $10. Also living in a rural area makes it more cost effective as you can use an 800 number to access MCI Mail, making the call toll free instead of a long distance call to gain access at a remote city. You can also fax with no phone charge to anywhere in the US (foreign access does carry an extra charge), and the fax is sent in a matter of moments.

Email services also provide for teleconferencing. If you have several parties in several locations, the logistics of a phone conference can be difficult. On-line services such as Compuserve etc. do offer a conferencing feature that allow people to share in a discussion in real time (computerese for talking at the same time). Several people enter a conference area and simply type messages on-line. As you send the messages they appear on each persons screen simultaneously, identified by the ID of the person who typed it. Of course it does take a bit of savvy to figure out the conversations sometimes as a line may refer to something someone said a few lines back. You do have the advantage that you can read everything each person says and save it to your hard disk for later reference. This may prove particularly useful, for instance, in interviewing a potential witness.

LOCAL AREA NETWORKS

Most attorneys will probably still feel more comfortable sitting at their office desk rather than their patio chaise lounge, and for them one of the most important forms of communication will be between office computers. Large firms with large computers can easily communicate between terminals since they are all being served by a central processing unit. There is, however, a strong movement to link PCs together. This has some advantages as well as some serious drawbacks.

Even if you start out with only one PC, it will not be long before the competition for that computer requires a second or a third. Larger and more powerful PCs are often used as fileservers to store data used by several people in an office. Fileservers allow common access to the same data as well as a means of exchanging data between other PCs. Active client information and in-house work products can be centrally stored and updated. On the other hand, each individual PC user has the option to continue to use their terminal as an independent unit, with separate software and stored information when appropriate. If one of the PCs fails, the others will still function, avoiding the frightening "total shutdown" syndrome which can occur if there is a central computer which supports many separate "dumb" terminals.

A second attribute is the ability of PC users to send information back and forth within the office without producing any printed copy. An attorney may choose to edit all his dictation in this fashion and send it directly to the printer, or attorneys and paralegals can send documents back and forth for revision and further editing, saving several steps in the production chain.

A third advantage is that other electronic equipment, such as the letter quality printer, can be included in this network so that it can serve many PCs. The printer must be equipped with an appropriate buffer (extra memory) so it can line up (spool) the printing jobs it receives.

Remote Access to a LAN is becoming more widely used today, especially with the increased number of portable and notebook computers. By connecting a portable computer to a modem and the office computer to a modem, the two machines can be connected over the phone line. Once connected files can be exchanged and documents can be printed at the office computer. This is extremely useful for retrieving information while in the field and then having them ready when returning to the office.

Local Area Networks or LANs are now an essential part of an office computer system. LANs enable computers to send mail back and forth with email and allow many computers to share a device such as a modem or a printer.

Types of LANs

File Sharing software: Servers and Clients
>   Dedicated
>   >   Novell
>   >   AppleShare
>   Peer to Peer
>   >   Personal AppleShare
>   >   TOPS
>   >   LanTastic

Network protocols
>   AppleTalk
>   EtherNet
>   Token Ring

Typology or physical layout of network
>   Daisy chain
>   Backbone
>   Passive Star
>   Active Star

Mixed LAN
>   Multiple computer operating systems on the same LAN

File Sharing

A LAN may allow files to be shared in either of two ways: peer to peer (i.e., between any two machines), and with the use of a dedicated file server (i.e., one machine dedicated entirely to sharing files).

A dedicated file server is a computer set up to perform a single function: serve files over a LAN. It cannot be used as a regular computer to run programs such as word processing, because the file server software takes over the entire machine. The dedicated file server may be referred to as a server. Personal computers which are connected to the server over the LAN are often referred to as Clients. With this system if you wish to send a file to another computer on the LAN, you have to copy the file from your own computer to the file server. Then the person requesting the file, copies the file from the file server to his own computer. However, dedicated file servers permit centralized storage of a single database or important information that many people need to access. Such databases or information may simply be too large to comfortably put on each machine or are being updated so frequently that to duplicate the data on each local machine would be a waste of time. File sharing via a file server are thus an important function of a LAN. Additionally dedicated servers can be optimized for simultaneous access by several users with the server software. Examples of dedicated file servers are Novell for MS–DOS and Macintosh (Novell may also be run on a UNIX file server as well), and AppleShare for Macintosh computers.

Peer to peer file sharing software uses each machine as both a Server and a Client. By doing so it is possible to copy or retrieve a file directly from one computer to another. Because the computer is performing two tasks, i.e., file serving and running a normal program such as word processing, there is a slight decrease in the performance of the computer. Peer to peer file sharing is more commonly used on Macintosh computers since it is built into the current operating system (Personal AppleShare), or is inexpensively set up with other software programs such as TOPS or EasyShare, or AllShare. On the MS–DOS side the relatively inexpensive LanTastic does the same function. Essentially the same network as used to share a printer allows you to send a file directly to another computer on the network. The advantage of this system is that every machine is used as a terminal and there is no expense incurred in having to buy a machine which does nothing but act as a file server. The disadvantage is that whatever machine is accessed to send or receive a file will be slowed somewhat. Generally this type of peer to peer serving is used in smaller offices of less than 10 machines or in which there is no single file (such as a large database) which everyone needs to access all the time.

Some technical information is required when setting up an office to determine the exact type of network required. Setting up a network can be complicated if you are not experienced with computers. This is one area of computers that it is best to contact an expert consultant. The determination of the type of network is based on the number of computers to be linked, the type of work to be done, and the physical layout of the offices.

Network Protocol

There are several network protocols available today for personal computers. The most common are AppleTalk, Ethernet, and Token Ring. The differences between them are the speed with which the data is handled by the network, the cost of the network hardware (cables, connectors, special cards which are added to the machines) number of machines which are optimally connected, and complexity of the system. These types can also be mixed so that a system may have several machines on AppleTalk while the backbone (see description in discussion of topology below) may be running on Ethernet for higher speed. At the bottom end of the network protocols is AppleTalk on Macintosh computers and now available for MS–DOS machines as well. It is simple and inexpensive until you try to have more than about 10 computers hooked up. The hardware for AppleTalk is built into each Macintosh and a simple cable is needed to connect the machines. For MS–DOS machines, a card must be added as well. The largest problem is that with this kind of system you are essentially using a 1 lane highway for all the network traffic. Computers send packets of information out over the network. With AppleTalk only one packet (a unit of data) at a time can go over the network. So if you are doing a lot of printing to a network laser printer, and trying to access a large multi-user database, an alternative solution is better.

The next alternative is Ethernet. Ethernet runs many times faster, but is considerably more expensive to install. All machines require an adapter card in them for the cable to attach to. Cables come in three types: thick wire, thin wire, and phone cable (twisted pair). The longer the distance between computers the more expensive the cable type is required. Also with Ethernet all machines must be connected to a star controller and the wires run from the machine to the controller. So our network with phone wire may be a maximum of 300 feet total, but one with thick wire can be 1500 feet. The gains in speed usually offset the cost by far. Ethernet is like a 10 lane freeway compared to AppleTalk. Information from many computers can be sent simultaneously without the network slowing down.

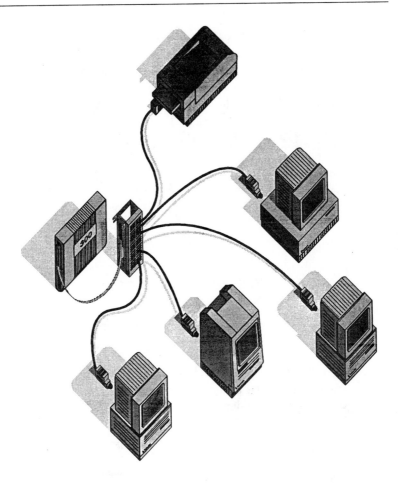

Ethernet with StarController

Courtesy Farallon Computing

[G19617]

More sophisticated networks can be Token Ring. These are very expensive requiring expensive hardware and wiring but allow for very fast networks with little or no speed decrease with the number of users on the net. The topology for this is a circle and information is carried around by attaching our little packets to a "shuttle" or electronic token that is constantly racing around the circular network. The Token Ring protocol is only used in the largest of networks today.

Network Topology

In addition to the network protocol there is the topology of a network to be considered, i.e., the physical form of the network.

Some network protocols such as Ethernet only work effectively in a layout called a star configuration where all the computers are linked to a central controller and exist as spokes on a wheel.

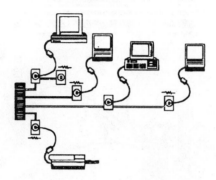

Passive Star Topology

Courtesy Farallon Computing

[G19718]

Others can be a straight chain, etc. With only a few computers they can all be linked in a daisy chain or along a backbone. A daisy chain simply links from one to the other.

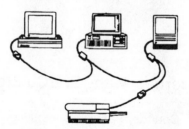

Daisy Chain Topology

Courtesy Farallon Computing

[G19719]

With a backbone, there is a cable put in and the machines can plug into the cable at an outlet. Generally this type of system is linked using phone wire, from computer to computer or in the walls.

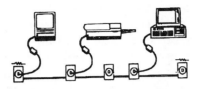

Backbone Topology

Courtesy Farallon Computing

[G19720]

The network hardware is built into the Macintosh, as well as the software (system 7 operating system). With more computers and traffic, a star controller is added that allows for several backbones to operate. A total of 250 computers can be linked this way.

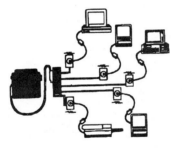

Active Star Topology

Courtesy Farallon Computing

[G19721]

Mixed LAN

LANs often serve as a way of linking together PCs that are different types. We generally call these "Mixed LANs". For example, you have several MS–DOS machines which run dedicated legal systems or a substantive program for your law specially. The machines run fine, though they are showing some signs of aging technology. You decide to add several new machines. You choose Macintosh because of the ease of use, and because you now want to do more graphic work and require a better display of what you want to print. You also want the machines to be able to access a common mail system and to share a printer as well as accessing a Foxbase Database the office has running. You can set up the Macintosh computers with Ethernet and connect them to the MS–DOS machines. For more sophisticated larger networks, a Novell file server can be set up and run on a dedicated MS–DOS machine. This type of network is a dedicated server type. The MS–DOS computers are all connected with Ethernet. The Macintosh computers can be added as well and see the files on the server with Novell for the Macintosh. Today there are many solutions to running on a mixed LAN which allow for different computers to be all hooked up together. It does not follow that one must buy the same type of computers in order to extend a network. It makes more sense to buy the type of machine that will do the best job for the function that is required.

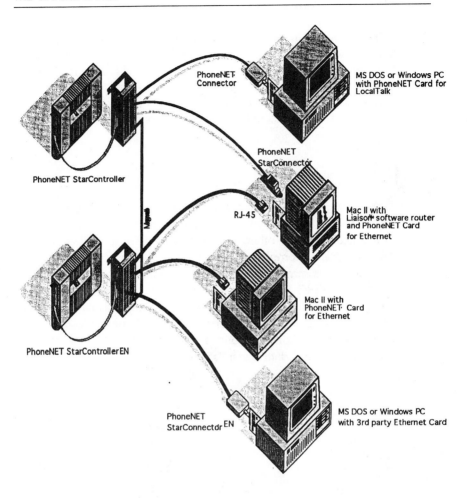

PhoneNET Connector

MS DOS or Windows PC with PhoneNET Card for LocalTalk

PhoneNET StarConnector

PhoneNET StarController

RJ-45

Mac II with Liaison™ software router and PhoneNET Card for Ethernet

Mac II with PhoneNET Card for Ethernet

PhoneNET StarControllerEN

PhoneNET StarConnector EN

MS DOS or Windows PC with 3rd party Ethernet Card

Mixed LAN (Graphics Courtesy Farallon Computing)

[G19722]

It is important to design a system that will include room for expansion. If you underbuild, you may have to do a costly overhaul as the system grows. One way to handle growth is to separate the network into regions that are logically connected and share most data. For example you might create a region (called a zone) for the graphics and design team that does the brochures etc.

This team has its own laser printer and spends most of the time only sending files back and forth in that zone. It can link to other zones when necessary, but this way the traffic is limited to the local traffic within that zone. AppleTalk could be fine and inexpensive here. The backbone could be Ethernet and files are then sent from their zone to the accounting department on Ethernet.

ON THE ROAD

Toting a portable (about 4–7 pounds), the attorney can travel from Toledo to Timbuktu and be able to retrieve information from his office library or other electronic data bases as well as send in notes or other completed work products via telecommunications. Existing telecommunications, which are mainly the telephone lines put up by AT&T for voice communications, often provide maddeningly slow data transmission, but with the deregulation of the national telephone system many commercial companies are competing to set up communications systems that are suitable for very speedy computer data transmission.

[G19618]

Apple Macintosh Powerbook-notebook computer with modem/fax modem built in.

CASE STUDY #1

Sole Practitioner Criminal Practice

Kent Clark has a solo practice in criminal law and has practiced law for the past 15–20 years. He has a practice in a small building which he shares with several other lawyers, thus dividing the cost of the secretarial staff and the law books etc. Kent began to practice before computers became popular, and developed his own system of analyzing information for litigation which includes file numbers, notes and references with outlines and summaries. Kent uses an MS–DOS system and has seven computers in the office. Because of the nature of the independent associates he does not use a network for file serving. Two other machines are networked to a printer, and there are two laser printers and one dot matrix. He has a computer at home with a modem and two modems at work. He does some forms on the lasers, but these are mostly templates from past motions. The civil lawyers in the building use the forms more. He stores the motions in compressed format. He has a 100 MB hard disk, two systems with 100 MB hard disks, 200 MB for his secretary, and a 100 MB at home. Most of the software he has seen for the legal profession is geared toward civil litigation, not criminal and so off the shelf software was not as useful to him as his manual system. He uses computers for word processing, database storage for clients and for case organization, and telecommunications primarily.

Telecommunications:

One associate has a secretary across the country to whom he Fedexs his dictation. She receives it in the morning and by the time he gets to the office she has emailed the typed file back to him taking advantage of the 3 hour time difference to complete the work. Kent uses WESTLAW for Shepardizing. Using it for research proved too expensive for his small practice. He says that he could not learn to use it in a cost effective manner in his solo practice.

TIP: When Shepardizing or checking on court decisions that may or may not still be valid, Kent finds WESTLAW extremely useful. In a matter of minutes he can find a list of references about a case, log off WESTLAW and then look up the actual citations from the printed volumes in his office. Kent also uses it to look up information about other lawyers and judges and how they have practiced law.

TIP: He uses his own computers for a BBS (bulletin board system, i.e., computer software which allows you to call your computer via the phone lines and a modem and leave messages or transfer files) to send files back and forth. He does not use the email on commercial services, but has other attorneys send files directly to his system and vice versa. On the road he uses a lap top or borrows a computer. For example he had a case in another county and had access to a computer there. He was able to download his files from his office machine when he needed to get them. He sets his office up with auto answer but uses password protection and phone back.

He has just started using Windows 3.1, but finds it less powerful than MS–DOS for him. It uses a lot of disk space, and has memory problems. However, it is good for multitasking such as downloading email in the background, though WordPerfect in the foreground does slow down.

Kent creates indexes to crime reports and summarizes the crime reports. For database he uses Evidence Master for depositions and litigation support and a shareware program called PC file. With Evidence Master he has someone manually type information from depositions.

TIP: Kent uses WordPerfect as a database to file information. He goes through depositions and marks the material he wants entered. He creates an index to the deposition with the material he feels is relevant rather than loading the whole file into a program. Using the whole transcript imported from ASCII files and then searching often gives you too many references and you have to eliminate all the unwanted ones. So he finds the programs that automatically search not as useful because they do not do intelligent searches. By reading the printed deposition and marking it, he chooses to database only the relevant material. He makes an index by page number and then one by witness which requires he review the crime reports. Then he makes an outline of each report. While he uses WordPerfect for storing much of the material, it does not allow for multiple or logical searches and that is the advantage of databases. For that he uses PC file. PC file is handy for databasing his archived files which are filed in numbered boxes and cross-referenced in the database. He uses case numbers and the year and date. He does not record the detailed information on the cases anymore, though he used to (i.e., motions, disposition etc.)

He does not do the billing on the computer but does his annual profit and loss on the computer. He does his bills and checks manually. Most of his cases are lump sum cases. He can estimate very well how much a case will cost. For the court appointed cases where he has to log his time, he does this in WordPerfect as well.

Back up is mainly by floppy disk and redundancy among the machines and at home. Backup is performed weekly and there is offsite storage. He mostly backs up data files, and not the application (program) software. Two machines are on a tape device. They are on an Ether network, and use LanTastic software to access the other computers. Each machine is backed up independently. Eventually he will add a dedicated file server for storage and archiving.

He is not using any disk or CD service for law updates. There are motions published on disk he is thinking of getting, but they are not very good and take up disk space. Criminal jury instructions are on disk; he uses this product but he cannot get it to work very well. He feels that if he were just starting out he would probably get the case law on CDs, but since his library is intact it is not what he wants now.

He organizes each case in a separate sub directory. When the case is closed he moves this to an archive sub directory. When he needs the space he moves the oldest cases to floppy for storage.

He uses an automatic optimizing for his hard disk that optimizes once a day. His current system has been in use about 7–8 years though he has upgraded the hardware.

At home he uses graphics and animation programs, Dollars and Sense for his personal check book, and is on Compuserve (*C*ompuserve *I*nformation *S*ervice). He sometimes follows things related to travel on CIS. He also uses a shareware program for figuring the costs and maintenance of the office building.

He uses a calendar program on his secretary's machine. He marks entries during the week in his book and then gives her the entries. She enters them and on Monday gives him a print out of the week. There are features in multi-user calendars that may be nice, but he feels most of them are too complicated to use. There is one master calendar that includes each person. He doesn't need to pull it up on the computer since his practice is not that hectic. Mostly he enters time in a file at home in a subdirectory for WordPerfect for his times. Then he has a status file that determines which version at home and office needs to be updated. He uses sneaker net to transfer them. For these functions he finds DOS easier than Windows for copying all the files to floppy. Windows makes everything run slower.

One of the big peeves is the expense in constantly upgrading software. Trying to choose a system or a product becomes very difficult. Then there are the conflicts to worry about. With Windows memory management has become a real issue regarding conflicts.

He really enjoys the use of modems and communications. He feels people using BBS's are people who enjoy being there.

Critique: It would be advantageous to switch the machines to a dedicated file server network, even if the lawyers are not practicing together. The system can be installed to allow privacy with passwords for each lawyer. This would make the system smoother and more efficient. In addition automatic tape back ups can be performed. The redundancy and floppy system would be difficult to use for restoration if a crash happened. With a LAN file server, and call in he could efficiently communicate memos with his secretary and himself.

For a solo practice lawyer, Kent actually utilizes his system very well. He has experimented with state of the art systems and over the years has been able to use the computers in a very cost efficient way.

CHAPTER THREE

How Computers Work

AN INTRODUCTION TO THE COMPUTER FAMILY

For most law offices, the versatile microcomputer, standing alone or attached to others, will be the computer most often used. But computers come in a variety of shapes and sizes which offer a wide range of different services for different sized law practices. An understanding of the various members of the computer family will help you make choices for your law practice.

Mainframes

At the head of the family is the mainframe. This is the computer used by your bank to send you monthly statements. As you know it is not infallible but it is certainly efficient. Mainframes are very powerful and can support many, many users and often perform many different tasks at the same time. They can also store huge amounts of information for fast retrieval, like the whole of American case law which is stored on mainframes for WEST-LAW, LEXIS and VERALEX. Mainframes can support thousands of users at the same time in what is called a time-sharing arrangement, which means that the user pays only for the time used. Mainframes range in price from a low of several hundred thousand to millions of dollars. The more powerful the mainframe the higher the price. Usually, specific software must be written for mainframes, and the software can be even more expensive than the computer itself. Organizations that have hundreds of users or have an enormous amount of data that must be stored and retrieved, must have the capacity of a mainframe within the organization.

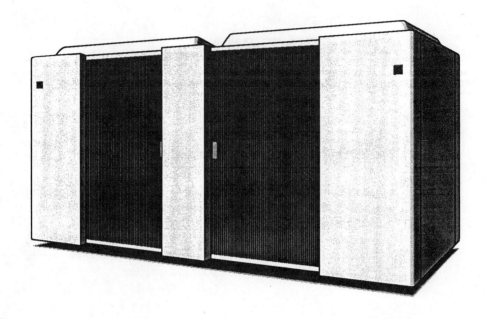

I B M   M A I N F R A M E
[G19619]

Lawyers do not usually fall into this category, and are not likely to have mainframes in their offices unless they are the corporate counsel for a large company. Lawyers will use remote mainframes however, when they access WESTLAW or LEXIS, or when they use the information services of nonlegal data bases such as NEXIS or DIALOG. They may also use the services of a mainframe if they send out their payroll or perhaps their billing and timekeeping to a service bureau that supports a mainframe. If a law firm has an enormous law suit in which many thousands of documents and many firms are involved, a litigation support service vendor with a mainframe may be employed. And finally, there is a slow, but potentially explosive movement toward electronic mail between lawyers and clients in which a mainframe serves as a computer message center. The ABA/net uses a mainframe to serve lawyers in this fashion, and several private vendors, such as MCI provide similar services.

Some of the leading names in the mainframe hardware world are: IBM, Digital Equipment Corporation, AT & T, and UNISYS.

Minicomputers

The lines are being redrawn in the computer family almost daily. What was considered to be a minicomputer several years ago is now considered to be a workstation. Minis generally fill the category between workstations and main frames. They can support many users, some as many as 100 or more, and have the capability of performing many tasks at once. They range in price from tens of thousands to hundreds of thousands. Customized software must be designed specifically for a manufacturer or a customer. Many large firms do use minis in-house. If they have several hundred clients and are supporting 15 workstations or more, a mini may be the appropriate choice. It will be capable of handling the firm's word processing, timekeeping and billing, and storage and retrieval of large or small amounts of information and work products.

Well-known names in the mini manufacturing world include Hewlett Packard, Wang (VS–100), Digital Equipment, Prime, and IBM.

Work Stations

This is a relatively new subspecies in the computer family. Basically a workstation is similar to a personal computer with a more powerful CPU. Often these workstations use a type of processor called a RISC processor. RISC stands for Reduced Instruction Set Computer. A personal computer is generally powered by a CISC or Complex Instruction Set Computer chip. The difference is that the RISC processor contains fewer commands or instructions and therefore is able to process the data from 5–50 times faster than a personal computer. In many cases these computers operate using UNIX as the operating system, however IBM and Apple computer are very hard at work to write a new type of operating system that will run on these machines as well as MS–DOS machines and Macintoshes. This new system is called Taligent and will allow programs written for the other platforms to run on these new faster machines. Currently running software developed for other operating systems requires running a system software emulator, which often degrades the performance. Workstations are multi-user, multi-tasking, which means that people at different terminals can be doing different tasks simultaneously. It should be able to support all the computer tasks appropriate for a small to medium sized law firm.

N e X T

[G19620]

The great differences between a workstation and a mini are expense and processing power. A workstation may begin at under $10,000 and each additional terminal may cost $5000 or less. The great saving is the relatively inexpensive software.

The workstation may have a great future in the small to medium-sized law firm. It can provide more terminals per dollar than individual personal computers and the file sharing allows for utilization of centralized information and communication among the terminals. The potentially fatal flaw is that if the central computer fails, every terminal goes dead. This, of course, is a problem with personal computers and mainframes as well.

Some of the noteworthy competitors in this new field are: Sun, IBM, Hewlett Packard, and AT&T.

Personal Computers

This is the little computer that has made it possible for small and humble law firms to have the power that was previously available only to the large and the well off. PCs can support almost all the same tasks that the much larger computers do, albeit with more effort on the part of the user. PCs are usually single user and can perform only one task at a time, however improvements to the operating system now allow for multitasking on these machines as well. They range in speed from 8 bits to 32 bits in main memory from 640 kilobytes to more than 128 megabytes, and in price from about $800 to $10000 or more. These numbers indicate that it is a subspecies in transition, growing larger in terms of power and speed each year and growing less expensive in price. All PCs can support all of the tasks generated by the average small to medium law office and can also communicate with the large, far-distant mainframes of WESTLAW, LEXIS, ABA/net and other services.

[G19621]

PCs can be linked together in local area networks to share stored information and printers. A variety of network solutions is available which with increasing cost provide greater speed and allow for the connection of far larger numbers of machines than before. In addition Wide Area Networks provide links between offices in several locations.

There are hordes of competitors in the lucrative PC field, a short list includes: IBM AT or 286 machines, 386 and 486 machines as well as various clone manufacturers such as Compaq, AST, Dell and many more; AT&T, Radio Shack, Hewlett Packard, Tandem, and too many to name. These are all PCs which use the Intel family of 8086 to 80486 CPUs. Apple with its line of Macintosh computers from the Mac Classics to the powerful Quadra systems offer a competitive line of PC that use a different CPU based on the Motorola 68000–68040 CPU and are optimized for graphic user interface. Amiga and Atari offer computers but since the installed base of these machines is quite small their use in the legal profession is rather limited.

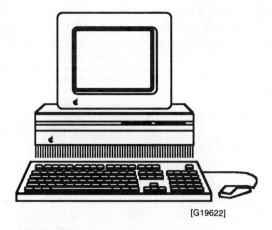

[G19622]

Dedicated Word Processors

Most attorneys and legal workers have had experience with dedicated word processors. This was the first piece of computer equipment for many well established firms. Dedicated word processors are a dying species. Most law firms today have switched to a more versatile, true computer system. They have been offered in many sizes, from stand-alone, to multi-terminal, but all have been characterized by a small memory, and software to accomplish only word processing, usually built into the computer at the factory. They have been more expensive than PCs, but accomplished their single task of word processing very competently. Some companies such as Radio Shack offer dedicated word processors in a very light weight portable.

Some of the leading manufacturers in this field have been: Wang, DEC, CENTREX, IBM, Radio Shack, and Royal.

Transportables

These are basically PCs with handles. Advertised to be portable they are usually too heavy to port without a sherpah. As a subspecies they are fading away since their utility is not clear. Leaders in this field have included Apple and COMPAQ.

Portables

Portables are machines which as powerful as many of the desktop PCs and weigh in the range of 6–9 pounds and are powered by batteries. These machines include a full hard disk and floppy disk and full sized keyboard. Almost every manufacturer has a machine in this category or in the one below. Many of the Japanese firms such as Toshiba, NEC etc. have made a strong showing in this category and the notebook sized machines.

Notebook Computers

These are truly light weight fully functional portable computers, weighing five pounds or less. This subspecies is rapidly developing its technology and is already able to perform most of the tasks accomplished by the desktop microcomputer. Very efficient for traveling or for taking to court, these machines are definitely the in the future of law offices. Some of the currently popular brands here are: IBM, Toshiba, Radio Shack, Apple Macintosh, NCR, AST, Texas Instrument and too many to name. The Apple Powerbook (notebook) in one year has become the largest selling notebook (see picture below).

Powerbook 145
[G19623]

WHY COMPUTERS?

Whether they are housed in a huge computer facility, or fit into your briefcase, computers are useful because they perform two functions at incredible speed, and with almost total accuracy: the storage and retrieval of vast amounts of information, and the computation of numbers. Almost all of the tasks that an attorney performs requires the creation, storage, and retrieval of information. Most of the functions performed in his law firm's back office involved storage, retrieval, and computation. Broken down into these two categories, the tasks that attorneys and legal workers are called upon to perform daily include:

1. Storage and Retrieval of Information.

Legal research

Factual research

Storage and Retrieval of litigation documents

Creation, Storage and Retrieval of memoranda, pleadings, forms, and other office work products

Calendaring and Docketing

Conflict of interest checks

Client mailing lists

Personnel records

Legal education

Tracking legislation

Electronic Mail

2. Computation.

time-keeping

billing

accounts receivable

general ledger

financial management reports

tax preparation

amortization schedules

estate planning

financial modeling

A combination of these two skills is applied in the newly developing area of decision making or artificial intelligence. This can be put to use in law practice in predicting the outcome of litigation, choosing juries, and potentially in making decisions regarding legal strategy.

HOW DO COMPUTERS WORK?

Fortunately, the lawyer or legal worker does not have to have much understanding of the way in which computers actually perform their functions of storage and retrieval or computation in order to apply them to daily legal tasks. He also does not need to know how to program a computer since there are trained programmers who can put together sophisticated, ready-to-use packages for legal use, or who will design a custom package for individual needs. In fact, since a new program can take months of a professional programmer's time to produce, it does not make sense for an attorney to put billable hours to this use.

What an attorney or legal worker does need to know is what time-saving tasks computers can perform for him, and what kinds of computers, or configurations of computers, can best accomplish this. To make these assessments, however, it is useful to have some understanding of the actual technology.

HARDWARE.

The term computer really describes the entire system, which includes both the machinery, called hardware, and the instructional programs which operate the machinery, which are termed software. The hardware of different computer systems may look like members of entirely different species, but whether the computer system is designed to read the prices on cans at the supermarkets, monitor a spacecraft to Mars, or edit a standard contract, there are common principles in its operation.

In all computer systems, the machinery, or hardware, can be conceptually divided into three parts: the central processing unit, the auxiliary mass storage devices, and the input and output apparatus.

Central Processing Unit

The central processing unit, or CPU, as it is commonly referred to, is truly the brain of the computer. In modern computers it is made up of silicon chips that are about one-quarter inch square in size to about 2 inches square. Each chip is a complex semi-conductor containing thousands of transistors and other parts commonly referred to as Large–Scale Integrated Circuits or LSI's. The CPU performs all the arithmetic and logical functions of the computer, it has a memory to retain information for instantaneous retrieval, and it provides the control mechanism to regulate all the other functions of the computer. The operational divisions of the CPU are the Arithmetic/Logic unit, the Main Memory, and the Control unit.

Arithmetic/Logic Unit (ALU) and Floating Point Unit (FPU)

The ALU of the Central Processing Unit, commonly referred to as the microprocessor, or processing chip in microcomputers, performs arithmetic functions and makes logical decisions, based on the instructions given to it by a program. It carries out these instructions by breaking a task down into logical operations that can be carried out on binary numbers—strings of 0's and 1's—and doing hundreds of thousands, or millions of such operations each second. Many CPUs today have a second chip associated with them which perform this function faster than the CPU and free the CPU up for other functions such as the control functions. These chips are known as FPU for Floating Point Unit or in nontechnical terms, math co-processor.

Main Memory, or Storage

Bits and Bytes

Information is stored in main memory or storage of the CPU in binary format; this means that the smallest element of computer memory can be in only one of two electronic states; "on", or "off", which corresponds to the binary numbers 0 or 1. This smallest element is called a binary information digit, commonly abbreviated as "bit". In most microcomputers it takes eight binary information digits, or "bits", to represent a single character, such as the letter "q", or the number "8". Data is stored and transmitted between main storage and the Arithmetic and Logic Unit, (ALU), for mathematical and logical operation in multiples of eight bits, or "bytes".

When describing the power of a computer, the terms "16 bit", and "32 bit" are often used. This represents the amount of information that can be processed in one machine cycle. The more bits that can be processed in one machine cycle, the faster, and therefore more powerful the machine. The amount of information a computer can hold in main memory is also determined by "bit" size, (See RAM and ROM below). Computers for scientific purposes are often "32 bit". Most computers for law office applications are "16 bit", but there is a trend toward more powerful "32 bit" computers even among microcomputers.

The speed with which computers operate is difficult for ordinary human comprehension. Machine cycles are measured in nanoseconds, or millionths of a second. For instance, an "8 bit" computer accomplishes approximately two million cycles per second, while a "16 bit" machine performs four million cycles per second. The speed at which a computer operates is the most important factor in determining the number of user terminals that can be connected to it. WESTLAW's computer can handle thousands of user terminals, while most microcomputers give reduced performance with more than two or three.

Personal computers today are generally based on either the Intel family of CPUs—8086, 80286, 80386 or newer 80486 CPUs, or the Motorola family of 68000, 68020, 68030, or 68040. Each CPU is progressively faster than the preceding one, however with the faster CPUs there may be a problem of compatibility. Caching (a specialized form of high speed memory in which repeated actions of a program are stored for faster processing), page memory management etc., are increasingly integrated into the CPU rather than sent to another processor. With the increasing complexity the software has to be rewritten to operate with the new CPUs. If you have an office, for example, with 386 machines and you add a new 486 machine to your system, you may be forced to upgrade your word processor to run with it. Once you do that you may be forced to upgrade the other machines to maintain compatibility. In addition, it may be necessary to upgrade the operating system as well. One must be very careful then, to not upgrade simply because it is the trend, or you want to have the fastest most powerful machines around. The cost of the upgrades, plus the time for a consultant to reconfigure the machines for compatibility can become very expensive. Also in the process of upgrading system software, you may lose compatibility with other software that you have enjoyed using. The CPU generally lives on a printed circuit board in the computer known as the Motherboard. It is possible to increase the speed of the computer by adding an accelerator board. These boards have a faster CPU chip on them and are added to the computer in one of its slots or in some cases clipped to the Motherboard directly. The accelerator can take over as the main CPU in these cases. Newer technology is now coming from the UNIX operating system and the Macintosh operating system which will allow Multiple CPUs to function at the same time, or in parallel. In these cases computer tasks may be sent to one of the CPUs while the other is still available. Traditionally this is useful for such things as graphics programs which require intensive processing to render an image in 3D. However as the technology takes advantage of these systems it will be possible to have computers in which activities such as database searches are handled by one CPU while the computer is still available to do word processing without any decrease in performance.

RAM and ROM

Bits of information are stored in main memory or storage in one of two forms on additional chips: RAM, or random access memory, and ROM, or read only memory. The information bits that are stored in RAM memory can be accessed in any random order, without having to search the memory serially, or bit by bit. This makes access almost instantaneous. The time taken to get a bit out of memory can be as little as ten-millionths of a second. RAM is used to store data and programs that may change. For instance, if a legal worker uses the computer for word-processing on Monday morning, and for time-keeping functions on Monday afternoon, he will be using different programs, and different data. This information will be stored in RAM memory so that it can be removed when programs and data are changed. All information in RAM memory is extinguished when the computer is turned off.

[G19624]

Since many programs take a great deal of RAM memory, this is a number you will see advertised when looking at computers. RAM memory is measured in thousands of bytes, or kilobytes, normally referred to as K or in megabytes which are millions of bytes, normally referred to as megs. Therefore, when a computer manufacturer advertises that its product has 2 megs of RAM, it is saying that the computer has 2,000,000 bytes of random access memory in main storage. Most PCs today come with a minimum of 2 megabytes of RAM. In general, computers with larger memories can handle more sophisticated programs. The huge computers owned by WESTLAW and LEXIS run programs that must retrieve information from millions of documents.

Computers have been designed so that RAM memory can be added. In some cases the operating system may have to be upgraded to be able to access the additional memory. RAM chips usually came in 256k strips or SIMMs (single in line memory modules) but more recently 1 megabyte chips have become so cheap they are standard. Now there are 4 megabyte and 16 megabyte chips. In order to upgrade a computer for more memory, you often have to remove and discard the chips you have and replace them in the same slot on the motherboard with a SIMM strip that has more memory. Often the memory must be upgraded in certain configurations. For example on some Macs you must install 4 chips at a time and they must be the same size chip. So if you have a 4 slots with 256 kilobyte chips for a total of 1 megabyte, in order to upgrade you will need to add 4–1 megabyte chips to get a total of 4 megabytes. With the newer chips that have more memory, however it is necessary to check with the version of the operating system to be sure that all the memory can be addressed.

Multitasking is the process of running two pieces of software at the same time. UNIX allows for this, the MacOS permits a simplified version called multifinder in which you can have several programs loaded, but they are not running exactly at the same time. Whenever you add this type of functionality to your system additional RAM or memory is required. For example if I needed 4 megabytes before to run the word processor and the operating system, now I may need 6 megabytes if I am going to simultaneously use a simple graphics program. Why would I want to do this? If I want to copy and paste a diagram from a drawing program into my word processor or I am preparing a report and the data is in a spread sheet, I will want to copy and paste the data into the word processor as a table. In these instances I will want to have both programs open at the same time and simply go back and forth. Otherwise I would have to open one program copy the information, close the program, open the other program and then paste it in. Most often this type of activity is done when using graphics programs and Desktop publishing, however it can easily be used when preparing financial data, or when using litigation support software. There may be a database in use for the filing of documents that permits locating the documents and you don't wish to quit the word processor program to do this. More memory is the solution in these cases. Increasing memory does not usually make things go faster or improve performance as a general rule. It simply allows you to perform more tasks at once. (The one exception to this may be some graphics software in which the entire file is loaded into memory).

ROM, or read only memory, is electronically similar to RAM. The only differences are that the information stored in ROM does not change, and is not extinguished when the machine is turned off. ROM is a type of static RAM, that is RAM that does not need constant refreshing. The information is written in at the factory and cannot be altered. Software programs work by addressing software code that is in the operating system and in the ROMs of a computer. ROM chips are usually not accessible to the user and are not generally changed during the life of a computer. The ROMs in an IBM AT (a 286 machine) are as good the day you buy it as they are 4 years later. There may be some limitations—you may not be able to format a new higher density disk or perform a task that has been added to the newer faster machines.

Some computers perform only one function; like dedicated word processors, or pocket calculators. The programs for these computers are kept in ROM memory and cannot be changed or taken out. They also cannot be updated, which can be a serious disadvantage. These machines normally have little or no RAM memory.

There are also unchanging functions that control the operation of a computer that are stored in ROM memory in all computers. This might include at least some of the most fundamental "systems programs", such as those that get a computer going when it is turned on, or interpret a keystroke.

Most modern computers have what is called MOS memory. MOS is an acronym for "metal-oxide semi-conductor". Information stored on MOS chips is volatile, which means data is lost when the power to the computer fails.

Since the memory on most RAM chips is refreshed constantly this is called Dynamic RAM or DRAM. This type of memory consumes power and would shorten the life of portables. Therefore many portables use "pseudo static" RAM in which static RAM is used that is updated periodically.

Control Unit

The control unit of the CPU monitors and supervises the operation of the entire system. It includes a cycle clock, counters, and decoding circuits, which enable the unit to direct and schedule movement of data within the CPU and between the CPU and the various peripheral devices like the printer, or terminal. The speed at which the cycle clock operates, as well as the "bit" size, determine how fast information can be processed. A faster clock and a larger "bit" make a more powerful computer. Clock speed is measured in Megahertz or in thousands of cycles per second per second. A fast Intel 80486 CPU runs at a clock speed of 50 MHz. The fastest Motorola 68040 chip today runs at 33 MHz. For example you may use a 68030 that is 25 megahertz or one that is 50 megahertz. Generally the upgrade in speed causes less problems than the change in the basic CPU, but there are instances of problems in which the software will not run with a faster CPU. The CPU speed (both in terms of the number of the CPU and its clock speed) will affect certain types of software more than others. CPU speed will affect word processing very little, but graphics software is affected more. Databases can be affected, but are generally more affected by the amount of memory and the speed of the hard disk (which I will discuss later).

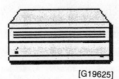

[G19625]

Auxiliary Mass Storage or Storage Capacity

After the CPU, the next most important component of computer hardware is auxiliary mass storage, also referred to as storage capacity. Main memory storage or RAM is expensive. In addition the contents are lost when power is shut off. Although it is necessary to store the programs or part of programs that give instructions to the CPU in main memory, it is usually not necessary to store more than a fraction of the data you are processing there at any given moment. For instance, if you are using a word-processing program to draft Points and Authorities on a personal computer, the computer may only take the specific part of the program that you are using, say the editing function into RAM memory and it may only take a few hundred words of the text you are editing. The remainder of the program and the text will remain in an auxiliary storage medium, probably a hard disk. There are only a few types of auxiliary mass storage in common usage today. Generally these are hard disks or some other type of medium such as optical disks. A few manufacturers have produced mass storage that are based on RAM chips combined with circuitry that retains memory even on shut down. Access time to RAM is from about 25,000 to 75,000 times faster than access time to a hard disk. For many functions, however, like editing a document, the access time to a hard disk is still so fast that this does not present a practical impediment. For other functions, such as searching a hard disk containing several hundred documents to find a specific piece of information in preparation for trial, lack of speed may become a problem with a small computer and the alternative is to either have sufficient memory on the CPU to load the data into it for searching or to use one of the newer but still very expensive storage devices which incorporate RAM chips into them.

There are several existing varieties of auxiliary storage and more in the development stages. The larger the amount of data storage which is "on-line", i.e. can be accessed by the CPU, the larger the variety of functions that can be performed. For instance, while it would not be necessary to have access to a large amount of data when editing a will, or drafting a pleading, it would be essential to have a large "on-line" data base for storing and retrieving hundreds of documents in preparation for litigation.

Disks

A disk is a device that stores large amounts of data in a manner that allows fast access. The disk is the medium of storage, and a disk drive is the machine that makes it work. Data is stored on disks similar to the manner in which music is stored on records. The surface of the disk is coated with magnetic compound, and electric signals representing the data are fed onto the surface using a read/write head similar to a tape recorder. The disk is divided into concentric rings called tracks, like the tracks on an LP record. Each track is divided into sectors. Each track and sector have an address so that individual pieces of information can be readily retrieved, as one can pick out a song on a phonograph record. The disk is spun at high speed and the head moves across the disk medium in a straight line to access the data, locating the information desired.

The amount of data that can be stored on disks is measured in bytes, as it is in main memory or RAM. Since both are measured with the same units it is often confusing to the beginner. It is best to think of the RAM in the computer as your brain capacity and the size of the disk as the capacity of your filing cabinet. Disk storage is usually expressed in thousands of bytes, (kilobytes, or K), or millions of bytes, (megabytes, or MB or megs) or now in billions of bytes (gigabytes, or GB or gigs). The capacity of disk storage is far greater than main storage; even with PCs it is possible to have hundreds of megabytes of disk auxiliary storage or even gigabytes. At this time, disks usually come in several varieties: floppy disks, which are removable and small in capacity, and hard disks, which are usually permanently sealed in a case because they float in a bath of oil and the slightest dust will cause a disk to not read properly. There are also several varieties of removable hard disks which combine the unlimited storage of a floppy with the speed and capacity of a hard disk.

Floppy Disks

Floppies are so-called because they appear as a flexible plastic disk contained in a square envelope. They may be either 5 and ¼ or 3 and ½ inches in diameter. The total storage of a floppy disk varies according to the density of the data stored along a track, and the number of segments into which each track is divided. Most floppy disks now have a capacity of from 360K to 2.8 MB: there are some new floppy drives which now claim storage as high as 20 megabytes. Five hundred kilobytes represents about 140 printed pages. The access time for retrieval on floppy disks is relatively slow since the disk drive is generally not very fast. Floppies are usually found on PCs and larger machines, like dedicated word processors, where it is not necessary to store and retrieve a large amount of data for any single task. Floppies are easily removed for off-line storage and are an inexpensive way to back up a computer. Therefore it is possible and convenient to archive hundreds of forms and old client files on floppy disks.

Floppy disks are good for loading software you buy, transferring data from one machine to another (a machine at home etc.—

this is affectionately known as sneaker net), storing files for later use, and an inexpensive way to back up the system.

Floppy disks originally came in 5.25 inch disks that were really floppy. You stored them in a paper jacket and the disk bent in your hands. There were usually 2 sizes, 360k and double density 720k. When the Macintosh was introduced it used a different type of floppy disk that was 3.5 inches and was encased in plastic with a shutter. When inserted into the disk drive the shutter was opened and the floppy disk inside was read by the drive. These first disks were 400k.

D I S K E T T E

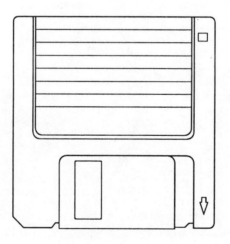

D I S K E T T E
[G19626]

A few years later MS–DOS machines started using the same size disks. Then other machines adopted them as standards. Gradually the capacity increased. Macintosh disks became 800k and MS–DOS became 720k. Then MS–DOS disks increased with new high density capacities to 1.2 megabytes. Macintosh then increased to 1.44 megabytes. MS–DOS disks are now available in 2.8 megabyte sizes and Macintosh will soon follow suit.

You may think all of this is just to play catch up with each other but as the operating systems continue to grow in size and complexity the disk capacity must increase with it.

Hard Disks

Hard disks are used in applications that require large data storage and fast retrieval facilities, like searching and retrieving hundreds of documents for litigation. Most large computers today employ hard disks. Hard disks are now also a common feature on personal computers. A single hard disk can have a storage capacity of from 20 to several thousand megabytes (gigabytes). The single disk can be joined with others in one disk drive to produce millions more bytes of memory storage, and with still other disk drive configurations to produce billions of bytes of storage. Several disk drives can be linked to the same computer at the same time by daisy chaining the cables from one disk to another. This chaining is accomplished because of the SCSI (pronounced Scuzzy) interface now built into PCs. SCSI stands for Small Computer System Interface. Generally up to 6 devices can be attached to a computer and can include several kinds of storage devices. Most everyday tasks in a legal practice do not require billions of bytes of storage, but with the recent increases in sizes of the system and applications as well as the sizes of large databases, a gigabyte storage device on a file server is not an unreasonable purchase today.

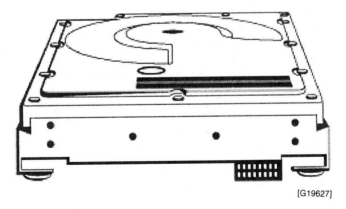

[G19627]

The disk drives which run hard disks are far more powerful than those that propel the floppies. Therefore the rate at which the information can be retrieved ranges from hundreds of thousands of bits per second in floppy-disk systems to 10 million bits per second for hard disks.

Hard disks are permanently sealed in the disk drive in order to prevent any dust from causing the head to crash. The disadvantages of hard disks are that they are considerably more expensive than floppies, and since they contain so much data and cannot be removed, they must normally be backed up, or copied, by some other medium, like floppies, or tape.

Today hard disks are reasonably priced so that they are the preferred medium for storage on a computer, though most PCs still have floppy drives so that software can be installed and information can be transferred for storage. The ability to add additional hard disks by chaining them greatly increases the flexibility of the system. Networking several small computers around one or more commonly shared hard disk is also commonly done to increase the storage capacity of an office system either with a dedicated file server or by the use of peer to peer networking.

Removable Hard Disks

Recently advances in technology have led to the popularity of removable hard disks. There are several types commonly in use today which employ different methods. One of these developed by Syquest is available in 44 and 88 megabyte cartridges. Syquest is now about to release a newer smaller cartridge with a 105 megabyte capacity. When the cartridge is inserted into the drive, the disk accelerates to reach the operating speed. As it does this air is blown across the disk to remove any particles of dirt that may cause the head to crash. A competing technology developed by Bernoulli uses a flexible cartridge that changes shape as it accelerates to operating speed. It is available in 45 and 90 megabyte capacities. In either case these disks may be used to substitute for a second hard disk for running software or for backing up systems for storage. These disks are very convenient and reliable. Many graphics service bureaus today use the 44 meg Syquest as a standard instead of floppies for receiving data because of the ease of use. Since the cartridges for either of these costs much less than buying additional hard disks and because they can be carried off site, many offices today purchase these drives as a standard part of their office equipment.

CD–ROM

The technology of auxiliary storage has advanced dramatically in the past decade with the widespread adoption and improvement of the hard disk and it continues to progress. However the hard disks are not a good medium for distribution of large amounts of data because of the expense. Even removable hard disks are not cheap enough for distribution of published information. Today CD–ROMs i.e. compact disk, Read Only Memory, are increasingly being used for the distribution of large data files such as the contents of a library of several thousand books on a single disk.

Unlike microfilm, where print is simply made smaller, all the powers of instant retrieval by key words or phrases are possible. The implications for the legal profession are staggering. Recently CD–ROM disks have been released which contain entire collections of law books and case law. (See Chapter 7)

In many ways the technology of the magnetic disks and CD–ROMs are alike. Both require disks and both require a head to "write" and "read" the data onto and off of the surface of the disk. In the one case, the head is an electromagnetic device that resembles a tape recorder head, and in the other, the head is a laser and its associated optics. CD–ROM disks resemble the CDs that are now popular in the music world. In fact the same player can be used to play music disks. However the reverse is not true. You cannot use a music CD player to read a computer CD–ROM disk because in order to be able to access the sectors on the CD–ROM a faster moving head is required, which is the principle reason why CD–ROMs cost 2–3 times what a music player costs. Today CD–ROMs cost $300–500, but with increased popularity these costs will decrease.

The main disadvantage of the CD–ROM at this time is that the laser burns a hole into the plastic disk medium. This makes it impossible to erase or alter the information burned into the disk. However the cost to manufacture the disk itself is so inexpensive (actual manufacturing costs are usually below $10 and can be as low as $1.50) that it is easy for vendors to send monthly updates containing new citations for very little expense. With entire law libraries available on CD–ROMs today it is doubtful whether a lawyer starting a new practice would want to purchase the books in printed form. Additionally the CD–ROM disks have the ability to perform rapid searches that would normally take valuable time away from one's practice. It is also possible to place the CD–ROM on a network so that several lawyers can access the information at the same time. If anyone has ever tried to use a law library only to find a volume checked out or in use by another lawyer, the advantages to this system are obvious.

In addition to the fact that these CD–ROMs are read only they are also considerably slower than hard disks. While each year the speeds increase, they are still not fast enough to be useful for anything other than storage of large volumes of information. Currently these CD–ROMs hold about 500 megabytes of data.

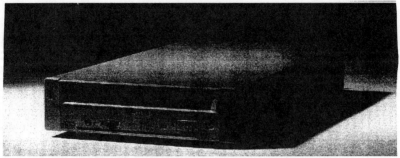

[G19628]

Optical Disks

A variant on the CD–ROM is the read-write optical disk. Optical disks provide a very large removable storage capacity. In addition they are very resistant to damage and are ideal for archiving data. Today they are available in large 5.25 inch disks which store up to 650 megabytes on a single cartridge. More recently 3.5 inch disks have become popular which can store up to 128 megabytes of information on them. Access times have been steadily increasing to the point where they now rival the speeds of all but the fastest hard disks. While the cost of the mechanisms are still fairly high ($4000 for the larger capacity and $1600 for the smaller ones), the cost of the medium is less than that of removable hard disks. Optical disks are becoming the medium of choice for the storage of scanned images. Firms using scanners for document storage usually use this medium because of the large size of the scanned images. Once archived to optical disks images can be retrieved at a later date.

Silicon Wafers

A new technology is being developed which may make hard disks obsolete. Information is written to a multilaminate card. Since there are virtually no moving parts with this technology, it is potentially a more trouble free system. The expected costs of the hardware is about $1500 and each card will cost about $20 and be available in varying capacities for an additional cost. Speed of retrieval with this system is almost instantaneous.

Magnetic Tape.

Magnetic tape is both the least expensive and the slowest medium for retrieval. Information on magnetic tape is stored and accessed sequentially, while on disks it can be accessed at random. In that sense disks are like LP phonograph records, where the needle arm can be placed at any point, and tapes are like audio cassettes where one must play through the whole tape in order to locate a particular song.

Because of the slow nature of the retrieval, tapes are most commonly used in law offices for back-up, off-line storage of large data bases, such as financial records, or out-dated material which is unlikely ever to be needed again.

It is likely that the law office of the future will use a variety of storage mediums. Optical disks may be used for archival storage, including reference libraries; hard disk storage will be used for projects requiring large databases, such as litigation documents, which must be continually updated; and floppies may continue to be used for routine text editing. The same computer system will be capable of handling all mediums.

Input/Output devices

Input and output devices, the third category of hardware, come in many different forms. The reader of prices on cans at the supermarket is an input device; the machine which prints your airline ticket is an output device.

Terminals

A keyboard is the most common type of input device in a law office. Often a combined video screen and keyboard are attached to a computer as a single unit. A video screen is sometimes called a cathode ray tube, (CRT), or as video display terminal, (VDT). The whole unit is referred to as a terminal.

[G19629]

While some computers have the video built in, such as the Macintosh SE series or the Classic series, most often with MS–DOS machines, UNIX machines and more powerful Macintoshes, the monitor is a separate device. A processor board is placed inside the computer to which a cable is attached and the other end attached to the monitor. In some computers there is a video processor already built onto the mother board and then the monitor is simply attached. Monitors come in black and white, gray scale, and color. Black and white is the simplest and requires the least processing—therefore the computer runs the fastest. As you increase the gray scale and color depth of the monitor, speed goes down. This affects the refresh rate—the speed with which the video screen is redrawn. With complexity it takes more time to refresh the page. The highest level of gray scale available today is 256 shades of gray. This is based on the fact that the human eye can discern a step change from one color gray to one adjacent to it. Add more levels and the eye perceives the step from one gray to another as no change at all. In color, the eye is capable of seeing the same step change with 16,000,000 colors. This is referred to as 24 bit color. For any pixel or dot on the screen there are 24 bits of color information associated with it. Since processing of color at that level is so intensive, the screen refresh on a complex color document can become very slow. To compensate for this, there are special video accelerators which speed up the graphics processing.

If a computer is to be used only for word processing or database work, and color is simply an esthetic it does not make sense to install a 24 bit color graphics card on a color monitor. An 8 bit card with 256 colors is sufficient. A 4 bit one with 16 colors may even be adequate. Color systems on MS–DOS systems are very inexpensive, but add little functionality. Color is nice to the eye and may be helpful for sorting documents (for example in the MacOS you can label your folders different colors and different label priorities. You may choose to have all active case files a certain color, or all the client files a particular color. You can then easily find by color all the related material for a particular client. You can even back up all the files of certain color.

A lawyer contributing to a national computer magazine described using color text within the word processor. He found colored text valuable in writing long appellate briefs and in identifying and organizing the summary of evidence culled from thousands of pages of testimony. Sometime later when he worked on some documents in a work group, each person edited it on screen with a different color.

The same color monitor may be capable of different levels of color by simply adding a new graphics card to the CPU. A Sony made Trinitron monitor is capable of supporting 4 bit, 8 bit and 24 bit color. Whether you can display the 24 bit color is simply a matter of the video card. Sometimes even the same video card is capable of displaying the 8 bit color and by simply adding additional video memory or video RAM, it can be made to display the greater number of colors.

Dumb Terminals

A "dumb terminal" is a terminal that must rely on the CPU of a central computer; it has no memory or logic of its own. When several terminals share the same central computer the configuration is called a "shared logic" system. This configuration is currently popular in law offices which have a large central computer with several "dumb terminals".

Intelligent Terminals

An intelligent terminal has some memory and can perform many functions without relying on the central computer. A system employing both intelligent terminals, and a central large computer is called a "distributed logic" system.

Personal Computers as Terminals

Personal computers, which are certainly intelligent terminals, and offer increasingly more memory, can be attached to one another, or "networked" to share databases, and to communicate; this configuration is sometimes referred to as a "shared resources" system or a "network" system. The network may include printers, scanners, fax machines and duplicating machines as well; each of these may have a very small memory of their own.

Optical Character Recognition Units (OCR)

An optical character recognition unit, or OCR, is an input device which converts printed characters to computer machine language for storage on magnetic medium, or for entry into the CPU for processing. The main mechanism of the OCR is an optical character reader, or scanner, which "reads" hard copy, i.e. a printed page, converting it to an electronic impulse for entry into the computer, or storage on a magnetic tape. Scanners work through the use of laser and photocell technology. They are currently capable of "reading" data or text at a speed of approximately two pages per minute.

The use of OCR in law offices has been increasing dramatically within the past few years. The principal use of OCR has been to convert documents received into word processing documents for adaptation rather than rekeying of the material, thus saving labor. In offices where documents must be read and changes noted, this saves on the processing of Xerox copies sent to each person and then trying to collate the modifications. Once the document has been read into a word processor it can be sent electronically to everyone and the changes noted by the secretary on receipt of them. One attorney would fax drafts of contracts to the other party, changes to his contract were received by fax, then OCR'd and a document comparison utility run in order to pick up the changes that were made. This saved in both labor and paper while increasing the accuracy of his work. Using OCR with faxes allows you to transfer data when the other law firm is not on email or is using a different system where the files were created in a different system.

In some offices the repertoire of the OCR has been expanded to include the "reading" of full-text deposition tapes into the computer.

[G19630]

The possible applications of OCRs are almost unlimited. Full text of client files, office memoranda, and litigation documents could be "read" into a central database. In short, all the documents which comprise the practice of law could be placed in a computerized database for rapid access and editing. Advances in software have increased the accuracy of OCR software to the point where it is now above 99% in most cases regardless of the typeface used or the source of the material. A common page will have no more than a few errors in it and combined with the built in spelling checkers, the error rate today is minimal. The cost of a good scanner with an automatic document feeder is now well under $1500 and good OCR software runs between $600 and $1000. Most firms today are including this technology in their budget for computer systems. Those who have included it are now finding it indispensable.

Automatic Speech Recognition

The ultimate fantasy of almost every attorney who has worked with computers, or who hopes to work with computers, is to speak directly to the computer in ordinary language. The attorney might simply say to the computer, "Find me all the cases in the federal court system since 1975 that have dealt with the issue of the pirating of computer software." The computer then will dutifully search its database and produce these cases on the screen, or it may respond with "Do you mean all forms of software, or would you like to limit your request to application programs?" Whether or not the computer responds in a human-like voice, or as a printed response on the video screen, is probably not such an important element in this fantasy; the important points are two: the attorney does not need to touch the keyboard, and the computer will make leaps in logic, which will allow it to conceptually limit a very broad request.

Of course the applications of such a capability are almost limitless. The labor-intensive task of typing or entering words and numbers would disappear. An attorney could dictate the document into the computer which would print it on the video screen. Alterations could then be made by simple voice commands. Bookkeepers would enter the numbers with their voices and make corrections orally as well.

The technology to accomplish some of this is just around the corner. Apple Computer has been working on a system of speech recognition that does not depend on training the computer to recognize your personal speech pattern. Apple has done limited demonstrations of this technology and is prepared to place this system into their line of hand held Personal Digital Assistants which will be released in 1993 and will recognize several thousand words. Larger versions capable of increased vocabulary (i.e., greater than 10,000 words) will be available for their desktop machines.

The problem of speech recognition is compound. The core of the difficulty is the complex and variable way linguistic messages are encoded in speech. Computers do not live in the world of people and learn from everyday experience. Therefore, for a computer to "know" a natural language, it must be provided with an explicit and precise characterization of the language. At the present stage of understanding of language this is possible only to a very limited degree. A second major difficulty is that human voices are remarkably different. Anyone who has attempted to learn a foreign language from one teacher is always dismayed to learn when visiting the country that the same words sound very different with different speakers. It will be a very revolutionary advance when speech recognition technology is available because it promises to be independent of pronunciation.

For attorneys and legal professionals, however, even very limited voice communication capabilities may be useful. It might not yet be possible to draft a trial brief by voice, but it would be a dramatic advance if one could use key words to call up cases from a database. Unfortunately, the keyboard itself often keeps attorneys away from computers. Many attorneys learned touch typing quite proficiently at some point in their adolescence but are unwilling as adults ever to approach a keyboard again. This means that they must depend upon others to perform the simplest computer tasks. Even limited voice recognition could break this keyboard barrier.

Pen Based Operating Systems

Pen based systems permit the user to handwrite with a simple stylus on an interactive screen, generally an LCD (Liquid Crystal Display). The system turns the handwritten characters into type on the screen automatically, independent of handwriting style. Technology is progressing very rapidly with this problem. The written word is obviously a less complex phenomenon than the spoken word, although there is still the problem of individual differences. Pen based systems are now being used. GO has a working system available and the technology has been licensed to several others. Microsoft is incorporating this as well as Apple. Apple will be using it in the new Personal Digital Assistants to be released shortly. NCR has a pen based system out now. At the most primitive level these systems simply record the information and store it. The most sophisticated translate the handwritten text into a word process document and run the entire operating system without a keyboard. For use with compact hand held devices this eliminates the bulk of a keyboard. These systems are increasingly used by delivery services such as UPS for receipt of packages, and by law enforcement for data entry by police.

The capability of reading handwriting and putting it into machine-readable form is a useful one, but obviously far less significant than voice recognition. For experienced typists it takes much longer to hand-write a document than to type it. It may be most useful, however, for those attorneys who either cannot, or will not, use a keyboard.

Printers

The three major output devices used in a law office are the video display terminal, the printer and the fax machine. Until paper is eliminated in the practice of law, the printer is an essential ingredient of computer hardware. Since law practice generally demands a very polished finished product, the quality of the printer is an important issue.

Printers are generally classified as either impact or non-impact. An impact printer creates a printed character by striking the paper with some device. A non-impact printer creates a character by some other means, for instance, spraying with an ink jet, or fixing toner onto paper with heat. The major considerations in choosing a printer have to do with: speed, quality of print, noise level, reliability, and cost (See chapter on Buying Hardware and Software).

Impact Printers

Today impact printers cost the same as the least expensive ink jet printers and are no more or less reliable. For this reason they are rarely chosen today as the main printer for a system. In one area they do have an advantage: they are capable of output onto multipart forms. They are, however, also slower and noisier. Before the revolution in laser printers, most law offices used either Selectric printers, which are very slow at 15 characters per second, or Daisy wheel printers, which are speedier at 30 to 55 characters per second. For law firms that require forms in multiparts there is no substitute for a dot matrix printer. The real choice is in the quality of the output. The standard 9 pin produces a rather crude output compared to the 27 pin printers. These 27 pin printers are available at very reasonable prices today and are even networkable so that standard forms can be placed on a dedicated dot matrix printer and accessed by anyone on the network.

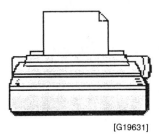

[G19631]

Non–Impact Printers

Laser printers have become the de facto standard in law offices. The least expensive machines now sell for under $1000. Laser printers, which do not strike, but rather heat toner onto the paper in the same fashion as a copier, offer outstanding quality and high speeds. More expensive machines offer faster output, network ability, a wide variety of type faces and multiple bins for letter head, envelopes, and plain paper.

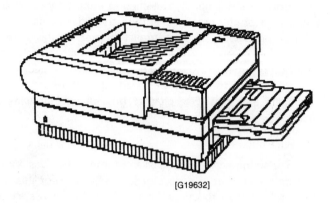

[G19632]

SOFTWARE

Although dramatic advances have been made in virtually all areas of hardware over the past ten years, the machinery is useless without the proper instructions to run it. Good software, that is "de-bugged", i.e., well-tested, is extremely difficult and time-consuming to produce. Programs to perform complicated tasks may take months, or even years, of a talented programmer's time. Unfortunately, some law offices have had the experience of buying the hardware first and then hiring a programmer to produce customized software. Several years, and many thousands of dollars later, the programs may still be filled with "bugs".

Software, or program instructions, come in several forms, each providing different functions. These are termed: operating systems; language assemblers, compilers, or interpreters; utility programs; and application programs. The attorney will really need to become familiar only with application programs, which instruct the computer to perform specific tasks like word processing, or accounting; all of the other programs usually come with the computer and are "transparent", i.e., not visible to the user.

Operating Systems

The operating system software serves as the traffic director of the computer system; it controls the flow of data entering and exiting the entire system. The flow of its instructions may be seen in the following sequence: it relays information from input devices to auxiliary storage devices, it transfers the information from the auxiliary storage devices into the main memory, it orders the execution of arithmetic and logic functions, it orders the processed information to be out-putted, usually to a printer, and if communication to another terminal, or by telecommunications is desired, it gives the necessary command.

For large computers, a specific operating system is usually designed by the manufacturer for that specific hardware. Among the PCs, however, there has been a distinct trend toward using the same operating system, currently MS–DOS, UNIX, or MacOS, in order to make use of the same application programs.

Language Assemblers, Compilers and Interpreters

Programs must be in "machine language", (a string of binary digits), in order to be executed. The translation from a higher level language, like BASIC, C, Pascal, FORTRAN, or COBOL, to machine language is done by programs called assemblers, compilers, and interpreters. Assemblers and compilers translate the entire program before it is run, interpreters translate each instruction in turn as it is being run.

Utility Programs

Utility programs are routine programs that are used to perform system-related maintenance functions and tasks. An example of a utility program is Norton Utilities which protects against data corruption and fixes problems that occur with directories on hard drives.

Application Programs

Application programs are what make the computer useful (see Chapter 4). These are the programs that the user deals with directly. Instructions on different application programs allow the same computer to perform such diverse functions as drafting a pleading and computing a time sheet. All the other programs merely prepare the computer for these complex applications. Often application programs which give instructions for sophisticated tasks can be more expensive than the hardware which performs them.

Some computers, like dedicated word processors, perform only one application, and the program is permanently written into their ROM memory. The trend in law offices, however, is toward multi-use computers. Their use may be limited only by the available application programs. For instance, the same computer may be able to perform word processing activities, time-keeping and billing functions, but cannot perform the calendaring functions because the appropriate application program for calendaring has not been written for that computer system. Some computers can accept more than one application program at the same time. With this computer system, one terminal can be performing editing functions and another can be performing accounting functions, or both can be performed on the same terminal with a split screen.

Currently, application programs for law offices are available from software vendors which provide either packaged or customized programs, from computer retail stores (packaged programs), or from an individual programmer hired to develop customized programs in-house. For personal computers, there is a tremendous cottage industry of individual entrepreneurs who develop application programs and market them through the computer trade journals, or legal periodicals. Because of the tremendous growth and increasing competition in the area of packaged application programs, the costs to the consumer have been steadily declining.

Communications Programs

Communications programs enable one computer to talk to another computer, or another terminal, whether it is in the next room or the next state (See Chapter 2: The Virtual Office). This can be done with in-house wiring or by hooking up to a telecommunications network. When a computer communicates with another computer very far away, as when a legal worker uses WESTLAW, the communications must also pass through a modem in order to send the computer signals across the telephone lines. If compatible computers are communicating in the same room or building, a modem is not necessary. Different communications software is used to link computers in a close network than is used to communicate by telephone lines over long distances. Some of the problems of communicating among computers were discussed in "Chapter 2, The Virtual Office".

CHAPTER FOUR

Choosing Software

It has become an almost established truth in the computer business that choosing software must precede buying hardware. The rationale is that although almost all PCs are theoretically capable of performing the same tasks; software, or the instructions to run the computer, is not available for all tasks on all computers. The initial rush toward IBM compatibles at the PC level for some time diminished this conflict between hardware and software, since most new business software is written for IBM's operating system (MS–DOS), but the rise of the Macintosh and the more recent introduction of more powerful workstation computers again makes it very important to consider the available software prior to a commitment to a hardware system.

YOUR NEEDS

Preparation:

Before running to the computer store it is important to sit down with everyone in the office; attorneys, paralegals, and support staff if your practice is middle-sized, or just you and your secretary if you are an independent practitioner, and discuss what ways a computer could make the practice more efficient, more productive, and possibly more versatile. Remember, Start Small, but think ahead as well. (Look at Individual Task Survey and Software Needs Assessment Chart)

Review, Renew, and Expand

Many law practitioners who currently have a computer system in place should consider reviewing the software and hardware they are currently using. This is especially true if the system has been in operation for two or more years. Computer hardware and software improvements are so rapid that the review process should be ongoing each year. In some cases it may simply be a question of upgrading current software and system versions. Often a new version of software contains many new features that help increase the efficiency of the office. In some cases the process of renewing the system may be more involved. A software vendor may be out of business or a competitor may release a package which is so superior to the product currently in use that it is foolish not to change products. In addition to keeping up with new versions and new products, the review process should also be an opportunity to consider the entire system with regard to increased utilization, additional equipment, additional software, and network expansion. A law office which anticipates its needs can then plan ahead and add or change hardware and software at the best prices and with a minimum of interruption to the office routine.

Although each office will have different immediate and long-range needs, the nature of law practice, whether you are a tax attorney, or a family law practitioner, provides a certain common denominator. Every attorney produces volumes of paper in documents, letters and other work products and most attorneys have clients who must be served and billed. Therefore the immediate needs of virtually all law offices should include word processing, a data base management system (for general purpose organization), and the ability to communicate with computers outside the office. An electronic spreadsheet for financial planning and a time keeping and billing system may or may not be immediate needs, but they should definitely be included in the six month projection.

INDIVIDUAL TASK SURVEY

Each member of your law office (including all attorneys and law clerks) should be individually surveyed for present work patterns before any decisions regarding hardware and software are made.

Full-time___   Part-time___If so, how many hours/wk.___

Job title:

Job Description:

Word processor or Computer experience (including WEST-LAW or LEXIS):

How many hours per week (on the average) do you spend doing the following tasks:

1. typing:
2. organizing documents for trial:
3. performing legal research: (include travel time)
4. performing nonlegal research: (include travel time)
5. drafting legal documents, memoranda, briefs, or other forms of legal work products:
6. filling in printed forms:
7. keeping time accounts:
8. client billing:
9. general ledger and other accounting functions:

10. Any computational activity such as damage projections, mortgage amortization's, etc.

11. calendar maintenance:

12. Other activities (not including client contact, depositions or court appearances):

Carefully review the information gathered from this sheet before proceeding to the software and hardware assessment forms.

ASSESSING YOUR SOFTWARE NEEDS

Tasks you would like your computer to perform:

	One Month From Now	In Six Months
1. Word-processing (general)		
2. Specialized Automated Document Systems		
estate planning		
family law		
real-estate amortization		
incorporation's		
real estate closings		
pleadings and practice forms		
federal income tax		
other _____		
3. Calendar/Docket		
4. In–House Library		
5. Conflict of interest		
6. Litigation Support		
7. Case file index		
8. Electronic Spreadsheet for Financial Planning		
9. Time keeping and Billing		
10. General ledger		
11. Management Reports		
12. Electronic Mail		
13. Legal Research (WESTLAW, LEXIS, AMBAR)		
14. Factual Research (DIALOG, BRS, NEXIS, etc.)		
15. Desktop Publishing		

Following the START SMALL rule, you need only search for software which satisfies the one month requirement. In making this initial purchase, however, a few technical considerations are necessary in order to make the initial software work well together and to prepare for future software considerations.

OPERATING SYSTEMS

Each PC has an operating system which serves as the traffic director of the computer system. It controls the flow of data entering and exiting the entire system, including telecommunications and the printer. Unfortunately the micro industry has not been able to settle upon a single operating system, and software programs must be written (at great time and cost) for each operating system.

Today there are 5 basic operating systems in use for PCs and Workstations: DOS (or more correctly MS–DOS which means Microsoft Disk Operating System), Windows for DOS (soon to be Windows NT without MS–DOS), OS/2 for IBM PCs, UNIX (with several Graphic user interfaces such as Motif and SunOS), and Macintosh OS. The majority of the offices will use MS–DOS (and or Windows) and Macintosh. MS–DOS is used because the majority of computer users are trained in it. The majority of software vendors for the legal market have developed software on MS–DOS. Macintosh has made inroads into the market simply because the system is easy to use, applications are similar and allow you to cut and paste data from one program to another, and you see on the screen an excellent representation of what you get when you print.

There are too few applications for law practice available on the other operating systems to be used by the majority of law firms. While UNIX is an excellent operating system especially for large numbers of users on a network, and there are a few excellent programs for case management, UNIX is still a very complicated system to install and use. It requires very powerful hardware to support it. IBM's OS/2 has almost no applications available and seems to be generally lacking in support from the software developers.

There is truth to the issue of choosing the software programs first before choosing the hardware. You must also consider the operating system which will run the software programs. If there is a specific legal package that you must absolutely have, first find out what operating system is required. This will help in choosing the hardware, but it is not sufficient to determine the choice of the entire hardware system. For example there may be one particular personal injury system that is ideal for your firm to use. But this amounts to only a small percentage of the work. The PI application or program will only run on MS–DOS 3.3. Is it necessary to buy 12 machines which run on MS–DOS 3.3 just because this program requires it? Not today. Several options are open. Buy one MS–DOS machine just for that program and put it on a mixed network with other machines such as Macintosh or PCs that run Windows. These other machines require less training and the applications are more consistent which means greater use of the computer.

The choice might be to simply purchase a DOS emulator software package for the Mac to run the PI program; another solution is to add a DOS hardware card to the Mac. The same is true now for UNIX. Emulators are being designed for different operating systems so that you don't need to force a decision based on the absolute need to run one package.

The decision as to what software to buy thus starts with which packages are in your list, and which operating systems are required. If you only need generic word processing and calendars and billing, then it may not matter exactly which software you need since there are excellent products available for all operating systems. Keep in mind, the more useful, friendly and easy it is to use, the more use it will get, the less time it will take a new person to learn it, and the less dependent you will be on specially trained individuals to operate it.

The Macintosh (Lisa) operating system pioneered the Graphic User Interface (GUI) which is now being imitated on other platforms. Among the features of this system is a standard interface for ALL software which runs on Macintosh. If you learn a spreadsheet, you will use the same commands in a word processor for cutting, copying and pasting. As a result this makes it easier for someone to operate several different software packages with a minimum of training. Surveys done on the utilization of computers verify this, the average MS–DOS user operates about 1–2 software programs, while the average Macintosh user operates 6–7 software programs during a day's work. Windows for DOS and new graphic interfaces for UNIX are testimonials to the effectiveness of the Macintosh OS as computer manufacturers respond to the increasing sales of Macintosh computers. You might then consider early on that an easy to use interface would be the most important criteria when computerizing a law office. On the other hand most law offices have already invested in MS–DOS machines and there is a great deal of law office software written for the MS–DOS operating system.

The ability to run different operating systems on the same hardware is often the solution to keeping flexible. If you know that you need several machines in an office, but one is going to run MS–DOS all day long with a dedicated MS–DOS-only piece of software, consider using MS–DOS on a single IBM clone or IBM on a mixed Local Area Network. If it is only an occasional use of the program, then consider a machine with an emulator. If you are using a series of integrated applications that only run on MS–DOS, then all the machines should be running MS-DOS. Mixed operating systems are often used without the user knowing it. Fileservers may be set up on one operating system, and all the desktop computers operate using another system.

MAIN MEMORY REQUIREMENTS

More sophisticated software may require more main memory. Main memory is like the workspace inside the computer, and it is measured in bytes, the way that electrical light bulbs are measured in amps. Although it may be useful, it is by no means necessary to understand the workings of bits and bytes. You only need to know how many bytes are required for the software you choose. If you feel the need for a greater understanding of computer mechanics read the chapter on "How Computers Work".

RAM (Random Access Memory) chips are so inexpensive today that you should buy all the memory that you need to comfortably operate the system you are using. There are some caveats: it depends upon which operating system you have as to whether you will be able to address all the memory. An IBM with 4 megabytes running DOS 3.3 and no manager for the expanded memory may be a waste of money. A Macintosh with 16 megabytes of RAM installed may not be able to address it unless it is running under system 7 with 32 bit mode enabled. All this means is that memory chips are not the sole agents-memory depends upon factors in the operating system as well. Using the computer in multitasking mode will require more memory that in single application. Multitasking allows you to operate more than one program at the same time. For example you might want to print a mail merge document with 400 letters and that takes about 15 minutes to print. With the merge program running in the background and print spooling enabled, you could continue typing in a word processor if you had enough memory. These newer operating systems and newer programs tend to be memory hogs. You will need 4–8 megabytes today to run a Macintosh on system 7. If your machines are networked and have email and calendars and other of extras, you will need the memory to handle it. However nothing is as intense a requirement for memory as graphics software. If the machine is being set up for just graphics, it is not uncommon to have a 20 megabyte minimum configuration. Different software programs have different memory requirements so when purchasing the software check on what is required for a particular application, add to it what you will need to run the operating system (allowing for choice of fonts and system extensions), and add at least another 20–30% as a minimum configuration.

Today it is wise to buy a machine with at least 2 MB of RAM for MS–DOS and at least 4 MB for a Macintosh.

HARD DISK REQUIREMENTS

Hard disks provide a vast amount of additional, or auxiliary memory. Although these were not commonly found in the first generation of PCs that almost universally used the more limited storage of floppy disks, technology has advanced to provide more power at lower cost. Almost all computers sold today either come with a hard disk already installed, or with an easy option to install one.

Most often people are confused by the difference between the hard disk requirement and the memory requirement (RAM). (This is discussed in detail in the chapter on computer basics.) Both are measured with the same increments, i.e. megabytes, so it is easy to understand the confusion. Memory or RAM is the amount of space in the computer that is used by the application and the computer system to run and process information. As long as you use the same applications and the same system this does not change. Hard disks are the storage devices for the information you record as well as storing the application information. You install the applications on the hard disk where they are stored. When you launch them they load into the RAM or memory. When you then save a file or document, it is stored on the hard disk. As you continue to store documents or data on the hard disk, the hard disk fills up and you need to begin considering ways to handle the storage. Today hard disks are considerably faster and larger than ever before. A few years ago a 20 megabyte hard disk was considered a good starting drive. Today it would be between 40 and 100 megabytes and probably costs the same as a 20 megabyte did a few years ago. It is mandatory today to have a hard disk. You cannot consider a machine that has floppy drives only. A floppy drive is viewed today as a way of inputting data or new software, for transferring data to another machine, and for back up or archival purposes. The discussion of backing up and archiving will be discussed at length in Chapter 12.

INTEGRATED SYSTEMS

A leading buzzword in computer software is integration. The ideally integrated system is a total package where a user can simply choose from a main menu the application desired, such as word processing, electronic spreadsheet, or database management; and the commands are similar for all the applications, sparing the neophyte from mastering different languages. The information stored in the data bases can also be manipulated for different applications, i.e., billing and word processing, by-passing the labor-consuming task of re-entering information for different applications. There are two categories of integrated systems which are available: Integrated software for **general business,** and integrated **legal** software.

Integrated systems for general business which have received a good deal of attention include: Symphony and Works for MS–DOS and Works and Claris Works for Mac.

Integrated software is often the best choice when starting an office or when training someone new. The packages are usually an excellent value, but they have limitations. Often though the limitations are apparent with heavy use. You may find that doing a mail merge in an integrated package is easy, but you don't get all the formatting you would like in the printed output. Then it is time to consider moving to a more sophisticated database and word processor package. There are two types of integrated systems: one which is a general business package such as Microsoft Works and the second which is specific for the legal profession. Programs such as Works offer several less robust programs combined into one. Works has a word processor, a database, a spread sheet, and a telecommunications package. For a small office doing light work, this may be adequate and cost effective. However many of the day to day processes may be better handled by buying the more powerful individual programs such as Word Perfect or Microsoft Excel and Microsoft Word. Excel and Word have a significant amount of communications between them. Word and Word Perfect surpass the integrated packages in the macro creating features and in the template offerings by third parties. Pleadings, contracts, wills, etc., can be created as a template in Word or Word Perfect and used for many cases by simply changing a name once and the whole document is complete. Attorneys working in tax law will find spreadsheet templates available for various financial and tax preparation on Excel.

Integrated legal systems offer easy to implement solutions that generally cover the entire range of needs for a law office. A good integrated legal system should have the ability to communicate well with the different parts of a system. For example in an integrated legal system you might want to send a letter to certain clients pertaining to certain issues in a personal injury suit. With an integrated legal system, the merge features for including the clients and issues may be a simple matter of selecting them and the form letter will automatically include them. Also there might be a matter about a certain client that has a calendar date which you need to prepare for and requires advance warning. With an integrated legal system you might select the matter and choose a warning date for it.

The drawbacks to an integrated legal system are generally twofold. First, if the system is adequate for your general practice but lacking in the specifics you need for your specialty, then the whole system is viewed as weak. Second, integrated legal systems tend not to be very flexible. Because they are written specifically for a law practice with a certain size practice or type of practice, the integrated legal system may not be as applicable to your needs. In order to build a system for your office practice it may be advantageous to buy the specific software you need and then integrate them yourself. Of course this requires more information and skill. However you will have a substantive law package that is specific and detailed for your law specialty. For example, you might be working with bankruptcy and the integrated packages may not cover this area well. You might then choose to buy a specific bankruptcy program, word processing software, and legal billing package. By using the import and export features of the different packages you may be able to accomplish the same tasks as with an integrated package.

Another piece to the puzzle of choosing between an integrated package and separate software is the change in how operating systems behave with regard to software. Both MS–DOS and Macintosh OS have added features that increasingly allow different *unrelated* software applications to link together. Apple has implemented this on several levels: at the lowest level there is a function called publish and subscribe in which information is shared by compatible software. Users of Microsoft Excel and Microsoft Word can create a spread sheet which is published on a network. A pleading written in Word can subscribe to the spreadsheet and the information will appear in the Word pleading. If information is updated in the spreadsheet, then the next time the Word pleading is opened *it is automatically updated.* IAC (Inter Application Communication) and Apple Events allow a more direct approach. Software which use these features can actually read and write to data in another program which may be totally unrelated. Increasingly the distinction between fully integrated programs and those which are integrated via the system software will disappear. As a user you are freer to choose different programs that suit your needs. Such connectivity is beginning to appear in DOS platform applications as well.

Integrated programs are available specifically for law office application, which include word processing, time keeping and billing, accounts receivable, general ledger, management reports, calendar, and perhaps file management. For MS–DOS, Summation is one such application, and for MacOS, MacLaw is another example of a fully integrated legal package. These packages keep track of the clients, the matters which are at hand, the calendar, conflicts which may arise among various partner in the law firm, billing, etc. It is certainly an attractive concept, and in the future most software will probably appear in this form; but at present writing much of the best software may not appear in integrated form, particularly word processing, data base management systems and communications software.

The best available integrated systems for law offices, and probably the most useful, are the financial management packages, often available as separate add-on modules, that include time keeping and billing, accounts receivable, general ledger and management reports. While there is not much practical purpose in having your in-house library integrated with your billing system, it makes a great deal of sense to use the same data base for accounting, billing and financial management.

APPLICATION PROGRAMS

Now that you are alerted to looking for a consistent operating system, and noting the main memory and hard disk requirements, you must choose the specific application programs that will work for you at a price you can afford. In the rapidly expanding software field, any specific recommendations may be instantly obsolete, but the following comments provide some general suggestions:

Word Processing

Word processing is the heart of all business today. A good word processor should have all the features listed, be fast and easy to use, and accommodate the more complex needs of a law office. Word Perfect DOS is today the de facto word processor for MS–DOS machines in the law office. So much so that several software companies for the legal profession manufacture templates and forms only for this product. On the other hand, other word processors may be easier to learn and use, while offering advanced features which require less programming skills.

MS–DOS and/or Windows: Microsoft Word, Word Perfect, Wordstar 2000, AMI Pro

Mac: Microsoft Word, Nisus, Word Perfect

Features in a word processing package should include:

Line numbering

Tables

Calculations

Graphics

Document Preview

Cut and Paste. Complete editing capabilities, deletion and addition of words, sentences, paragraphs.

Move blocks. Whole sentences, paragraphs and files can be moved.

Global Search and Replace. A repetitive word or phrase will automatically be replaced by another word or phrase.

Automatic pagination. Pages will be automatically re-numbered after editing.

Storage and Retrieval. Text can be permanently stored on magnetic medium and retrieved for re-editing and re-use.

Merging. The text of one file can be merged with the text of another, or with information from a data base. Most useful for developing variables or alternate clauses in documents and in producing fully automated document systems.

Special function keys. A feature that allows you to use a computer's special function keys for such routine functions as centering, moving a block, etc., can be a good time-saver.

Floating Footnotes. A feature that allows easy placement of footnotes at the bottom of each page (or at the end of a section or document) that will move appropriately with editing, is particularly useful for formal briefs.

Sorting and Indexing. The ability to sort alphabetically and to automatically generate and index.

Spelling Checks. A built-in program to check spelling errors against a large dictionary. Some of these dictionaries feature legal terms as well.

Table of authorities

Thesaurus. Some programs include a full-scale thesaurus as well as a dictionary.

Data Base Management Programs

A general data base management system, like the popular Foxbase available from Microsoft which is available on both MS–DOS and MacOS can theoretically perform an almost unlimited number of organizational, computational and search and retrieval functions. For instance, all time keeping and billing, financial management, calendaring, in-house library, conflict of interest and even litigation support tasks could be performed by this one program which costs about $700 or less.

However each of these functions must be individually developed, which takes some skill and a lot of time. For some functions, like billing and financial management, discretion is probably the better part of valor and the user should gracefully submit to purchasing an already packaged program, even though it costs a great deal. Unless you have a real understanding of accounting principles, and many hours to offer to the computer, developing these systems will be out of your league.

On the other hand, it is a relatively simple task to set up an in-house library, a simple litigation support system, a calendar, a new matter memo, and a conflicts system. Specific advice on how to do this will be offered in later chapters. Because the nature of law practice requires organizing a great deal of information, a data base management system seems obviously invaluable, yet at this point few lawyers make full use of its powers.

Database programs are composed of records divided into fields. Data is entered into the corresponding fields which can be searched, sorted and formatted. Sometimes information is filed using another type of software called hypertext. Hypertext systems store all the information in each record without using fields. When a search is performed, it is done on the entire record. The advantages and disadvantages of each system will be discussed in Chapter 7: Database management systems: Finding needles in haystacks.

True database programs can be divided into two basic types: Flat file and relational. With a flat file database all data is at the same level. This makes the database easy to construct, the program runs fast, and is simple to use. However as soon as you try to look up information on more than one field with qualifiers, you run into problems. For example: search for all the companies doing a specific volume of business, in several industries in a range of zipcodes. This is very hard to do unless you use a relational database. Relational databases are like several flat databases connected together. So in this example you might have a field for company name, size of the business, type of industries, where there is a second database of industries connected to this field, and finally a zipcode field. When entering the type of business it would be one which is contained in the list in the related database business types. A search on this relational database could give you ones which are of the correct size etc., and a range of industry types. If you were to use a flat database they would all be mixed together or you could only get one type at a time in a report. Relational databases are the basis of many custom applications built for the legal profession today. They are especially useful for substantive legal work. For the everyday tasks such as mailing lists, and other issues, flat databases are preferred. The speed and ease of use make them preferable.

MS–DOS

For many years dBaseIII was the dominant software in the MS–DOS world. More recently the rise of Foxbase which reads databases written in dBase has eclipsed the former dominance. Foxbase is a cross platform product (i.e., same information can be used on a Macintosh or MS–DOS machine) and runs faster and more efficiently than dBase. Paradox is another example of a well known MS–DOS database which is extremely fast and rather easy to use.

Macintosh

The major flat database is Filemaker Pro from Claris (also available on Windows). There are four major relational databases: Helix Express (formerly Double Helix), Omnis 5 or 7 (also compatible on MS–DOS machines), Foxbase, and 4th Dimension. Of these 4th Dimension is the most popular.

UNIX

On UNIX systems, Ingres is the major relational database.

Mixed platform integration on a Local Area Network for larger networks

Larger firms may use mixed networks with different operating systems and use SQL (Structured Query Language) on a mini computer serviced by PCs. A high speed VAX computer becomes the file server for the multi-user SQL database and a Macintosh, for example, may become the user's terminal as well as a fully functional PC for other work.

Communication between computer systems today makes the choices more one of how many users will be accessing how much data at any given time. Then the system is chosen. If you have a small to medium firm you will not need anything very sophisticated. A simple local network and file server with a multi-user flat database may be all you would ever need.

Time Keeping and Billing Systems

It is here that the buyer must linger longest. There are now over several hundred software packages for PCs that claim they are the ideal solution to lawyers' time keeping and billing woes. They span the price range from $300 to $3000 and offer everything from no-frills straight billing to five billing options accompanied by a general ledger, a docket control system and a smorgasbord of internal management reports.

Aside from being assured that the package you choose claims a compatible operating system with other software you desire, there are at least two other considerations in addition to pocketbook to keep in mind.

1. Is this software really designed for a law office? The reason that there are so many available software packages for this application is that a law office is considered an easy variation from a general business billing program. As you well know, however, law offices are quite unique in terms of how they arrange their billing rates and how much detail they provide in the billing statement. Make sure the package you choose really suits a law office, and even more importantly, can accommodate your own billing idiosyncrasies.

2. Take a small bite first. In keeping with the "start small" rule, it is wise to choose a package that has expansion modules. You will pay less and have a chance to become accustomed to the billing module before deciding to expand to the general ledger, accounts receivable, docket, management reports, etc. You may even decide you do not like the software well enough to buy additional modules and would rather purchase separate packages. It is useful, but not required that all the parts are integrated, and can share common information.

The choices include legal solutions which have time and billing incorporated into a larger practice management system for lawyers, or more flexible stand alone systems. Programs which are built into complete solutions are often not the best for general accounting, though more than adequate on the billing side. General accounting packages frequently have time billing and job costing modules that are flexible enough or customizable enough to be more than adequate for a law firm. Because they are sold to a larger market than attorneys, they often are better priced. Be sure that your needs are met by the software. Firms which pay the partners on the basis of the receipts of the clients will want software which reports this information. Law firms that post the non-billable as well as the billable hours will want software that does that easily. If accounting data is reported on a regular basis to the partners, then a general ledger with adequate financial formatting of the reports may be important as well. When operating on a network with many lawyers it is crucial to have a system that provides time sheets electronically for processing by the accounting staff without having to perform data entry. Sophisticated time billing software often allows the practitioner to time the phone call or visit or time spent working on a project by typing a simple keystroke to initiate the time keeping function.

Time Billing vs. Job Costing

One of the primary uses of computers in law offices continues to be for managing billings. There are different levels of accounting and integration between billing software and accounting software. Complete packages as far as accounting are concerned will have time billing integrated with the Accounts Receivable and in turn to the Accounts Payable and General Ledger. At the simplest level, time billing is just what the name indicates: a billing software that records and bills time and reimbursables to a client. A more sophisticated type of software adds the ability to track hours and expenses to a specific job for a client; therefore with long term clients who have many projects ongoing, you are able to get a cost breakdown by project. Cost breakdowns enable you to determine where you are with the budget allotted for the project. In addition to including the hours billed and reimbursables for any one project, job costing software usually incorporates the billing and expensing of cost items at a single entry point. In one example a cost is entered into the payables for printing. The payable is entered into Accounts Payable and the proper amount allocated to a job for subsequent billing. The job costing software automatically adds in any overage factor (flat or percentage). When the billing is printed and posted it will include any sales tax necessary where applicable (more states are requiring sales tax on various printing and imaging documents). It will accrue the receivable as well as the payable in one entry (well, maybe 2 postings, but at least there is no discrepancy between the figures for the expense and the billing).

For internal use at a law firm, reports can be generated in sophisticated job cost packages that show the performance of other attorneys in billable hours, unbillable hours, and the receipts against hours billed. Payments and disbursements can be made in relation to the cash received on projects. Bills to vendors and contractors can be paid when clients pay invoices for them. Profitability can be used to determine whether a project is worthwhile pursuing. Good software will even allow for graphing the data for reports. Information over time is plotted.

Job costing and billing software contain options to bill clients on the unpaid balance. By charging interest on unpaid balances the aging is reduced. Regular statements generated by the accounting software facilitate the cash flow problem when interest charges appear. As the cost of running and operating a law practice increases, more office services are itemized and billed to the client to offset the overhead. Charges for reproducing or sending material are billed. Computers and document imaging or other technology are amortized over the use and a figure billed that reflects the cost of these assets to reduce the capital investment in equipment.

The choice of which system is best really depends on a combination of your requirements and what your budget allows.

Timeslips has long been a standard used by many law practices and it is reasonably priced. However it is not a full accounting system and must be mated to the accounting software if that is required. Fortunately Timeslips has a package called Timeslips Accounting Link which automates this process.

Electronic Spreadsheets

An electronic spreadsheet is a widely useful computer application that allows future projection of financial or numerical data. It allows the attorney to play the "What If" game. For instance, an estate plan that is based on the client surviving to 90, could be almost instantly modified to consider the results if the client only survived to 80, or if he gave away half his estate at 60, etc. Laborious calculations that might previously have taken hours, if they had been attempted at all, can now be accomplished in seconds.

This software package may not be a first round draft choice for many or perhaps most attorneys. It depends on the nature of your practice, and the amount of time you are willing to spend playing with developing a system suited to it. Estate planning and tax consultation are obvious candidates for a spreadsheet, but personal injury damage calculations, real estate development and family law are also in the running. If in doubt—wait it out—and consider this a second round purchase.

At the simplest level a spreadsheet can be used to calculate figures. The ability to change the information and result in a single keystroke make them ideal for the "What If" inquiry. On the higher end, spreadsheets like databases, can be customized for substantive legal work. With powerful database and macro functions built into such powerhouses as Excel and Lotus, forms and legal documents can be generated with the simple entry of the few requisite items. Mail order catalogue companies offer inexpensive templates for standard forms and calculations and often can replace the purchase of more expensive dedicated software.

More than just mathematical results are generated by the spreadsheets of today. Excel or Wingz or Lotus have very powerful graphing tools built in and can be customized for a graphic output. Microsoft has built special links between Word and Excel so the spreadsheet information can be placed into the word processor i.e. for a report. Then if the information is updated on the spreadsheet it is simultaneously updated in the word processor.

Some leading software packages are:

MS–DOS: Lotus 123, Quattro Pro

Windows: Excel, Lotus

Mac: Excel, Wingz, Lotus 123, Spreadbase (a relational database in spreadsheet format)

UNIX: Wingz

Communications Software

Whether you want to transmit and receive data across the street or across three continents you will need a communications software package in addition to a modem (to be considered in hardware). You may not consider electronic mail or WESTLAW to be among your first priorities. Think again. There is literally a whole world of information available through telecommunications and you don't have to start with an expensive subscription service like WESTLAW or LEXIS. Begin with sending information and receiving helpful information through the relatively inexpensive ABA/net. Take advantage of one of the commercial electronic mail services, such as MCI Mail to deliver documents to clients or colleagues across the country in two hours. Once you become accustomed to the idea you can expand your net to include legal and factual information databases at your own pace.

Communications software itself is not expensive and there are many competitive brands focusing on a general business market. Both WESTLAW and LEXIS offer their specialized communication software to more easily access their data bases at a low price. The required hardware, the modem, is more expensive (less than $500), but a good investment.

To be able to communicate across the office rather than across the street, you may need different communications software with cables that link PCs together within the office. You do not need a modem for this since you are not using the telephone lines. If you are buying more than one PC initially it is wise to make certain that software and hardware are available to develop a local area network, even if you have no immediate plans to link them together.

Fax Modems

Fax modems can be extremely useful. In most cases you are able to send a well formatted document to a fax machine with extremely high resolution. Sending it to another fax modem device allows that person to print it to a laser printer for maximum resolution. The software for this in most instances allows you to simply issue a print command and instead of printing to a printer, it is sent to the fax modem.

Modems

Modems are the heart of the telecommunications from your computer to the telephone. The software you use to command the modem is often very powerful and can be very bewildering to the beginner. We call this configuring the software for your modem and the particular other party the modem will be contacting. Each modem manufacturer requires a special set of instructions for the modems they make. General modem software therefore will require that you do this before you can use the programs. You will have to do this for each person or email service or information service. Inexpensive software often requires that you reprogram this each time. Better software allows each to be saved and when you call that person the next time, you merely select that person's phone in an address book and use the settings you need for them. In many cases it is the same setting so there is no problem. As modems increase in speed and power, the complexity of their instructions also increases. There is a trend now for these to be built into software so that you merely select the type of modem.

Specialized on-line services frequently offer custom software. While you may use the general software as well, the customized software may allow you to navigate easily throughout the service while the general software either requires that you learn the command language of the system, or that you learn a sophisticated scripting language in the general telecommunications software and program the scripts for the work you do on that service. Personally I would recommend spending the extra money and use different software for each of the separate services that I belong to.

Local Area Network (LAN)/Email software

Communications between computers on a LAN inside the office requires an entirely different type of software. To understand the difference between email outside your office and within the office, remember this: to communicate on email outside an office a modem is required which converts the data into sounds that are transmitted over the phone lines; a LAN based email system requires no outside connection. The physical LAN within the office is sufficient to carry the information. The physical part of the network (the wires and connectors) is called the Local Area Network Architecture or Topology. Next is the file sharing device or method: dedicated, or peer to peer. Dedicated file serving software is Novell (DOS and Mac), or AppleShare (Mac). Peer to peer software is LanTastic (DOS) or TOPS (DOS, UNIX, or Mac). These systems will allow for transferring documents or sharing them, but are not convenient for sending memos to someone which require a response, nor are they convenient for sending a document *directly* to a particular person on a network. Either method uses a type of software to allow use of the data or software over the network.

For sending memos and files between different computers within the office, email software is also required if not built into the file sharing software. Such software as Microsoft Mail (MS–DOS,

UNIX, and Mac), QuickMail (Mac and Windows), and cc:Mail (MS–DOS and Mac) are optimized for sending memos or files to individuals or groups easily. These programs also log the mail sent and can request responses from the recipient as well as notifying him when mail is in his inbox. These system based email programs can be used to link to affiliates or branch offices at other locations automatically via modems. By bridging two or more email networks with modems, email can be sent directly to another computer in another office automatically. By adjusting the priorities, this can be done immediately or programmed to wait until there is a certain volume of mail or at a certain time (when rates are off peak, etc.). In addition LAN based email software may link to email on the on line services email. For example it is possible to have QuickMail on your office machine dial up MCI Mail, collect your mail automatically and distribute it to the appropriate person in your office. Newer versions of LAN based email even allow you to record voice messages along with the written message so you can pass along the appropriate tone with the message. Email is one of the most used software programs in office with more than one or two computers.

Specialized Legal Software

We are in the midst of a boom in legal specialty software. Tax packages, which appeal to a large business market, have been available for several years, but now we are now seeing offerings in litigation support, real estate amortization, family law, estate planning, corporate law, will drafting, fiduciary accounts, etc.

Specialized law software is usually built in three ways: Software written from scratch in a programming language, software that is a customized database package, and finally forms. Forms may be templates made for a word processor program or they may be designed in a forms design program, with or without a database behind them for storage of information.

If you are buying a PC specifically to enhance your specialty practice in say, estate planning, then you certainly want to consider available estate planning software in the first round. If you are not sure how a specialized package might fit into your practice, *wait*. When you become more familiar with the system, you will have a better idea of how to make use of specialized software.

With specialized applications which require complicated computations, like tax or estate planning, it is probably wise to select already developed software. With other specialty areas, such as family law or will drafting, it may be preferable to develop your own specialized system with a general word processing program. A general data base management system can be used to develop your specialized requirements for litigation support, calendars, and general case management. The advantage of developing your own specialized systems is that you do not have to change your habits. If you spent 10 years developing some good will forms you probably do not want to adopt someone else's work product. A new calendaring system could initiate chaos in your office, while automating the old system would not. Every lawyer prides himself on his individuality and automation does not require crushing that quality.

If you do have the need for a specialized package, first be certain that it will function with your operating system and then insist upon a thorough demonstration of the system. Money should not be the primary criteria in evaluating this software. If a system does not work well it will cost you a great deal in wasted labor and frustration.

Finding Software

Most applications in a law office can be handled by general business software such as word processing, data base management systems, and electronic spreadsheets. These will be available at all computer stores. Most computer stores will carry at least one time keeping and billing package for law offices, but you can also order almost any package through them. Ask for recommendations from friends, look at bar journal reviews and reviews in periodicals like the ABA's *Law Office Economics and Management,* or other technical periodicals for lawyers. *The Lawyer's PC,* published by McGraw Hill offers regular reviews and a yearly catalog of legal software.

Litigation support packages are a popular new software product and are being widely advertised. Other substantive packages such as specific packages for tax or trust accounting, for family law, estates, etc. are more difficult to find. A general software catalog will include them, and these catalogs are usually available at your computer dealer. The ABA *Law Office Economics and Management,* and *The Lawyer's PC* are valuable references for this software as well. You can always write directly to the software manufacturer if you learn of a particular specialized product that interests you. Again, it is always possible and often preferable to develop your own systems rather than relying on packaged systems.

A general rule with all specialized software is to insist upon a complete demonstration and references from other satisfied users. There are too many get-rich-quick software entrepreneurs offering products filled with glitches and bugs.

Finding Software:

Legal Software Review–Lawyer's Library, 12773 New Halls Ferry Road, Florissant, MO 63033 (800) 875–5649

Locate–ABA, Order Fulfillment 511, 750 N. Lake Shore Dr., Chicago, IL 60611 (312) 988–5555.

Law Office Computing: 3520 Cadillac Ave., Ste. E, Costa Mesa CA 92626 (714) 755 5466 Published 6 times per year/ $39.95 per year by James Publishing Group

**All computers
today need
virus protection!**

[G19633]

CHAPTER FIVE

Choosing Hardware

Technically speaking the computer is the little box which contains the brain, or Central Processing Unit, everything else is a peripheral device, including the keyboard, the disk drives and the screen or CRT (Cathode Ray Tube, also called a VDT or Video Display Terminal).

[G19634]

Sometimes when a computer is advertised at an outrageously low price the disappointed prospective buyer realizes you only get the Central Processing Unit for that price and the addition of the necessary peripherals brings the cost up to the old familiar range. In the case of compact machines such as the Apple Macintosh Classic or many of the laptop computers, the keyboard, CRT and disk drives are all included into one box and offered for one price complete.

Classic II

[G19635]

Normally the purchaser buys the entire package, CPU, keyboard, disk drives and CRT from the same manufacturer but will look to other manufacturers for other peripherals such as the printer or the modem. But it has become popular for computer retailers to assemble their own systems, using components from different manufacturers. These systems are called clones and often carry no brand name.

As discussed earlier with regard to software, if you already have computer hardware and it is two years old or older, it is essential that you review the hardware, compare it to what is now available, and make decisions about renewing the system and possibly expanding it. For example, a single attorney law practice with one older computer that leased a computer for $180 per month took 45 minutes *machine time* for the accounting software to produce the monthly statements. A newer faster computer could be leased for $155 per month and produced the same statements in 5 minutes! Obviously even a loss in paying off the lease and selling the old machine was a worthwhile investment if that 45 minutes saved could become a 45 minutes per day savings. At a rate of even $16 per hour, this means the new machine saved $12 per day or $60 per week. In addition there is the factor of the user *feeling* more empowered by increased productivity. Tools which increase the perception of being able to accomplish tasks in less time, make office staff feel more important, with the sense of being able to accomplish more.

When choosing new hardware systems or when considering adding to your current system, the first consideration must be the operating system. If purchasing for the first time the decision is usually made based on the software available, and the ease of use of a system. When upgrading or adding machines, you might consider adding machines which have a different system than the original ones. There may be an advantage to running certain software packages on one operating system while new machines are used to perform different functions. A law office with 4 partners chose to keep their accounting running on the MS–DOS clone they already had because it served their purpose and there was a trained person who operated it. The firm decided to purchase additional Macintoshes for the secretaries, office manager and partners because of the ease of use and networking capabilities. A network card was added to the MS–DOS clone which enabled it to communicate on email with the Macs, and to use the same printer as the Macs.

Once you have chosen your operating system, and decided upon your first round software purchases, you will start to investigate computer hardware which will support your choices. The reassuring news here is that any system which supports your operating system will probably do the job well. Although computers are technically complex, they are quite uniform; there are only a few processing chips shared by all manufacturers, and more problems are likely to occur with the software than the hardware. This does not mean that you should not be concerned about warranties and availability of parts and repair, but most dealers and repair services handle many different brands, and it is not necessary to go with the most famous brands, i.e., IBM, APPLE or Compac to get good service and repair. With hardware, more than with software, you can shop with your pocketbook.

If you are looking for the rock bottom bargain, you should investigate the clones put together with no manufacturer's mark. The things to watch out for are:

1. Is there a one year warranty on parts and service from a reputable local dealer? (This eliminates many mail order models)

2. The system should include a minimum configuration of 2 megabytes of memory for a MS–DOS machine and 4 megabytes for a Macintosh, one hard disk and one floppy disk drive, and both a parallel and a serial port, one for connecting the printer and one for connecting the modem (Macintosh computers all have 2 serial ports and do not require a parallel port to connect to a printer).

BITS AND BYTES

There are some general technical issues to consider in purchasing the computer unit and the peripherals such as the printer and the modem.

Anyone who has followed computers at the most novice level, including reading computer news stories in the local newspaper, knows that both bits and bytes seem to be growing larger. PCs used to be advertised as 16 bit with a memory of 640 kilobytes, and are now advertised as 32 bit with 2 megabytes to several megabytes of memory.

What does this all mean to the potential buyer? Basically, without a complex explanation of how computers work, it means that computers with larger bit sizes operate more quickly and with more kilobytes they can handle more complicated commands and more data in their main memory. For the legal professional it means that certain applications, particularly those requiring large databases, such as litigation support, or those requiring complicated computations and large data bases, like large office timekeeping and billing, can be more efficiently handled by 32 bit machines with at least 2 megabytes of memory.

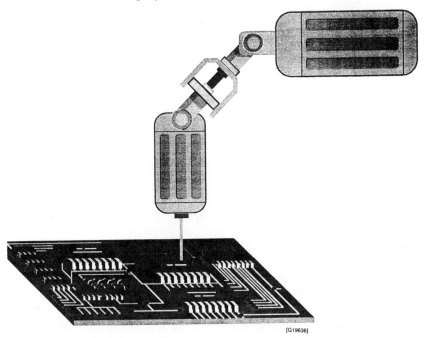

[G19636]

The trend is obviously toward the more powerful machines, rendering the first generation of 8 bit, 64 kilobyte computers obsolete since software is no longer written for these machines. But the fact is that no matter what you buy, it will probably be obsolete in a few years and if you still get service from an old-fashioned, out-of-date computer, it may not be a good idea to turn it in just to be up to date.

For most offices a 16 bit IBM–286 or 386 compatible which runs on MS–DOS or a Mac Classic or Mac II series which is expandable will be a good choice for virtually all of your law office applications. If you plan to develop a very large database of information for a large case, or if you have more than 100 clients to bill, the more expensive IBM–386 or Mac II, with its larger main memory, larger hard disk capacity and greater speed is a good choice. Many prefer the compatibles, such as COMPAQ and Dell. Clones with no brand name produced by your local computer store will be the least expensive choice, but you must pay attention to the guidelines offered above. Other manufacturers, such as APPLE, may be expanded (at additional cost), to handle an MS–DOS operating system or Windows.

DISKS: FLOPPY OR HARD?

Briefly, magnetic disks are the storage medium where all information and program instructions are stored when not being actively processed in the main memory of the central processing unit. First generation 8 bit computers almost universally offered storage only on floppy disks, usually 5 and $\frac{1}{4}''$ in. diameter that were put in and taken out of disk drives with each computer use.

[G19637]

Newer floppy disks are 3.5 inches and hold much more data.

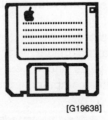

[G19638]

The most efficient of these hold at most about 120 pages of text. The second generation of PCs often boast hard fixed disks which can hold several million bytes of information, or several thousand pages. It is rare that a single legal document will extend beyond 120 pages, but it is not so rare to have more than 120 pages of documents, even in abstract or index form, in preparation for trial. If there are several billing attorneys or paralegals and more than 100 clients, the billing information will certainly take up more than 120 pages. Floppies however are becoming more and more interchangeable. All MS–DOS floppies except the 2.8 megabyte floppies can be read by both Sun UNIX machines and Macintosh floppy drives. With the Mac you may need file translation software to bring the drive up, but there are vendors which produce utilities for mounting the MS–DOS disks on the Mac. Sun OS has that built in now. By the summer of 1992 there will be software available to run the Macintosh disks and software on UNIX based machines. There are programs which will mount Macintosh disks on MS–DOS machines now. The lines between operating systems are becoming less well defined with time and compatibility between systems is less of an issue. There is even a software program that runs MS–DOS on the Macintosh and it formats the MS–DOS disks in the same disk drive on the Mac as is used to run the Mac system. Because hard disk storage has become so inexpensive it makes sense to purchase a computer with one hard disk drive and one floppy disk drive. The floppy disk will be used to load information and to back up the information on the hard disk. Years ago people were able to operate machines with just two floppies; one usually contained the data and the other held the operating system and program. Today this is not feasible. Each computer must have its own hard disk. A beginning computer today should have at least a 40 megabyte hard disk; an 80–100 megabyte disk is preferable.

Since the hard disk is where all the programs, system, and data are stored, you want enough space to easily accommodate the information you will be working with for some time into the future. As a hard disk gets full, it slows down and problems may occur with the software. Files usually become fragmented, that is pieces of the file are written to various places on the hard disk where there is room, and the hard disk has to search over the whole disk medium to assemble all the data into memory (RAM) in order to work. It is a good idea to not let a hard disk become more than $\frac{2}{3}$ to $\frac{3}{4}$ full. When a disk becomes full, you have several options. You can buy a larger disk and replace it (there is almost no resale value in used hard disks however), you can add a second hard disk to the system, that is daisy chain them together, or you can move some of the information that you do not need currently to floppy disks or some other storage medium.

If you have a very large database, it might make sense to purchase an additional back up system, perhaps a magnetic tape system (see discussion chapter 12). The one story that seems universal among all computer users is how they lost two days, two weeks, or two months (the stories vary slightly) of work when the power went out, or the coffee spilled on the disk, etc. You should always make a copy of your disk after each working session, insuring that barring extreme disaster, or extraordinary clumsiness, the work will always be preserved on at least one disk. For most of your law office applications, however, one floppy disk drive will be sufficient for this purpose.

Hard disks are by no means infallible. A regular back up of a hard disk is mandatory (for a detailed discussion, see chapter 12). How often you make a back up depends on how important it is for you to try to recreate the lost data. For accounting software it is essential that a back up is made every day. That way if something goes wrong with the data all you will need to reenter is today's data.

HOW MANY COMPUTERS?

The minimum number of computer terminals and supporting hardware you must purchase depends on the tasks you are currently performing. Begin with an individual task survey and a software needs assessment presented here, before you attempt a hardware needs assessment.

When configuring the office, if there are to be more than 4 or 5 computers, one should think about adding a file server to the system. A file server is a high speed computer with a large storage capacity that only runs file server software. It is used to store data that several people need to access. This data may either be files that are stored for later use by someone else on the network, or for storing large files such as databases. A file server may be the only way to tie all the information together. Multi-user databases often require as much speed as possible because they are used by many people at the same time. Therefore the file servers are often optimized for this kind of work.

ASSESSING YOUR HARDWARE NEEDS

(This must be done in conjunction with your individual task survey and your software needs assessment chart)

1. Number of computers:

a. How many computers do you have in your office that are used more than 40% of the working day? _____

(This is the minimum number of PCs that you need)

b.   Do you plan to computerize your litigation support functions?

If so you will need to equip one PC with a suitably sized hard disk. (This PC may double for word processing functions, if it is not used more than 50% of the time for that function).

c.   Do you plan to computerize your timekeeping and billing functions?

If so you will need at least one-half time use of a PC for this function. If you have more than 100 clients this computer should have a hard disk of at least 80 megabytes.

d.   Do you plan to use WESTLAW or LEXIS?

e.   Do you plan to join ABA/net or subscribe to another electronic service? If so you will need at least one-half time use of a PC. This PC must be outfitted with a modem.

The above are the minimal guidelines for computer purchase. Ideally each attorney and each legal worker would have a terminal, but it is not necessary to begin in this fashion.

2.   Number and quality of printers:

A heavy-duty laser printer with print spooling can run all day (and even into the night if necessary). It can probably support the output of many attorneys (up to between 5–10 depending on the work load); if multipart forms are to be processed then a good quality dot matrix printer may be required as well. Additional less expensive slower laser printers or ink jet printers may serve as additional or back up printers where heavy usage on a main computer is required. If usage is very heavy you may wish to limit the number of computers to laser printers to a **7 to 1** ratio.

3.   Other hardware:

Your office needs at least one modem for electronic mail or for accessing information data bases such as WESTLAW, LEXIS or ABA/net.

You may wish to link your PCs together using local area network hardware and software systems as such Ethernet on MS–DOS systems or AppleTalk on Macs.

MODEM?

Computers can communicate with each other over standard telephone lines. Telephone lines are set up for voices, naturally, and send an analog electrical signal which is continuous in form. Computers communicate in a different electronic mode and their signals are digital, or on and off, in form. The word modem means modulate de modulate. It is a device that enables you to translate the digital information in a computer to the analog tones and pulses carried over the phone lines. A modem is required at both ends of the process; it must be attached to both computers—the one sending the information and the one receiving it as well.

You may say that you can pick up a telephone to talk to another attorney, a client, or the court, or you can use the mails or a fast courier service to deliver documents; or you might connect to your office via your lap top while traveling. Like many new devices its usefulness is not always immediately apparent. However, it is probably the communications ability of computers that will ultimately change the nature of your law practice most significantly. Not to list again the great variety of applications made possible through communications (See Chapter Two: Law Office Without Walls), but a modem can bring almost all the world's legal and technical knowledge to your desk, and it has the potential of almost eliminating paper from law practice, as courts and clients accept electronic documents.

Yet it is possible to start very small and a modem should be included with your initial purchases, unless your budget is truly rock bottom. Fortunately the price of modems has decreased significantly over the past few years and for a few hundred dollars you can purchase a powerful modem (9600 baud) with automatic dialing capacities; this permits an almost instant connection to computers you deal with frequently, like WESTLAW. You may begin with modest attempts, like taking advantage of the relatively inexpensive ABA/net to schedule your airline reservations, but you can expand your net at any time to include sophisticated information databases and electronic exchange of documents.

The speed of a modem is measured in Baud Rate. This is the transmission of how many bits of data can be transmitted per second over a phone line. When modems were first introduced many were 300 baud and a fast modem was 1200. Today these rates have increased dramatically through increased transmission as well as a technology known as data compression. A standard modem today is usually 2400 baud and a fast modem is 9600 baud, with some capable of transmitting 14,400 baud over the phone lines. When you read the specifications of these new faster modems they will often say things like 9600 baud capable of 57,000 bits per second throughput with v.42bis and v.42 error correction. This means that there is in the hardware of the modem the ability to collect the data from the computer, compress it into small packets and send it out at high speed. The actual transmission over the phone may only be 9600 baud, but the amount of data sent is much higher because the modem has chips that receive it from the computer faster than the modem can send it, and at the same time reduce the size of the data to be sent using special technology. To receive the data from the computer as fast as it can, these modems also require special cables that enable what is known as hardware handshake. This allows the modem to tell the computer how fast and how much data it can receive before sending it over the phones.

Computers can send data to the modem many times faster than the modem can send it over the phone wires. In order for this high speed technology to work there also has to be error correction. When modems were only 300 or 1200 baud, the error correction was usually handled by the telecommunications software in the computer. With higher speeds of transmission the software could not keep up, so more sophisticated modems also do their own error checking. Error checking sends a signal out to the modem at the other computer to see if the packets of information that were sent were received correctly. Sometimes noise and interference on the phone lines causes the packet to be damaged in transmission. The error checking tells the computer to resend the data. The amount of data or information in each packet can be varied by the software for the telecommunications. Packets are usually 128 bytes, 512 bytes or 1 kilobyte. Naturally the larger the packet the fewer number of times that error checking will occur so the transmission is faster. Of course when a bad packet is found, more information has to be resent. When purchasing a modem it is important to consider the quality of the modem especially if you live in an area in which the phone lines are not as clean. Areas with fiber optic and modern equipment have cleaner phone lines and better transmission of data. As you move farther into the countryside, it is a wise decision to consider purchasing a better quality modem. The extra money spent on the hardware saves on phone bills that result from errors in transmission.

A standard has been developed for the commands that are issued to the modems by computers called the Hayes Commands. Modems that are Hayes compatible ensure a standard for communications. However there are varying degrees of compatibility. Your best assurance that a modem is compatible is purchasing one of the standard name brands such as Hayes, US Robotics or other similar companies. These modems are often the most expensive, frequently 2–3 times more expensive than other ones. If you wish to save money on purchasing a modem, you may have to spend extra time configuring your telecommunications software. This can be very trying, but once you have it configured you will never need to do this again. You will need to configure the software for the particular service or computer you are communicating with by setting various parameters and commands to the modem. If you set your modem to a faster speed and it connects to one that is set slower, the modems usually adjust the rate, but just about everything else must be set manually. This mystifying process may require that you call in a specialist to set up your telecommunications the first time, but after that you will generally have no problems except for the phone lines.

Modem vendors are now providing many new features with their products. Many modems today include fax technology. This enables you to send and receive faxes from the computer. A file created in a computer is printed to the fax modem instead of a printer. The resulting output to a standard fax machine is far superior to the normal fax transmission. If a fax is received either from a fax machine or another fax modem, the output can be sent to your standard laser printer to produce a high resolution output. In addition the file can be stored and archived in the computer for further use without having to use paper output if so desired. This is a very cost effective way to add fax capabilities to an office since you can usually purchase a modem-fax modem for less money than you can buy a stand alone fax machine. The main drawback is that you need to have the computer on in order to receive the fax. Also some of the fax modem software may interfere with certain other programs since it must be running in the background.

Fax modem-modems (modems which have fax capacity) can be extremely handy when used with portable notebook computers. With this combination in a portable you can call your office to get electronic mail, log onto a service such as WESTLAW to get your mail or other data, and if you are traveling and in a hotel you can use the fax machine in the hotel lobby as a printing device instead of having to carry a printer or locate one. If you need to print something at your office, there is software available such as AppleTalk Remote that enables you to log onto your own computer machine at your office and print to the computer attached to it or on your local area network. In addition to fax capabilities, new modems are adding voice mail technology as well. These modems can distinguish between incoming fax, incoming computer data and a phone call from a person. In addition cellular technology has been added to modems which will allow you to communicate without the need for plugging into phone jacks (a handy feature if you stay in one of those motels where the phones are permanently wired into the wall). Or you may simply be in some office where it is not practical to break into their phone service to get a file you badly need from your office.

Recent developments in phone company service have paved the way for even faster communications between computers than standard phone lines are capable of providing. These newer phone lines are of two types: dedicated digital networks and switched networks. Digital networks provide the same kind of digital transmission that your computer uses. One example of this is a standard called ISDN (Integrated Services Digital Network). In order to operate, your computer must be attached to a special phone service line that provides this service and a card or circuit board on the computer that can access it.   In the US this is in limited use in Silicon Valley.   In France the national phone service Minitel has provided this service to every phone user in the country.   The result is that very high speed data communication is possible everywhere in the country.   This system provides very clear communication and the type of error checking necessary with modems on normal phone lines (and the resulting slow down in communications) is absent.   Recently several areas of the US have implemented a mixed technology called switched networks: Switched 56.   In March of 1992 California implemented this service over the entire state.   It allows for the use of phone lines to transmit data in digital form by activating switches at the phone company switching office.   The user must be within 8 miles of the center, sign up at a cost of $1250, and add approximately $1500 of communication hardware to his computer.   Considering this same equipment cost about $5000 a year ago, you can expect to see the prices of this same service and hardware drop dramatically as the number of people using it increases.   What this means to the end user is that the cost of accessing on line databases will come down dramatically.

LOCAL AREA NETWORKS

You do not need a modem to connect computers together within an office, but you do need specialized cables and communications software.   If you are purchasing more than one PC, it is useful to have them communicate with each other to exchange documents, or perhaps to share a common hard disk.   The subject of networks is a very complex issue.   The simplest form of network is called a LAN or Local Area Network.   Several computers linked to a common printer is a LAN.   The same LAN can be used to connect several computers in such a way as to share data or to access a file server with common data stored on it.   By adding additional software the same LAN can be made to do several things.   As the LAN grows and more people use the network, performance usually declines.   When it declines to an unacceptable level, then a faster network type must be used.   For example, all Macintosh computers come with networking built in, called Apple-Talk.   By adding wires and a simple $35 connector to each machine AppleTalk can be installed.   The physical hardware of the network is called LocalTalk and the software protocols are the AppleTalk.   This is a reasonable solution that is very inexpensive. It allows you to connect several machines to a common printer, communicate between machines (i.e. send files, electronic mail, etc., depending on the software) and to access a file server.   When there are more than a handful of users the performance declines.   Think of AppleTalk as a 1 lane highway.   As the network traffic increases, the data lines up behind each other and waits its turn to be processed. If many people are accessing a multi-user database it can become maddeningly slow to look something up or to add a new record.

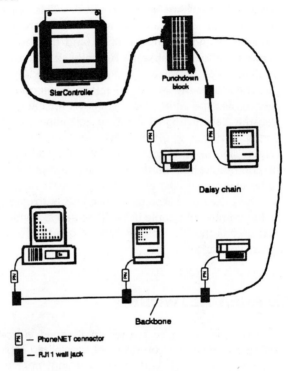

StarController connecting daisy chain and backbone branches
[G19639]

The network can be speeded up by changing the configuration. We call the map of a network the topology. A single wire running through an office is called a backbone topology. Computers can be attached off this singly or in side chains. Moving up the ladder is a star topology—either passive or active. In this configuration all the computers are wired to several backbones that radiate out from a central point—usually located where the telephone wiring punch down blocks are in an office building. An active star has the same topology but a star controller is added. All the backbones connect to this electronic device that sorts out the traffic to the different spokes in the star. By using the star configuration traffic can be isolated in such a way as to keep the heavy users from interfering with other people on a network. If changing the topology does not solve the speed problems on the network, then a faster network is required. Ethernet is the next level up from AppleTalk. Try to think of Ethernet as a 10 lane freeway in our example. If you are sending a lot of traffic out on the network, there are passing lanes available so that someone else using the network is not slowed down. Again topology plays a factor. You can run Ethernet in a backbone topology, but the distances allowed are very short. Ethernet can be cabled using thick wire (coaxial cable), thin wire, or phone wire (called 10 base T). You could make a backbone with thick wire up to 300 feet; with thin wire the total is 75 feet. An active star topology changes that. Each run of a 10 base T off a star can be up to 300 feet. There is a large difference between installing a simple AppleTalk network for $35 per node plus some phone wire, to several thousand dollars for merely a few computers to install an Ethernet with special cable, a $2000 star controller and a person to wire it. In addition each machine also requires an Ethernet card @ $300–400 each and depending on which wiring is used, an additional transceiver for another $175 per machine. Initially Ethernet was not as popular: if one machine went down or was removed, a special terminator had to be manually installed at that node to prevent the network from going down. More recently "Plug and Play" style Ethernet now allows you to disconnect a machine without any problems.

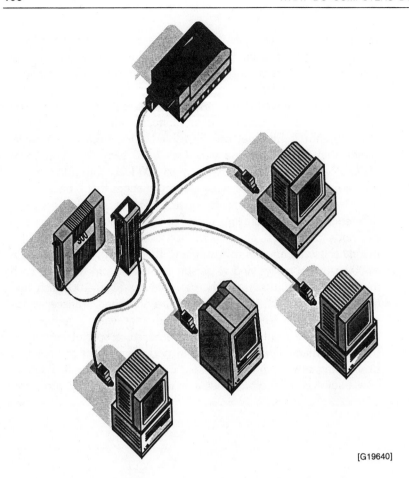

[G19640]

Larger and more complex LANs require even more sophisticated networks than Ethernet can provide. Generally these alternate networks are not used with systems having only PCs but are
used in networks which combine minicomputers with PCs. One of
the more sophisticated networks is called Token Ring. In this type
of network packets of information race around the network at all
times and when data is sent on the network it is simply attached to
these racing packets called Token. It is extremely doubtful that
these systems would be seen in a law practice except in very large
corporations in which the legal department is operating on a
corporate network.

WORKSTATIONS

There is a powerful big brother to the personal computers of
today. These machines are called Workstations and are usually

many times more powerful than the personal computers of today. They may become the personal computers of tomorrow as the technology improves and the prices to manufacture them decreases. These machines are based on a technology called RISC technology or Reduced Instruction Set Chip. A normal PC (Intel 80X86 or Motorola 680X0) is powered by a CISC technology or Complex Instruction Set Chip. CISC chips have a large number of instructions built into them that can be addressed by the operating system and the programs you use. RISC chips have far fewer instructions and as a result are able to process data very rapidly. Today there is less software available for these machines as the programming required is more complex and so they are not as suitable for general use. Advances by such leaders in RISC technology as Sun Microsystems and third party vendors are creating interpretive software that will enable many of the standard MS–DOS and Mac software to operate on these machines. IBM and Apple have signed a joint agreement to co-produce such an operating system for the newer higher speed RISC machines. Code named Taligent, the venture is hoped to further integrate hardware so it will run on any machine which runs UNIX, MS–DOS, or MacOS etc. in a user friendly environment that will make programming easier and additions or specializations to the operating system more available. While these new machines are faster and more powerful than the personal computers, the main advantage to their use is either with graphics programs or in network functions. Since graphics use is generally only of limited specialized use in the legal profession, more often these machines are used where a more powerful file server is required for a network situation. Corporate law firms with 200 attorneys and 300 staff users who are required to access a common set of files or data would be the main application of these machines.

PORTABLES

The largest growing segment of computers today is actually in the opposite end of the spectrum from the workstations—the portables. Only a few years ago portables were expensive, heavy devices with limited capacities. Today portables are decreasing in size and weight while increasing in power and function with each passing year. Portables are fast with 386 or 68030 CPUs and hard disks in the 100 megabyte range weighing between 4–6 pounds. Screen technology has developed dramatically with back-lit active matrix technology providing extremely sharp resolution. Color screens have recently begun appearing although in limited use because of the drain on batteries. Rechargeable batteries for laptops provide from 2.5 to 6 hours on a charge depending on the manufacturer.

A portable computer will be in the future of most computer users, but it may not be the first purchase unless you have special needs. (For example, if you travel more than 25% of the time, and your office is literally your suitcase.) For daily intensive use the stability and comfort of a well-designed desk computer will probably never be challenged by portables. And of course you need a larger scale letter quality printer for any work product that is sent to clients or courts. When you do buy that portable computer you should be certain it is compatible with your office computer so that you can transfer data from one to the other without complicated manipulations. You should also be certain the software programs it uses are the same or similar to those on your office computer or you will have a frustrating experience transferring back and forth.

In addition to providing the ability to work in any environment, from airplanes to hotels, laptops enable attorneys to communicate with their office either with fax, or modem —via email, or by direct connection to their office network. Connection via modem to the office network enables you to either access or copy files that you may need while away from the office, send memos to the office members via a local email network in the office, or to print directly to networked printers in your office. Connection to major email services are extremely handy for communicating with other people and for such services as on line travel services. Flight reservations and scheduling can be made directly over the modem. Weather information at remote locations can be found. Checking and banking services are even available on line for payments and financial information. Newer cellular modems allow this type of linking even while traveling in an automobile or in an office or motel where phone communication may not be feasible. Documents that have to be filed in courts can be faxed directly to the court in areas where the court accepts fax input. Notes in courtrooms may be entered into portable computers for use in witness examination. Notes taken during a deposition can be referenced to transcripts obtained on disk from a court report. Portable technology is constantly moving in the direction of smaller size and ease of use. New portables are being manufactured with fewer features to decrease the size and weight. These portables then plug into desktop docking stations for added functionality. In addition to adding disk drive, larger monitor and extended keyboard functions at the docking station, it is possible to add overhead projection for meetings and discussions. Portables are plugged into overhead projection units at local sites and all the data is conveyed in the portable. MS–DOS portables today are well under $2000 for 386 machines with an 80 meg hard disk and active matrix screen, weighing between 4–6 pounds. Apple Computer has a series of Powerbook portables which weigh between 6–7 pounds cost between $2500–$3500 with 80 megabyte hard disks and excellent display. Plans from all manufacturers include smaller, faster, lighter portables, with new machines including color displays on the higher end.

[G19641]

Apple computer has announced plans to manufacture new devices called Personal Digital Assistants or PDAs. These are hand held devices so small that keyboard entry will not be practical. Instead Apple has announced that input will be with pen devices or via voice. Within the year Apple will be producing voice recognition independent of accent and capable of fast input. The information in these PDAs, can be uploaded directly into a office computer or a portable notebook computer for further processing.

HEALTH AND SAFETY FACTORS

Ergonomics is the fancy computerese term to describe the "science" of making the computer user comfortable. The eyes, neck, and back are the touchy areas, and a badly designed system can cause a great deal of discomfort and therefore inefficiency. Since it is not really the computer but rather the computer furniture in an office that often dictates the positioning of the computer with respect to the user, careful consideration should be placed on the purchase of this equipment as well.

Positioning the Monitor and Keyboard

When computers were first introduced, the only history that people had relating to the positioning of the human body with keyboard devices was typewriters. It took several years before accumulated data revealed the effects of continued use of computers. Seating and positioning of the monitor and keyboards were among the first items that were determined as important. Seats for continued computer use must support the lower back; a good chair with lower lumbar support is essential. There are several devices that can be added to normal chairs that help with that. One simple device called a Nada chair is a sling arrangement that supports the lower back by strapping it to the knees and supports the back in a firm position eliminating the need for the muscles in the back to have to support it. Keyboards must be set slightly lower than a 90° plane with the body. Since almost all computers have a detachable keyboard today this is easy to do by adjusting the height of the chair relative to the desk. In addition it is advisable to have the monitor slightly lower than level with the eyes—about 15° lower so the neck is not strained. As the demand for more ergonomic tables and chairs increases better designs are being produced. Tables which allow for height adjustment of the keyboard as well as the adjustable height of the chair allow for individual configurations. In addition monitors can be set to different heights with floating platforms that telescope for fine tuning the height in relation to the other adjustments.

[G19642]

Repetitive Strain Syndrome

Most important the wrists must be supported when typing. Inexpensive wrist pads are available which are placed on the desk at the bottom edge of the keyboard for resting. Repetitive strain syndrome is a common result of improper support of the wrists and is becoming more prevalent as computer use increases. Since portables generally have the keyboard attached to the computer it is often difficult to configure them in a way to reduce the possibilities of strain. However, when Apple introduced the Powerbook series of notebook computers, they took special care in designing the keyboard to reduce this possibility. Instead of the keys being at the bottom edge of the computer as other manufacturers had done, Apple moved the keys up closer to the screen and left a platform at the lower edge of the computer for resting the palms. In addition, lifts were provided that raised the rear of the computer off the table slightly so the wrists were in the proper position for minimizing the strain. The same principles apply to desktop keyboards. Inexpensive support pads may be purchased to elevate the palm of the hands to the same level as the keyboards. In some states and cities, laws have been proposed in some areas to make it mandatory for employers to provide furniture that will minimize strain.

Radiation and Emission

In addition to the height adjustment there are considerations regarding the distance from the screen. Aside from the discussion of visual acuity, there is the issue of the radiation. It is well known that radiation from the screens of color monitors is far greater than that of black and white monitors. In addition, the radiation from the sides and back of the monitor is many times higher than from the front. It is recommended that you position yourself no closer than 12 inches from any monitor and certainly farther if you use color. There are devices that attach to the screen to reduce the radiation especially the EMF (electro magnetic frequencies) and the elf (extra low frequency). However these filters also reduce the brightness of the display, often increasing eye strain. In general, the normal display of the cathode ray tube or CRT (as in a television) is more of a strain than the LCD (liquid Crystal Display) of the portables that are backlit. Sweden has developed the most rigorous requirements for the maximum allowable emissions from monitors and all new monitors are now conforming to these standards.

The size of the monitor can also be a factor in ease of use. Many monitors are 12–13″ displays, following the example of the television industry. Full page display and 2 page display provide a better viewing area, enabling you to see a whole page at a time. This gives a better approximation of WYSIWYG (what you see is what you get). Combined with the type face representation, full page display enables you to view the complete document was it would print out, reducing the need for printing drafts.

A high resolution gray scale monitor is often sharper and easier on the eyes than a color monitor for long term use. Macintosh pioneered the black characters on a white background while most other manufacturers displayed white characters on a black background. The Macintosh display is far easier on the eyes over a long period and now other systems are beginning to display the same way. With the introduction of Windows for the MS–DOS operating systems, the traditional white characters on a black, amber or green background has been changed to the same as the

Macintosh. Whenever possible it is best to use black characters on a white background.

PRINTERS

Until the day of the paperless law office dawns, the attorney's major form of communication with the outside world will be printed text, or "hard copy" as it is called in the computer world. Law firms have always maintained a high standard for the quality of a finished product that leaves the office, both in content and in appearance. The arrival of almost universal word processing capacities makes that standard even higher. No longer will the discrete "white-out" or even the self-correcting strike-over key pass inspection. A document must now be letter perfect in all respects. It would therefore be a small disgrace to send out a document printed by a dot matrix printer, featuring the square sorts of letters that are popularly associated with computers.

Impact: Dot–Matrix and Daisy Wheel

Before dismissing the lowly dot matrix, it should be mentioned that these printers are inexpensive ($500 or less), and very fast, (up to 340 characters per second). For a second printer used only for in-house, or first draft purposes it is an acceptable choice.

Impact or dot matrix printers in law firms today are generally relegated to writing checks or forms where duplicate or multipart forms are processed. Daisy wheel printers, while higher in type quality, are almost never used.

Lasers Et al.

Today's law firms depend almost entirely on laser type printers. The prices of these printers has dropped to the point where an entry level laser printer will cost only about $900. Ink Jet technology has also become popular. The result is the entry level price for high quality printing is now under $400. Ink jets use a flow of ink through a fine jet nozzle to print. These printers are quite slow compared to lasers (ink jets produce a page every 1–2 minutes compared to lasers which offer between 4–16 pages a minute).

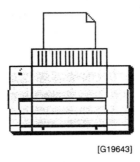

[G19643]

The resolution of ink jet printers is approximately equal to the standard laser printers however at about 300 dots per inch. One word of caution should be mentioned regarding the ink jet printers. The ink used in most of the printers i.e., the Hewlett Packard Ink Jet or Desk Writer etc., is partially water soluble. Output from the first versions of ink jet printers could be entirely made unreadable by smudging with water; newer versions have improved somewhat. For legal work this may be a problem. What if you were to write a contract only to have it disappear when it rained! Of course the alternative to this would be to take the output from the ink jet and Xerox copy it, but that is rather impractical. The inexpensive pricing of the true laser printers today makes the laser printer the first choice for the law office.

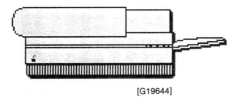

[G19644]

Newer laser printers have increased font resolution that approaches image setter (typesetter) quality. Hewlett Packard, IBM, and Apple all have laser printers now with 600 dots per inch resolution. Traditionally laser printers were fine for letters and communications, but if you wished to have something printed on a high speed printing press, the 300 dpi (dots per inch), the type could look a little fuzzy or bleed. Therefore for print ready brochures etc., the document was sent to a service bureau to be photo type set or image set at 1200 or 2400 dpi. With the increase in Desktop publishing, 600 and 800 dpi printers that are more affordable have been introduced, though significantly more expensive than the standard laser printer.

More recently, however, standard 300 dpi laser printers have been upgraded in a sophisticated way to approximate the output of these higher resolution printers without the substantially increased cost. This has been accomplished with new software built into the hardware (software that is permanently imbedded into chips is called Firmware) which changes the way the dots are shaped as they are output to the paper. One type of firmware smoothes the edges of the fonts since all font edges have jagged edges when magnified because they are composed of dots. This smoothing process is called anti-aliasing and is available on the newer genera- tion of printers. Another technology even changes the shape of the dots as they are printed. If all the dots are round, then there are spaced between the dots and edges of the dots can stick out or be curved inward. By changing the shape of the dots so that some of the dots are round and some are flattened like a cat's eye, the spacing can be changed and in a given space there can be more dots actually printed with the same basic laser printer. Since the same hardware is actually used these newer laser printers cost about the same as the old ones. The advantage to the law firm is that much of the material that previously had to be sent out to a service bureau for output now can be done on the same laser machine as the normal printing, reducing the overhead. In addi- tion some of the newer printers are using faster CPUs (central processing units—yes even the laser printers have CPUs just like the computer you use) which mean that the documents take less time to format until they are printed. On a network this can mean a reduction of the time spent waiting for the output.

Buffers=Print Spoolers

In the early days of word processors it was commonplace to see the word processor operator reading a book or staring at a blank screen while the work that he had typed was being printed. Usually the computer had so little memory that it could only perform one task at a time, and could not print while information was being entered. Most laser printers (and many of the ink jet printers) are network ready as they come. This enables several computers on a network to use the same printer, thereby dividing the cost of the printer by several computers. Normal use would require that each person wait until anyone else who is printing finish printing before they can continue using their computer. However there are software and in some cases hardware solutions that permit print spooling. When a user selects the print spooling option and then chooses to print a document, the document is stored on a hard disk in the background until the printer is available for use. The computer then sends the document to the printer selected. This is accomplished without interfering with the normal use of the computer by the user; the user is free to use his machine to continue doing other tasks.

A print spooler is a necessity for word processing, which is one of the major uses of your PC. In addition to freeing the word processor operator, it also allows you to share one printer among several microcomputers. The text from each PC is lined up (spooled) and printed in order (or out of order for rush demand). In addition to print spooling software you will need cables and appropriate software to share a printer, generally this is part of a LAN set up. There are many competing software packages at low price for this practical application.

OF MICE AND PENS: INPUT DEVICES

For those of you who are already computer users, it is difficult to appreciate the charms of mice or any other mechanical gadgets that get between you and the keyboard. For those who have a fear and loathing of the keyboard, which includes many attorneys, a mechanical helper may be useful. All the mechanical devices are based on the same principle. The computer user physically manipulates a mouse-like object either on a ball or on a specially lined board. This action moves the cursor on the screen and with specially designed software can perform fairly complicated commands. Some word processing programs even allow the mouse to perform editing functions.

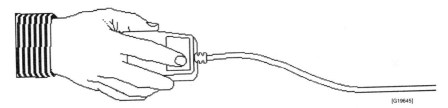

[G19645]

Several years ago you were limited to only a few brands of computers that used a mouse as an additional input device to the keyboard. The popularity of the GUI (or graphic user interface) has meant a rapid increase in the number of people using them. With a mouse you have less dependency on having to spell out the commands to the computer to perform system functions. In addition the mouse is helpful in working with graphic files. It can also be helpful for use with word processors and spread sheets for selecting text or a range of text. Newer versions of word processor software allow you to select text and grab it to move it to another area of the document, making the process more intuitive.

Touchscreen input has not been really accepted as a popular implementation for input. Original developers of this technology thought it would be friendly and accepted as it is very intuitive, but the displays tend to be less accurate than other input devices. Pen devices are gaining in popularity in many forms. Many graphics users are utilizing pressure sensitive tablets that permit the use of a pen device on a flat tablet. The harder you press, the greater the color that is produced.

Recently computer developers have been working on pen based systems for input and several are now available. These devices use an operating system where icons are selected with a pen instead of commands. In addition they recognize handwriting for creating word processing documents and within a year almost all major computer manufacturers will be producing them. The devices will be smaller and lighter than normal computers and in many cases will be useful for specialized applications. Already some courier services are using them for signatures and other data collection by delivery agents. Some of the devices such as the forthcoming PDAs from Apple (personal digital assistants) will be able to store personal data such as calendars and Rolodexes and allow the user to upload the information to a Desktop model. For an attorney on the go these pocket sized devices will be quite handy for accessing Daytimer information.

Input from voice is the newest frontier in input technology. Previous implementations either had to be trained to the dialect of the individual or were extremely limited. Within the next year several new devices will be marketed that recognize voice without having to be trained and will do so in varying degrees of vocabulary. At the lowest level these devices will recognize several hundred words and be portable hand held devices. At the higher level they will be able to recognize thousands of words. While not yet replacing the secretary, voice notes that input directly to a word processor represents a breakthrough. This will reduce the errors created in dictation and in the ability to create notes while in situations where normal typing input is not feasible.

Bar code devices are in wide use today for handling files and recording time use on files. Much like the scanners in wide use at the super market, files in a law office are labeled with a bar code. When work is performed on that case, a code reader is used to enter the code into the computer. This can be tagged for such tasks as image file storage of the entire document, OCR of the document, coordinating data entry to a file into a database storing the information about the case such as transcripts etc., and even for time billing. When an attorney or associate works on a case the beginning time is entered by scanning in the code. When work is finished another scan is made of the bar code. Active files can have their codes printed out so the entry of the time is easily available. The readers can be attached to the computer or they can be hand held devices that store the information for later uploading into the main computer. Billing can then be generated from the time use automatically.

Pressure sensitive tablets with pens are useful for graphics and although graphics may not seem to be essential for lawyers, there are some instances, such as trial simulations where they may have a place. Graphical productions look easy on television ads, and they are, but they usually require more hardware and software than your basic starter set. Special printers, color monitors and sometimes additional graphics hardware in the central processing unit are usually necessary. Some computers, like the Macintosh are specially developed to handle graphics, with most, it means additional expense. Consider graphics devices for law offices that require presentations on a regular basis.

Scanners

Scanners come in several designs and are useful for either creating an image of a document for storage and retrieval or for further processing by OCR (Optical Character Recognition) software to translate the contents into a text or word process file. For example, the firm of Johnson and Smith obtained some documents concerning correspondences during discovery. The documents were scanned using a document scanner and the images indexed and stored. They could electronically reproduce the document with signatures, etc. Several months later the exact wording contained in these documents were necessary to a further action. The image file was opened and OCR software then converted the image to text for use by the attorneys.

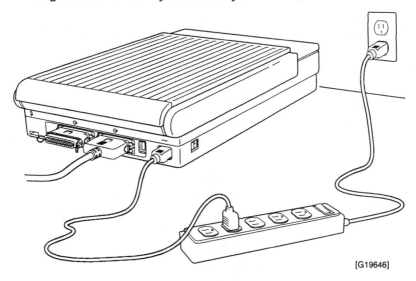

[G19646]

Flat bed scanners such as the Hewlett Packard IIp or the Apple OneScanner are fairly inexpensive today costing about

$1000 and often bundled with OCR software. Scanned material can be archived and stored electronically for document management in such a way that it is easy to locate without having a person find the file in a filing cabinet, physically give it to someone, or make multiple copies if several people need to see it. A scanned image or OCR document created can be stored in a file server and whoever needs to work with that file can retrieve it simultaneously. Flat bed scanners can take a whole page at one time and efficiently scan the image. Many models have a sheet feeder attachment so a multipage document can be loaded automatically. In addition to the flat bed scanners, there are several models of hand held scanners now available. They cost about ½ to ⅔ of the price of a flat bed scanner and are somewhat slower but are less bulky and can be easily used to scan parts of a document. Either type of scanner is able to provide graphic input or text input as well. A good black and white flat bed scanner will cost under $1000, and a document feeder can be added for another $300–400. Color flat bed scanners are also available for about 2 times the price of the black and white scanners.

PUTTING IT ALL TOGETHER

Once you have decided which software and hardware will be appropriate for your needs you must determine whether in fact it will match your budget. The good news is that computer hardware and software have steadily decreased in price and increased in power each year. By the time you purchase your system these tentative estimates will probably be out of date—but on the good, not the bad side of your budget.

Any budget estimate, of course varies widely depending upon the size of your office, the number of attorneys and legal workers, and on the nature of your practice. But in very general ball park figures, here is Budget A: The Minimal System, appropriate for a sole practitioner, or a starter set for a somewhat larger firm.

BUDGET A: THE MINIMAL SYSTEM

HARDWARE

SMALL SYSTEM–MS–DOS CLONE	
Packard Bell 386/20 100meg HD	$995
Abonite 12″ Monochrome Monitor	$149
H.P. DeskJet 500	$399
Practical Peripherals FaxModem	$195
PrinterCable	$20
Windows 3.1	$95
Total	**$1,853**

HARDWARE

SMALL SYSTEM-MACINTOSH

Mac LC III 4/80	$1,250
12" Monochrome Monitor	$169
H.P. Deskwriter	$399
Global Village Sen/Rec. F.Modem	$249
Printer Cable	$16
Keyboard	$125
Total	**$2,208**

SOFTWARE (MS DOS AND MAC)

Word Processing package	$300
Data Base Management package	$600
Electronic Spreadsheet	$300
Communications package	$100
Timekeeping and billing module	$1,000
Total	**$2,300**
Hardware Total MS–DOS	$1,900
Hardware Total Mac	$2,200
Software Total	$2,300
System Total MS–DOS	**$4,200**
System Total Mac	**$4,500**

* This budget does not includes any subscriptions to LEXIS, WESTLAW, ABA/net, DIALOG, or any electronic mail service, but it does include a modem for access.

For larger firms of 5–10 attorneys, more powerful machines should be considered, especially for those situations in which the machine is used at least 40% of the time, the following budget, Budget B: The Medium System, might be considered. This takes into account the greater storage needs for time-keeping and billing and data bases for in-house work products and possibly litigation support. You might consider a combination of Budget A and Budget B machines and network them together.

BUDGET B: THE MEDIUM SYSTEM

HARDWARE

MEDIUM SYSTEM-MS DOS

486DX/50 120HD	$1,749
Sony 13" RGB monitor	$629
H.P. LaserJet IIp+	$829

HARDWARE

Practical Perip. F.Modem	$289
Printer Cable	$20
Windows 3.1	$95
Total	**$3,611**
* H.P. LaserJet IIIsi substitute	$2,870
Total	**$6,481**

* For a better laser printer with high quality type, net-workable which can be shared among several machines, substitute a Hewlett Packard IIIsi and add $2870.

MEDIUM SYSTEM MACINTOSH

Mac IIci 5/80 w Keyboard	$2,550
13" RGB Monitor	$600
LaserWriter NTR	$1,600
Global Village Sen/Rec. F.Modem	$249
Printer Cable	$16
Total	**$5,015**
LaserWriter IIF substitute	$1,054
Total	**$6,069**

SOFTWARE

Word Processing package	$300
Data Base Management package	$600
Electronic Spreadsheet	$300
Communications package	$100
Timekeeping and billing module	$1,000
Total	**$2,300**

Hardware Total MS–DOS	$3,611
Hardware Total Mac	$5,015
Software Total	$2,300
System Total MS–DOS	**$5,911**
System Total MS–DOS with Network	**$7,111**
System Total Mac	**$7,315**

COMPARING ALL SYSTEMS

1) MAC SYSTEMS

SMALL SYSTEM–MACINTOSH

Mac LC III 4/80	$1,250		
12" Monochrome Monitor	$169		
H.P. Deskwriter	$399		
Global Village Sen/Rec. F.Modem	$249		
Printer Cable	$16		

SMALL SYSTEM-MACINTOSH

Keyboard	$125		
Total	**$2,208**		
Medium System Macintosh			
Mac IIci 5/80 w Keyboard	$2,550		
13" RGB Monitor	$600		
LaserWriter NTR	$1,600		
Global Village Sen/Rec. F.Modem	$249		
Printer Cable	$16		
Total	**$5,015**		
LaserWriter IIF substitute	$1,054		
TOTAL	**$6,069**		

LARGE SYSTEM MACINTOSH

Mac IIsi 5/80 w keyboard	$1,900	5	$9,500
13" RGB Monitor	$600	5	$3,000
Mac IIci Server 5/80 w keyboard	$2,550	1	$2,550
12" Mono Server Display	$199	1	$199
Server Modem	$499	1	$499
PhoneNet Connectors	$30	8	$240
LaserWriter NTR	$1,600	1	$1,600
Subtotal			**$17,588**
LaserWriter IIf substitute	$1,054	1	$1,054
Total			**$18,642**

2) MS–DOS SYSTEMS

SMALL SYSTEM-MS-DOS CLONE

Packard Bell 386/20 100 meg HD	$995		$995
Abonite 12" Monochrome Monitor	$149		$149
H.P. DeskJet 500	$399		$399
Practical Peripherals FaxModem	$195		$195
PrinterCable	$20		$289
Windows 3.1	$95		$20
Total	**$1,853**		$95
			$2,142

MEDIUM SYSTEM-MS DOS

486DX/50 120HD	$1,749		$1,749
Sony 13" RGB monitor	$629		$629
H.P. LaserJet IIp+	$829		$829
Practical Perip. F.Modem	$289		$289
Printer Cable	$20		$20
Windows 3.1	$95		$95
Total	**$3,611**		$3,611
H.P. LaserJet IIIsi substitute	$2,870		
Total	**$6,481**		$3,611

LARGE SYSTEM MS-DOS

386SX/25 80 Meg HD	$1,099	5	$5,495
Sony 1304S13" RGB monitor	$629	5	$3,145
Vertos 486DX/50 120HD server	$1,749	1	$1,749
Abonite 12" Mono Server Display	$149	1	$149
Windows 3.1	$95	5	$475
Practical Perip. F.Modem	$495	1	$495
Artisoft AE–3 Cards	$595	5	$2,975

LARGE SYSTEM MS–DOS

Novell Ether Cards	$249	5	$1,245
H.P. LaserJet IIp+	$829	1	$829
Subtotal			**$16,557**
H.P. LaserJet IIIsi substitute	$2,870	1	$2,870
Total			**$19,427**

If adding more machines multiply the number of machines by the costs to arrive at total figures.

* If you are considering linking any of these microcomputers together in a Local Area Network, the MS–DOS clones require an added cost of **$800** per machine *and* the cost of a dedicated file server, approximately another **$1800** (See figures in Budget C below). This means adding a total of **$1200** per machine to network them. Financing is available for most computer systems and with the larger systems lease agreements are often available which will even include the software.

To simplify the calculations for a large firm, the following budget, Budget C should be considered. It includes the costs for setting up a network of 5 computers and a file server. This takes into account the greater storage needs for time-keeping and billing and data bases for in-house work products and possibly litigation support.

BUDGET C: THE LARGE SYSTEM—
5 COMPUTERS WITH NETWORK

LARGE SYSTEM MS–DOS

386SX/25 80 Meg HD	$1,099	5	$5,495
Sony 1304S13" RGB monitor	$629	5	$3,145
Vertos 486DX/50 120HD server	$1,749	1	$1,749
Abonite 12" Mono Server Display	$149	1	$149
Windows 3.1	$95	5	$475
Practical Perip. F.Modem	$495	1	$495
Artisoft AE–3 Cards	$595	5	$2,975
Novell Ether Cards	$249	5	$1,245
H.P. LaserJet IIp+	$829	1	$829
Subtotal			**$16,557**
H.P. LaserJet IIIsi substitute	$2,870	1	$2,870
Total			**$19,427**

LARGE SYSTEM MACINTOSH

Mac IIsi 5/80 w keyboard	$1,900	5	$9,500
13" RGB Monitor	$600	5	$3,000
Mac IIci Server 5/80 w keyboard	$2,550	1	$2,550

LARGE SYSTEM MACINTOSH

12″ Mono Server Display	$199	1	$199
Server Modem	$499	1	$499
PhoneNet Connectors	$30	8	$240
LaserWriter NTR	$1,600	1	$1,600
Subtotal			**$17,588**
LaserWriter IIf substitute	$1,054	1	$1,054
Total			**$18,642**

SOFTWARE

Word Processing package	$250	5	$1,250
Database Management package	$600	3	$1,800
Electronic Spreadsheet	$300	2	$600
Communications package	$100	1	$100
Timekeeping and billing module	$1,000	2	$2,000
Hardware Total MS–DOS			$19,427
Hardware Total Mac			$18,642
Software Total			$5,750
File Server Software (MS–DOS Only)			$1,000
System Total DOS			**$26,177**
System Total Mac			**$24,392**

IS IT WORTH IT?

The real issue is that you probably can't afford not to computerize. If other attorneys are going to become automated and therefore perform their work more efficiently and charge less for certain standard services, you will not be competitive unless you are computerized.

Some of the factors which will determine your increased profit include:

the efficiency of your computer system

whether you increase your volume because of greater efficiency

whether you reduce your personnel costs due to greater efficiency

whether your rate of bill collection goes up due to computerized billing whether your billable hours increase due to computerized management reports

In some cases your computer will allow you not only to take on more cases, but to take on cases you would not touch before, such as larger litigation matters or routinized procedures such as probate.

Without question, you will receive the greatest immediate rush of new profits as a result of a well-functioning timekeeping and billing system; particularly if you make use of management reports. Not only will your bills be paid more often and more quickly, but you will finally receive interest on past due accounts. Management reports often produce surprisingly speedy income increases. When attorney Jones finds that he is the low man on the billing totem pole, he will struggle to climb to the top. This will be especially true if your office determines profit sharing based on billable hours.

UNDERWARE

A computer consultant acquaintance began a lecture with the advice, "Forget about the hardware and software, if the underware falls down all is lost". He meant that if the support people in the office, and this could include attorneys as well as paralegals and secretaries, did not take well to the computer system it would become an expensive fiasco.

Consultants for computer set up and system installation can be both the best money spent on a system if the consultant is good, and the worst if the consultant is not suitable to your needs. However it is most important for the consultant to coordinate with someone in the law office who will become the person responsible for the operation and maintenance of that system. At the very least there should be one person in the office who is in charge of the system, who is trained and knowledgeable and responsible or the consultant will be a waste of time. At the high end, the consultant either becomes employed by the office full time for maintenance and support of the system, or part of a team that provides that service. In any case unless the attorney himself decides to spend a significant part of his time learning computer systems this is a job best left to others.

Today more than ever it is important to have someone who can support the system as it is installed. No one person can know all the answers to all questions. A good consultant will know who to contact to get the answers and be able to interpret the solution and help with the implementation. Along the way you may have to bring in specialists to implement various parts of the system. These additional people should coordinate with the person in charge of the general system. For example, when setting up accounting software packages, the information about a particular accounting package may be so specialized that an installer for that package is required. A particular hardware configuration may be required on the machine using that software, etc. Any changes to that configuration should then be discussed with the accounting software specialist or the software may malfunction. It is important then when deciding what software is to be used that discussions be made early to determine the hardware compatibility before buying the hardware.

Here are some tips to help avoid this disaster, but no guarantee that every employee will become a computer enthusiast.

EARLY INVOLVEMENT

Every member of the office team should be involved from the early planning stages. When a software needs assessment is performed, every person should review their own tasks and decide how a computer might aid them. A detailed examination of existing practices and possible improvements should be undertaken by the members who handle timekeeping, billing, and bookkeeping.

Although not everyone in the office can troop through the computer stores, the person in charge of researching the software and hardware should make frequent progress reports and receive suggestions from those left behind.

UNIVERSAL TRAINING

"Start Training" is one of our general Start–Up rules. As soon as the computer or computers are operational every member of the office should be given at least minimal training on each application. Those who will be using an application on a regular basis, like the billing person, should receive extensive training with that application.

How much training is enough? As much as it takes to make the user feel comfortable and to completely abandon the manual ways. With timekeeping and billing it is recommended to keep a back up manual billing system for at least two months to make sure the disaster of a month without billing out does not occur.

Many computer software packages now come with their own training disks. A good training disk is worth several hundred pages of a printed manual since it walks you through the steps directly on the computer. Private software companies also sell training disks for more popular software programs, such as Excel or Word Perfect. Because of the notoriously poor quality of many of the software manufacturers printed manuals a whole print industry has popped up to help train on popular software as well. Computer stores will sometimes offer courses or seminars to learn specific software as well. A major consideration in purchasing software should be the availability and quality of the training, and this should be tested *before* the purchase.

RE-SHUFFLING

It may be that even in a small office the advent of the computer may provide the opportunity to re-organize office tasks more efficiently. By eliminating many of the labor-intensive typing tasks the secretary may be able to be retrained to take on traditional paralegal tasks like organizing documents for trial with the aid of the computer. This transformation must occur slowly, however, allowing everyone first to become well trained on the computer. Some square pegs will never fit into the new round holes created by the computer, and it would be wasteful to force these efforts.

It is as important to choose the correct support system as it is to choose the right software and hardware. Often the difference between a system working and not working is merely the support personnel and not the fault of either the hardware or the software manufacturer.

[G19647]

PART 2

SETTING UP YOUR OWN SUB-STANTIVE SYSTEMS ON PERSON-AL COMPUTERS

A system is simply an organized way of handling any repetitious task, like organizing documents for trial or producing articles of incorporation. Any task that you perform regularly should be systematized. This can be accomplished with absolutely *NO PROGRAMMING SKILL*. Automated systems may be set up in two ways: 1) utilize general multipurpose software such as word processing, database management or electronic spreadsheet software to formulate a system that works for you or, 2) purchase automated systems that are already formulated, such as those for wills, probate, or real estate transactions. The first option offers you far more flexibility and efficiency.

There are two general rules that you should observe in designing your own automated systems:

Rule One: Begin with the system you already have. If you have a manual system that works for you, whether it is calendaring, or completing a probate procedure, you must take advantage of the speed and skill with which you can use this system and incorporate it into an automated system rather than start from byte one.

Rule Two: If possible, create your own system rather than buy an already packaged software system. This is of course, a corollary of rule number one. If you buy something that someone else has already programmed, it will probably not have much in common with the systems that you have developed. It will mean that you will have to retrain everyone in the office in entirely different procedures.

Creating your own system will take a certain amount of time up front but the results will be well worth it. The system will be entirely tailored to your needs and your clients' needs. In the long run it will be an investment of time that will pay off for you. This does not mean that you have to program your own software or create all your own databases. What it does mean is that you should organize your system the way *you* operate.

CHAPTER SIX

Automated Substantive Systems: Word Processing

Step One: Typewriter to Word Processing: The Big Leap

Word processing is where you should begin to design, or redesign your systems. The first step is to insist that *all* typing now be done on the computer rather than on the electric or manual typewriter. The minimum number of computer terminals that are required in a law office is the number of typewriters that are used at least 40% of the time. It is quite inefficient and therefore costly to have some work products produced on manual typewriters or electric typewriters and some produced on the computer. Not only is the original creation of the document far more time consuming with traditional typewriters but it will not be stored on a magnetic medium that can be retrieved for re-use.

In creating a document, you can delete, cut and paste, and move blocks of text around with the touch of a finger. Then you can edit, store, and retrieve. None of these capabilities are available on electric or manual typewriters. More importantly, the work product that is produced on the computer is permanently stored on that magnetic medium until you decide to erase it. This means that you do not have to re-invent the will or type that same form letter each time you have a need for it.

For these reasons, even the most basic simple typing jobs, like a note to your client describing the status of your case, should be produced on the word processing software of your computer. You may not wish to store that particular kind of work product for future reference. A Xerox copy in the file is sufficient, but the time it takes to produce it will be much less than with traditional typewriters or electric typewriters.

Once you have made the transition from producing everything on the word processor, it is time to tackle the form file. Every pleading, every contract, every will, every basic document that you have in your form file should be transferred to a magnetic medium, either a floppy disk or a hard disk, for future use and retrieval. Again, this may be initially a time consuming project but in the long run the availability of all of your documents and all of your forms on a magnetic medium is an enormous time saver. In making this transfer, it doesn't make sense simply to copy the documents as they were in hard copy in your form file into your computer. Here is your chance to become fully automated and develop automated substantive systems with your word processing software.

Step Two.   Automated Substantive Systems

Most law offices use word processing as super typewriting. This in itself is a huge time-saver, but it does not take full advantage of personal computer power.   By using the special capacities of your PC, especially the merge function, you can shave the time it takes to perform routine tasks in substantive areas of the law to a fraction of what it took in the pre-computer era.

A substantive system is the organization of all the documents normally required for each procedure in a routine legal transaction to assure greater efficiency and fewer errors.   An automated substantive system is making use of the computer to achieve the greatest efficiency and even fewer errors.   Certain areas of the law are obvious candidates for automated substantive systems.   These include: divorces, probates, real estate transactions, wills and trusts, corporations, bankruptcy, collections, worker's compensation and pleadings for certain common types of civil actions, such as personal injury.   These are all substantive areas where a very large percentage of the paper work is repetitious, or boiler-plate, as it is fondly called.

All substantive systems include the document form or forms which contain blank spaces which must be filled in with variable information.   This variable information falls into three categories:

1.   Standard variables.   This is the kind of information that will be the obtained from all clients in that particular legal transaction; such as name, address, names of children, name of spouse, etc.   These items can be typed in each time (only once) or pulled from a master client list which contains a great deal of information about a client, without re-typing.

2.   Unique variables.   This is the kind of information that is unique to each document, and may change with the same client; such or the name of the witnesses to a contract, or the date the document is signed.   These cannot be automatically pulled from a master list of client information since the exact information may not be known until the time the document is required, at which point they must be typed in.

3.   Alternative clauses or paragraphs.   In most documents choices have to be made regarding jurisdiction, appropriate statutory provisions, grounds for complaint, etc.   Usually there are only two or three possible choices, and these can be presented so that the person entering the data may choose a single number, like 1, 2, 3, or 4, or press an already programmed key without typing in the whole phrase or paragraph.   The text itself will then automatically be retrieved and inserted in the proper place.

In developing a completely automated document system, the merge feature of your word processing software will allow you to enter all of this variable information just once and the computer will do the rest by inserting that information into all the appropriate places in that document, or series of documents. It will also allow you to make choices between alternative clauses or paragraphs. Most importantly, it allows you to use employees who are not at all sophisticated about the law or about computers and who are therefore paid at a lower rate.

Let us take, for example, the 25 minute divorce. Roberta Lombard, married for ten years, with two children and a house, walks into your office. The factual intake interview is performed by your secretary or paralegal seated at the computer terminal. The interview sheet is not a piece of paper, it is a form on the screen which prompts him to enter such information as: name, address, children, income, real property, personal property, etc. This intake form becomes the master list, (or database), which when completed will include all the standard variables which are required in the eleven documents and marital settlement agreement necessary to complete this divorce. It may also include billing, statute of limitations, adversarial parties, information and other data useful to maintain. The total intake entry time is fifteen minutes.

Roberta Lombard is then ushered in to see the lawyer. The lawyer has a hard (paper) copy of the intake information and while discussing her case, checks off several variable clauses and paragraphs on a separate form. In an alternative scenario the lawyer reviews the information directly on the computer screen, and enters, with a single keystroke, the choices of variable clauses and paragraphs directly into the computer. When it is time to produce the documents the secretary or paralegal retrieves the word processing file, i.e., the documents, alternative paragraphs, and clauses, and uses it in conjunction with the file which contains Roberta Lombard's master list. The secretary or paralegal then presses the merge key and is prompted by a series of questions on the screen, such as "What are the Names of the Children?". For all the prompts which require information contained in the master list, i.e., the standard variables, the secretary merely enters the name or number on the master list which is assigned to that field of information; for the unique variables, such as the date, or the names of the witnesses, the secretary types the information in directly—usually these are very limited in number. For the variable clauses and paragraphs, the secretary uses the form which the attorney has checked off, entering the numbers of the chosen variable clauses or paragraphs. The total entry time is five minutes. Roberta's name, or her spouse's name may appear more than 30 times in the body of the documents, but the secretary had only to enter one number or a short word. When the questions have all been answered the requested variables and clauses are merged into the 11 documents and the marital settlement agreement (a total of 44 pages), and printed out as a finished product. The merging is instantaneous, the speed of the printer determines the final production time.

There probably will be revisions of the marital settlement agreement or other documents as the negotiating process of divorce ensues, but it will require less than five minutes to produce a revised version of any or all documents with this thoroughly automated system which has required no special programming skills to produce. The miracle of the 25 minute divorce has been created.

In setting up these forms, they should be made simple enough for a secretary or a paralegal to fill in the information. It should not require an attorney or a computer whiz. This will free the attorney from tedious drafting and ferreting in the form books and restrict the interview to relevant legal issues, not fact finding. Profits should rise with the virtual elimination of labor intensive typing.

Saving Time

How much time does word processing save? This is a controversial question. There have been a number of studies by law office management firms and the estimates range from 50% to 2,000% savings in time over typewriters. This may seem a ridiculous range but it depends on where you start from and how far you go. If you can produce twenty-five pages of documents by entering three or four pieces of information only once, you may cut the production time to a fraction of what it was previously. If you can save even half an hour of an attorney's time, you have freed him to expand his volume or to go sailing. The bottom line for any office, small or large, is that there will be a great reduction in overhead simply by this one computer application: word processing; and it will be progressively more valuable with the increasing automation of your substantive systems. The savings may come in personnel time but for a small office they may also come in the greater potential for more cases. A San Francisco probate specialist increased her volume threefold in two years with no additional personnel by automating the 56 standard letters and documents which she normally uses in the probate process. Higher volume will yield profits more readily than reduced personnel time and costs.

SOFTWARE NOTES

Word processing software for PCs ranges from the primitive to the ultra-sophisticated. (See Chapter 4 on Choosing Software). It is now possible to purchase for PCs the same features previously found only on expensive dedicated word processors; in fact many of the new software packages are careful copies of some of the classic dedicated word processors. The difference between crude and full-featured may be only $100 or $200; it does not pay to tighten your purse strings in this critical area.

Word processing software has evolved over the past several years to include many powerful features. It is no longer a question of substituting a word processor for a typewriter, or for that matter even using a dedicated word processing machine versus a word processor program on a computer. Word processing software on a PC is the only choice. While the de facto standard for the legal profession MS–DOS user may be Word Perfect, it is not the only option, especially when other features are considered beyond the normal word processing. The most commonly used word processors for Windows and for the Macintosh is Word. Although Word Perfect is available for Windows, it has not been as successful as Word for Windows.

If you choose to create your own forms for your practice with word processing software because you have a very specialized practice, or you have your own style, over time you will have amassed a library of material that can be recycled for other cases. Contracts which initially require research and context sensitive wording may easily be copied from one document to another with word processing software. The search and replace features lend themselves to an easy update of new clients involved. This feature alone makes word processing software on a computer superior to all other ways of handling text. These techniques may be mated to the scanning, optical character conversion and word process copying to eliminate a large amount of time spent entering text. Quotes and references are easily added to documents.

Today's word processing software contains spelling checkers and thesauruses. These features may be generic and you can add your own terms, or you may insert ones which are specific for the legal profession. Grammar checkers are also becoming more available. These will inevitably assist in the careful preparation of documents. Glossary features allow the entry of phrases which are time consuming to repeat and can lead to errors if re-entered anew. You can add macro capabilities to these glossaries by the incorporating of styles with text entries from the glossary. For example you can use a glossary entry for your letterhead.

For special documents and forms, word processing software allows you to create styles that can be invoked with a series of key strokes. These styles include ruler settings, type styles, fonts and sizes, leading, line spacing, etc. Substantive legal systems based on word processing software may utilize a combination of the style sheets in a word processor and the glossaries, macro functions, and merge capabilities. The merge features allow you to use a text document as a database with the field entries separated by tabs and records separated by carriage returns. The word processing form contains the information to which the specific field of a record in the database text document is referenced. Logic is used in the form document to determine whether or how the information is included at the point of merging. Initially word processors required special terms or punctuation marks to use the merge features. The evolution of the word processing software is leading to a more intuitive procedure which lists the fields in pop-up menus and offers a user friendly interface.

Merges can be used for simple functions such as personalizing a general letter to a mass mailing of hundreds to thousands of people. They can also be used for recording the information that will be placed into the appropriate empty spaces in a word processing form. The result is that the difference between the use of database management software and word processing software for substantive law is decreasing. Both word processing software and database software can be used to generate a word processed document. It is easier for you to create your own with a customized word processor, but a form oriented flat database will perform as well (see discussion Chapter 7). The word processing software is still more useful as text entry software.

Special Requirements for Automated Systems

Automated substantive systems require specific word processing features, and these should be carefully investigated before purchasing any word processing software.

1. Merge capacities. These are usually promoted in terms of mass mailings, but for law offices with repetitious documents, merging provides the greatest efficiency. It is the cornerstone of an automated substantive system. It allows you to insert all variable information without re-keying it in each blank. Not all word processing packages support merging; beware.

2. Merging data with text. Many PC word processing programs offer limited database capacities, often called list, or mailing list functions. These allow you to store client information for regular mass mailings. They usually allow you to do limited sorting and searching as well. Some of these databases are sophisticated enough to hold all the information necessary for a substantive system, like a divorce. This is the information that is

gathered at the intake interview. Others are too limited for that purpose. Some of the new integrated programs, like Symphony or Framework allow easy transfer of database information into a document produced by word processing. Some do not. Make sure your word processing program is compatible with a database.

3. Keystroke glossary. This function allows you to store frequently used text or series of commands. This can be useful for storing variable clauses and paragraphs, but they can also be stored as regular word processing files.

Looking Forward

Newer versions of word processing software are headed into two directions: the lean and simple version, and the sophisticated full featured. Of the new features perhaps the most significant features are the inclusion of more page layout features, obscuring the differences between a low-end page layout and a sophisticated word processor. New versions of software include linking to spreadsheets and other documents. Tables created in a spreadsheet and updated are automatically updated in a word processor. Text blocks may be selected and moved with the cursor instead of having to cut and paste the material. Graphics features have been added for both handling graphics pasted into the word processor, or for creating simple graphics with the tools now provided. Remember that the term graphics should not be limited to pictures when thinking of word processors. A document that has been imaged and stored may be included in toto (including the signature) rather than translated to text with an OCR (Optical Character Recognition software) package. With the addition of the new Quicktime file format, graphics included in a word processor document may be a sound recording, an animated 3D document or even a video. Quicktime is available as a Macintosh format and will be available sometime in the near future on other operating systems as a result of the joint efforts by IBM and Apple Computer.

PRE–PACKAGED SYSTEMS

Pre-packaged systems can be extremely useful if they fit the type of practice you have. Although we have recommended setting up your own system, there are many new packages on the market. You should investigate these as well. Beware—a fair number of prepackaged systems do not make use of complete automation by merging variables, but still maintain the paper and pencil mentality of filling in the blanks. An example of this is one created with Cowles Word Perfect system:

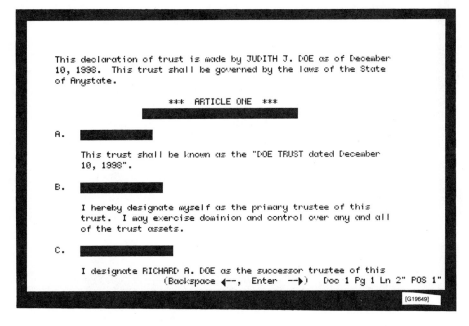

```
        Spouse:->
     Clientname:->        Ms. Judith J. Doe
     Dearclient:->        Judy

       Address:->         6010 Main Street
          City:->         Anytown
         State:->         Anystate
           Zip:->         55555
        County:->         Anycounty

        Notary:->         Jane Smith
Notary exp date:->        expires 12/16/99
      Attorney:->         Colleen A. Cowles

Socssr Trustee(s):->      RICHARD A. DOE
Alt Socssr Trstee:->      KAREN T. GESSLER
2Alt Socssr Trstee:->

      Guardian:->         RICHARD A. DOE
  Alt Guardian:->         KAREN T. GESSLER
 2Alt Guardian:->

  Test Trustee:->         RICHARD A. DOE
Alt Test Trustee:->       KAREN T. GESSLER
 (Backspace ◄--, Enter  --►)                    Pg 1 Ln 6.38" Pos 1"
```

[G19648]

```
This declaration of trust is made by JUDITH J. DOE as of December
10, 1998.  This trust shall be governed by the laws of the State
of Anystate.

               ***  ARTICLE ONE  ***

A.

     This trust shall be known as the "DOE TRUST dated December
     10, 1998".

B.

     I hereby designate myself as the primary trustee of this
     trust.  I may exercise dominion and control over any and all
     of the trust assets.

C.

     I designate RICHARD A. DOE as the successor trustee of this
              (Backspace ◄--, Enter  --►)   Doc 1 Pg 1 Ln 2" POS 1"
```

[G19649]

Many automated systems are put out by state bars, favorites are wills and real estate transactions. Legisoft is an example of an automated system for the creation of wills:

```
                        YOUR CLIENT'S COUNTY

       Enter the name of the county in which your client lives.

       Enter the entire phrase customarily used for the county
       (e.g. the County of Clear Lake  or  Santa Bonita County).

    ▶ Just press Enter if you don't want to mention the county.




     ┌ Your Answer Will Print As: ─────────────────────────────┐
       This trust agreement is made between John Smith, of
       Sonoma, California, Settlor...
     └──────────────────────────── Is This OK? (Y/N) _ ────────┘

                   Enter the Requested Information
              ── F1=HELP F2=BACKUP F3=MENU F10=QUIT ──
```

[G19650]

```
To see document, use these keys: ↑ ↓ PgUp PgDn Home End       To Quit: Esc
             John Smith and Sara Smathers Revocable Trust


                        REVOCABLE TRUST AGREEMENT

THIS TRUST AGREEMENT dated _____, is
made between John Smith and Sara Smathers of Sonoma, California,
called the "Settlors," and John Smith and Sara Smathers of Sonoma,
California, called "Co-Trustees," and referred to in this instrument
collectively as "Trustee."  John Smith is married to Sara Smathers.
John Smith's Social Security number is 123-34-5678.  Sara Smathers's
Social Security number is 234-56-9876.

FIRST: If at any time one of the original Trustees is unable or
unwilling to serve as Trustee, the other shall serve alone.  If both
of the original Trustees are unable or unwilling to serve as Trustee,
the Substitute or Successor Trustee under this Trust Agreement shall
be John Henry.
     The original Trustee and any Successor or Substitute Trustee
named herein shall serve without bond.
     Except as otherwise expressly indicated, each Successor or
Substitute Trustee shall have all the powers and immunities herein
given to the original Trustee.  No Successor Trustee or Co-Trustee
```

[G19651]

Although the general rule is to make use of your own systems, some of these pre-packaged systems might suit you. Try before you buy.

WHO'S AT THE KEYBOARD?

The question that is often asked is who should do the word processing? If it is simply a matter of inserting a few bits of information into a totally automated system, certainly the secretary, paralegal, or perhaps even the attorney himself or herself should perform this function. It may be possible to do it immediately at an intake interview. As a general rule, it is certainly useful to train everyone in the law office: attorney, paralegal, legal secretary, law clerks, bookkeepers, and occasional helpers in the art of word processing. Many attorneys today still insist on the old fashioned yellow pad for preparing notes and dictation for communications. Either they have not learned to type well, or they consider it a function beneath them. Although more young law school grads are passing the bar with typing and computer skills, they are still a minority. Those with the skills are often better able to handle the workload. Laptop computers with communications software allow for direct note input and interaction with files stored on the office system.

For the attorneys who still use manual input, pen based systems are now being readied for shipping. Several manufacturers (Go, NEC) already have units in production. AT&T and Apple will be releasing the pen based hand held computers this year, along with several other manufacturers later in the year. Lawyers will handwrite on a gray slate LCD, their handwriting interpreted and easy to read text printed out. Dictation entry will follow shortly. Dependency on the keyboard for data entry will become less of an issue. Those with typing skills will still be better qualified at computer work, however, and certainly nothing will replace the keyboard for speedy entry and for editing purposes; computer input by others will increase dramatically.

It will take a few weeks or perhaps even a few months for your office to become accustomed to word processing and to make maximum use of its powers. A built-in part of your procedure during the first year after the purchase of the computer should be a weekly or perhaps bi-weekly meeting to assess the progress of automation. At these meetings it can be determined how many of the old habits are dying hard and how much new efficiency has been brought into the office over the past week or two. A timetable should be set up for entering all forms onto disks for storage and creating completely automated substantive systems which will be used in your practice.

HOW TO CREATE AN AUTOMATED SUBSTANTIVE SYSTEM *

1. Collect all the possible documents and forms you might use in a particular transaction; e.g. bankruptcy.

2. Separate out the alternative clauses, paragraphs, or complete documents which you might use. Number them and indicate where in the text of the document or form they might appear.

3. Search the documents for all the factual variables which are required. Indicate whether they would be a "standard variable", i.e., one that you would elicit one time from each client, or a "unique variable", like the date which must be entered each time.

4. Type all the documents onto a floppy or hard disk. Name or number the variables, e.g. spouse, income, or 1, 2, 3.3 etc. and indicate where in the document they should be merged. Name the alternative clauses, e.g. jurisdiction 1, jurisdiction 2, or alt. 1, alt. 2 and indicate where in the document they should be merged.

5. Set up the prompt questions that request variables and alternative clauses, e.g.

"Spouse's Income?"

"Date of Marriage?"

Jurisdiction 1, 2, 3?

6. Develop an intake interview form based on information that you will require in the automated system, and any other information you would consider useful in this master list, or database.

CASE STUDY # 2

DISTRICT ATTORNEYS OFFICE PEACOCK COUNTY

Joe Smith is the Information Systems manager for Peacock County DA's office. The office is a mixed functions office, with two main divisions: Criminal Division (violent crimes), and Family Support Division which does collections for welfare department, absentee parents. The Criminal Division is concerned with victims and witnesses, consumer fraud, consumer protection, and has an investigative division. Both clerical personnel and attorneys are involved with this and they primarily use Macintoshes for personal computers. The Family Support Division in addition to the above personnel has a typing pool called the MAG room with a staff of

---

* Each word processing software system will require its own commands. This is a general description of the steps to automation.

10 people which processes a heavy load of forms and correspondence.

Computers:

An IBM 4301 mainframe does cradle to grave booking for the criminal justice system, i.e. the courts, the sheriffs and the police departments. There are 65 Macintoshes, 2 MS–DOS machines, and a UNIX mini computer, located in the Family Support Division. When computers of different types are linked together this is called a mixed LAN. In this case Joe accesses the IBM Mainframe by using dedicated terminals connected to the mainframe for those using the mainframe on a permanent basis. For research and sessions which are less than 30 minutes, Macs are used which run a terminal emulation program. They are seeking better connectivity between the Macs and the UNIX mini to be able to run X windows and the applications remotely from the Macs.

There are a total of about 65 Macintoshes of different configurations: 8 Pluses, 40 SEs, and the balance are LCs and SIs. LC is current machine of choice for purchasing. The servers are: a CX, an SE 30 and an SI. Each has 80 MBs or more. The main server has an additional 300 MB drive. The MAG room (typing pool) has an 80 MB hard disk plus a second 150 MB disk. Family Support has an 80 MB disk. Microsoft Mail email is on SE 30.

The Local Area Network

The Macs are connected using Ethernet, thin wire cabling. A Kinetics Fastpath is used to go from Ethernet to AppleTalk (LocalTalk). Soon this will be replaced by Liaison software for conversion from Ethernet to LocalTalk. The network is broken into smaller pieces with Ethernet as a backbone. The topology is a "mucked" up star. One Farallon StarController is for AppleTalk side, and 3 3Com multiport repeaters for the Ether star. The backbone comes down for computers off the repeaters. There are 5 arms on the star. There are parallel networks wired to the machines with Thin wire Ethernet and phone wire for the AppleTalk network. One printer and 4 Macintosh Pluses are on AppleTalk. The rest of the machines are on Ethernet. To translate the Ethernet to AppleTalk for the Laserwriter printers they use Dayna Etherprint. Each Macintosh computer has its own hard disk, and there are 3 file servers on Appleshare 2.0 (all Macintoshes on the system are running system 6—mostly 6.07 with some on earlier versions of system 6). They use folders on the file servers to send files to each other. Security is maintained on the server with some areas password protected—personnel and administration held back from most users, but the rest of the server is accessible to everyone.

Printing

The DA's office uses Apple built in print spooling. Each person chooses whatever printer he wants at anytime. They have 1 Laserwriter Plus, 3 Laserwriter NTXs and 7 Laserwriter NTs. They got the NTXs for faster output in the MAG room (typing pool). On the MAG room Laserwriters (2) are BDT 3 bin paper feeders. They have had a few software problems with these but they are minor. Mechanically it has been fine. An AppleTalk networked Imagewriter LQ is used for spread sheet reports which are too wide for other printers.

Databases

They are currently using Omnis software for their multi-user database. The database is one that has been custom built for tracking cases in progress. They use several versions of Omnis: v 3, v5, v7 for different databases. All will be eventually upgraded to 7. All material is entered manually. The main database is the juror-criminal list. This database records anyone who has been on a jury in the past, general demeanor of the juror, feelings about him, case type, anyone who has been contacted by the law, charged with a felony, or involved in any criminal activities. Information comes from the Jury Commission for potential jurors for any particular time and is compared to what is in database for that person. It is used for biographical information for the District Attorney for choosing a jury. Other Omnis databases are historical, i.e., databases of all the cases that ran through office which are still active. These include such fields in the database as: case number, defendant, aliases etc. This is strictly informational as the real material is on the county mainframe. Calendaring is also on the mainframe. They use Filemaker databases and Omnis databases for case-evidence, evidence numbers, discovery, and depositions. They use both Filemaker and Omnis for databases but if they have to do larger searches on the data they use Filemaker. For multi-user with Filemaker they put the data file on the server but use Filemaker's internal networking with some access restrictions. When they need to retrieve information from police reports etc., it is not printed but accessed via the Macs from the mainframe and read on the screens. The goal of the office is to reduce the number of print outs. All their databases are custom databases, nothing is off the shelf. When they set up their system there was nothing really available so they created their own.

Indexing

They use On Location software for building indexes for transcripts or depositions—anything read into the computer. The catalog is stored on the hard disk for future use.

Forms

The Family Support Division uses their Macintoshes to print forms on the Laserwriters. The forms are created using InFormed Designer to create the custom forms. They used the California Judicial counsel forms and then recreated them with InFormed Designer to make the forms interactive, setting them up as auto forms.

A number of the forms are generated in ask type statements in Word or Nisus. Nisus is the primary word processor of the DA's office. Nisus was added as a second word processor about a year ago. Nisus has very powerful macros and does incredibly fast searches. Nine months ago they replaced the dedicated Word processors with 6 Macs in the MAG room (typing pool) for the main word-processing tasks. The MAG room produces about 280,000 pages per year of hard copy. The volume of paper has been reduced since they installed the Macs because files are edited on the computers. They also use email for messaging. They use Microsoft Mail.

Scheduling

For scheduling, they make a different spreadsheet for each day's calendar. They tried Meeting Maker, but they couldn't use it because the various attorneys would not keep the calendar up to date. So scheduling became a hassle. So they resorted to hand scheduling with a secretary entering the data into an Excel template. The spreadsheet lists what attorney is to be in what courtroom on what day. Eventually it will be moved into a database. Docket and court calendar are on the mainframe system. When they put it into a database they will probably build one in Omnis or Filemaker if Filemaker becomes relational before they begin the project.

Email

Email has been very helpful for them. The attorneys and support staff do collect and respond to mail without a big back log. About 50 of the 60 Macs are on the email system. They use LEXIS as their on-line database for research. They have a dedicated terminal, but can connect via the Macs with either of two Shiva net modems—one is 2400 baud and one is 9600 baud. They use the LEXIS interface on both the terminals and the Macs. They use LEXIS for Shepardizing points of law. On-line research is mostly done in the large cases where it is critical. No email services used, but a few of the attorneys use dial in to leave messages or get files from the server. They do not use email for contact with outside attorneys, just for in house use. MacNet has a California DAs forum, but it hasn't been kept up so it has been used very little. Stand alone faxes are used independently of computers.

Portables are not used by county but a few of the attorneys have their own Mac Powerbooks they use to dial in when traveling or at home.

OCR/Scanning

OCR is heavily used. They use a Hewlett Packard ScanJet IIP with sheet feeder and Caere Omnipage 3 to scan mostly printed documents from communications and preprinted matter. They do not digitally store images yet. Translation from MS–DOS is done using Dayna drives (360K and 1.44 MBs) with MacLink Plus and Apple File exchange. When they transferred the jury instruction forms, they used SoftPC to run MS–DOS on the Mac and transfer the files by outputting the Word Perfect text as ASCII to bring into the Macs.

Graphics

Drafting programs are used for courtroom display material. They use Dreams for floor plans in court to show crime scenes. They may switch to Power Draw because California State Department of Justice has a color plotter that works with Power Draw. Department of Justice is mostly MS–DOS, but has a few Macs that use Power Draw. They exchange files currently by hard copy and then scan and or OCR the documents.

Backup

The backup is done with Retrospect Remote software and a 5 gigabyte Exabyte tape device. Daily backup is an incremental back up which takes about 2 hours to do all the machines. Once a month a complete back up is made that takes about 8 hours on Friday night. Back up is done automatically with timer software. Backup tapes are rotated off-site for safety. The same tape is for a week and then tape exchanged with an alternate. Only one tape is offsite at a time which is the alternate week tape. About once a month a tape is made which is stored for 6 months as a reference archive. Smaller 150 MB tapes are used for long term archive storage of inactive material.

Network Activity

For managing the network, Joe Smith uses Gracelan to monitor network activity. He also uses Traffic Watch II from Farallon. He found that network is generally used less than 1%, with a high usage of about 5%. They had printer problems with printers and the network until the printers were moved to Ethernet and Dayna Print because it was going down Fastpath to get to AppleTalk to get into printers.

Has had very few problems with network actually. Almost no hardware problems. Maintenance last year was less than $1500. Most of the problems he encounters are user problems, for example, someone forgets how to do something. Continuing training is the most time consuming activity in his department.

Training

They use MacAcademy tapes they buy for training of beginning Mac users.

Comments:

In the area of litigation support there are several products which would facilitate preparation for trial, such as Trial Maker and Ready for Trial for litigation support. The use of email and telecommunications from outside the office is another area that might be enhanced. As more lawyers in the DA's office begin using laptop computers this will become more attractive. The use of MCI Mail for text faxing is a large savings over traditional faxes with the $10 per month flat fee for domestic faxes. Fax modems with direct input to OCR would facilitate some of the OCR process. Currently documents are scanned and then OCR'd.

Overall it seems the DA's office has tried many of the solutions available for computerization and been able to sift out the ones which are very cost effective and efficient for them. Their use of computer technology is very high.

CHAPTER SEVEN

Database Management Systems: Finding Needles in Haystacks

When to Computerize?

It is virtually impossible to operate a law practice today without a database to file and store the information. It is entirely too time consuming to look up everything manually, much less remember where it is all filed. For you, using a simple PC based system, it is possible to enter each new document as it arrives just as you would in a manual index form. This gives you a great advantage if you are negotiating a settlement. It is possible for you to call up reports regarding certain factual issues which the other party may not be well enough organized to find.

For instance if you used the medical reports database suggested earlier, you would have instant access to the sum of hospital and doctors' fees at any point. You would have easy access to such information as how many times he saw Dr. Brown and what the prognosis was, etc. This information is useful in deposing witnesses as well as presettlement conferences, not to mention the trial itself.

How databases work

Database management systems are perhaps the least used but most promising personal computer application for law offices. With such systems as the pioneer dBASE, or Foxbase on MS–DOS, you can set up a variety of extraordinarily useful office systems to organize your information on personal computers. Recent upgrades of the leading database software today are far more powerful than ever and most are increasingly graphically oriented as GUIs (Graphic User Interface) become the standard interface. dBase (III or IV) has been supplanted by Foxbase and Foxbase Pro as the standard in the MS–DOS world with Paradox becoming more popular. On Macintosh the leaders are Filemaker Pro, Foxbase Pro and 4th Dimension. Foxbase (now owned by Microsoft) has become a leader in the MS–DOS environment because of its ability to read dBase information and process it more rapidly. The larger workstation computers and mini computers also offer more powerful, but more expensive database management software packages. Ingres is one of the leaders used on workstations which use UNIX operating systems. For the very largest cases, with many parties and tens of thousands of documents, the database management capacity of the workstation or mini computers (see Chapter 3) can be used as fileservers for personal computer networks.

Since law offices are in the business of producing and processing information, they are obvious candidates for information management. A database management system could prove to be the greatest leap forward since the introduction of the file cabinet. The applications which will be discussed in this chapter include: in-house work products indices, conflict of interest checks, client status files, and calendar and docket systems. Special attention will be paid to the management of documents for litigation—one of the primary uses of database management systems. Personal information managers are a second area in which database management systems excel.

All database management software packages have some common characteristics. They all allow you to create your own way of organizing your information, and they allow you to search and retrieve that information in a variety of ways. Beyond that there are significant differences among them in how much information you can store, how many ways you can search it, and how quickly the searching will take place.

A database is simply an organized body of information. A few terms are helpful when dealing with a database: a complete database is called a file, each entry in the database is called a record, and each individual item in a record is called a field. Your local telephone book is a database organized by four fields: last name, first name, address and phone number. The difference between the manual database of your telephone book and a computerized telephone book is that with your manual telephone book the only way you can access the information is by last name, since it is already presorted alphabetically according to name. With a computer you could access the information in your telephone book by any of the four fields, or combinations of fields. You could also retrieve it chronologically, or by numerical range. For instance, you could retrieve all the entries who live between 133 Elm and 244 Elm; or you could retrieve only the Martins who live on Birch, or all the Martins whose first name begins with J., but exclude the Johns. The permutations and combinations of retrieval are not limitless, but they may number in the hundreds with just these four fields. Consideration in creating a database should include whether it is a single user or multi-user on a network and with it the various levels of security. An additional consideration is whether to use a flat database or a relational database. A relational database is a collection of flat databases that are linked together. In other words one field in a relational database will be connected to a separate database containing all the types of information relating to the field in the first database. For example, you have a personnel database and within that database you have a field for job type, and the job type is also included in another database which list all the different job types and other related information such as pay rate, perqs, health benefits etc.

For most of the needs of a law office the database of choice will simply be a flat database; these work faster and are easier to set up.   Creating a relational database in most instances will require professional help.   In general these are of more use to larger firms which require more extensive reporting of information contained in the database.   An example of this would be a law office management system that kept information about clients, matters, calendaring, and conflicts.   Careful planning ahead of time to organize the type of material to be filed in the database will save time in programming later.   If you are not sure, you may try using a flat database in single user mode for your initial set up and graduate to a more powerful relational one later.   In most instances you will not have wasted your investment because the flat database will always be a useful utility for the creation of special small databases for client information or managing general office information.   When graduating to a multi-user relational database you will need to purchase a copy—what is called a "run time" version for each machine in the office.   A run time is a read-only form of the database program—as opposed to a full featured version required to program the database.   Run time software is considerably less expensive and allows you to install many copies of the software on your computer network at a substantial savings. Material created in a flat database can be exported to the relational one at a later date.   In addition the flat database can be used for activities that are relatively unsophisticated such as a Rolodex file.

An example of a relational database that can be used to store client/matter information might be one such as Law office manager for the Macintosh:

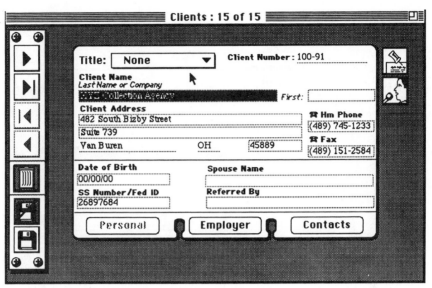

[G19652]

Client information is entered into the software (see above), which is composed of many databases linked together, that is in which the field of one is linked to the field of another. Information about documents which pertain to a matter for a client are entered (see below) and the link is provided by the client field.

[G19653]

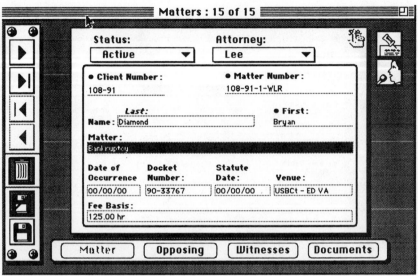

[G19654]

CREATING A DATABASE

Before we discuss the creation of a database, the first question to ask is whether there is a database in existence which already suits your needs. Some databases will satisfy most of your needs but not all and cannot be modified. The fields in these have already been set up for you. Some databases have most of the fields you require, but they can be modified by a programmer to include the necessary material which is lacking. In this case you would pay a programmer's fee for the modifications. And lastly you can create your own. A good rule is if the database does more than 80% of what you need, and you can accomplish the rest with other software, you should consider this software. The more generic and available the software, generally the less expensive it will be. Prices will be in the $100 to $600 range for preformatted software that performs general business tasks. Custom built software which is designed and written for your particular needs often runs between $2500 and $8000 for the initial 4–5 users. Building your own database will generally run between $250–$800 for the software, plus your time.

The procedure that you follow to create a database is similar no matter which software package you are using. First of all you create your own structure. This means you determine which fields you consider important for the body of information that you are organizing. With the telephone book the utility company has decided for you that the fields should be last name, first name, address and phone. If you are creating your own database you choose fields that will work for you. For a calendar/docket, for instance, you might choose the following fields:

case

date

time

attorney

activity

place

parties

opparty

comments

Creating a calendar/docket database using Filemaker Pro (for Windows or Mac) begins with defining the fields listed above:

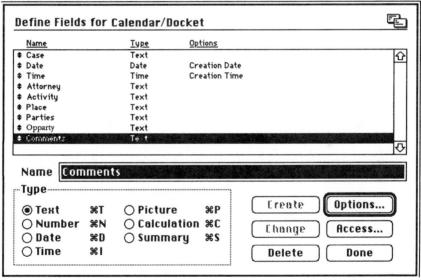

[G19655]

Once the fields are defined, you enter the first layout which is your record entry screen:

```
┌─────────────────────────────────────────────────────────────────┐
│ ▤□▦▦▦▦▦▦▦▦▦▦▦▦▦▦▦▦ Calendar/Docket ▦▦▦▦▦▦▦▦▦▦                   │
├──────────────────┬──────────────────────────────────────────────┤
│ ┌──────────┐     │   ▶                                           │
│ │ Layout #1│          Case  ┌─────────────────────────────────┐  │
│ └──────────┘          Date  │6/1/92 ........................   │  │
│ ┌──────────┐          Time  │12:52:33 PM ...................   │  │
│ │ ⌇⌇⌇      │      Attorney  │ ............................... │  │
│ │          │      Activity  │ ............................... │  │
│ │        1 │         Place  │ ............................... │  │
│ └──────────┘       Parties  │ ............................... │  │
│ Records:          Opparty   │ ............................... │  │
│ 1                 Comments  │ ............................... │  │
│ ──────────                  └─────────────────────────────────┘  │
│ Unsorted                                                          │
│                                                                   │
└──────────────────┴──────────────────────────────────────────────┘
                                                        [G19656]
```

It is important to be far-sighted in choosing fields for your structure since it is very difficult or impossible with most database management systems to change the structure once you have entered the data. The decision regarding which fields to develop should be made by all the parties who will be affected. For instance, an office calendar structure should be developed by everyone in the office, while the database structure for organizing the documents for a particular case should be made by the trial team for that case.

ENTERING THE DATA

After you have determined the structure, the second step in creating your database is to enter the data. This is obviously the most labor-intensive step. If you are trying to organize two or three thousand documents for trial, it will take some time, but probably no more than with manual indexing, and your retrieval powers will be incomparable. While manual indexing will allow you to retrieve documents only chronologically, or perhaps by the author, a computerized index will allow you to retrieve information by any number of combinations and permutations, chronologically and by range. It will allow you to find the proverbial needle in the haystack.

You can also edit your database and add new information readily on a computerized database management system. When a date in a calendar changes, as with a settlement, you can easily find all future dates related to that case and delete them. If there is a continuance you can find all future dates and re-date them quickly. This is a much more difficult task with a manual system.

WARNING! An absolute requirement in data entry is *controlled entry* and *controlled vocabulary*. One or two individuals should be in charge of entering the data and they should work closely with a carefully constructed controlled vocabulary so that the same abbreviations or the same codes are used consistently. A second reader should always check for errors. Because of the basic stupidity of computers, each entry must be exact. For instance, if you wanted all the records produced by John Martin and the data entry person spelled it Marten, the computer with its limited wisdom would not even consider that this may be the same person, and the record would be lost in computer limbo. The most important fact about using any database is that the data entry must be absolutely consistent. If you are going to do any sort of import or export in a database you must also consider the effect that a simple carriage return will have within a file.

The data entry person or persons are critical, but they need not be expensive. It is not necessary that they have any computer experience, or sophisticated legal knowledge. They do not even have to be crack typists. They must be able to follow instructions exactly.

RETRIEVING INFORMATION

Once you have entered your data you are ready to reap your reward by retrieving information in many formats. One of the most obvious ways is to sort alphabetically. You can sort the entire office calendar by all the attorneys or paralegals in the office alphabetically with a few keystrokes on most database management systems. You can also sort any field alphabetically or chronologically. For instance, you can sort the whole calendar alphabetically by client or you can sort it chronologically by date. The chronological sorts are of course critical for a calendar. New calendar items can be entered in any order and a chronological sort will instantly put them in place.

In addition to sorting alphabetically, you can retrieve information by any field or by any combination of fields. For instance if you wanted to retrieve all of the records in which Brown was the attorney, you would pose a command something like:

"find all records where Brown is the attorney."

Each database management system has its own retrieval language; some are very close to natural language and some are more idiosyncratic. Using a form oriented database such as Filemaker Pro we would perform the search for Brown by using the = sign:

```
▤☐▰▰▰▰▰▰▰▰▰▰▰▰▰▰▰▰▰▰▰▰▰▰▰▰  Calendar/Docket  ▰▰▰▰▰
┌─────────────┐
│ Layout #1   │
├─────────────┤        Case    [                                        ]
│  ╪ ╪ ╪      │        Date    [                        ]
│             │        Time    [                        ]
│          1  │    Attorney    [=Brown                  ]
├─────────────┤    Activity    [                        ]
│Requests:    │       Place    [                        ]
│1            │     Parties    [                        ]
│             │      Opparty   [                        ]
│ ┌─────────┐ │    Comments    [                        ]
│ │  Find   │ │
│ └─────────┘ │
│ ☐ Omit      │
│ ┌───┐┌───┐  │
│ │ ‹ ││ ‹ │  │
│ └───┘└───┘  │
│ ┌───┐┌───┐  │
│ │ › ││ › │  │
│ └───┘└───┘  │
│ ┌─────────┐ │
│ │= Exact  │ │
│ └─────────┘ │
│ ┌─────────┐ │
│ │..Range  │ │
│ └─────────┘ │
│ ┌─────────┐ │
│ │! Dupl's │ │
│ └─────────┘ │
│ ┌─────────┐ │
│ │// Today │ │
│ └─────────┘ │
└─────────────┘                                      [G19657]
```

Display or list is a simple command for any database system. The more sophisticated packages, however, allow you to sort by what is called Boolean logic. This means that in addition to finding a single field, you can find combinations or sets of fields by using connectors which define relationships. The number of fields you can combine in one search depends upon the sophistication of the software. The main connectors are: *and, or, not.* These logical operations may be expressed as find any, omit, or find only with symbols representing the logic.

The following is an illustration of how they would be used in Filemaker Pro:

```
▤☐▰▰▰▰▰▰▰▰▰▰▰▰▰▰▰▰▰▰▰▰▰▰▰▰  Calendar/Docket  ▰▰▰▰▰
┌─────────────┐
│ Layout #1   │
├─────────────┤        Case    [                                        ]
│  ╪ ╪ ╪      │        Date    [9/1/92...9/30/92        ]
│             │        Time    [                        ]
│          1  │    Attorney    [=Brown                  ]
├─────────────┤    Activity    [                        ]
│Requests:    │       Place    [                        ]
│1            │     Parties    [                        ]
│             │      Opparty   [                        ]
│ ┌─────────┐ │    Comments    [                        ]
│ │  Find   │ │
│ └─────────┘ │
│ ☐ Omit      │
│ ┌───┐┌───┐  │
│ │ ‹ ││ ‹ │  │
│ └───┘└───┘  │
│ ┌───┐┌───┐  │
│ │ › ││ › │  │
│ └───┘└───┘  │
│ ┌─────────┐ │
│ │= Exact  │ │
│ └─────────┘ │
│ ┌─────────┐ │
│ │..Range  │ │
│ └─────────┘ │
│ ┌─────────┐ │
│ │! Dupl's │ │
│ └─────────┘ │
│ ┌─────────┐ │
│ │// Today │ │
│ └─────────┘ │
└─────────────┘                                      [G19658]
```

The = symbol is a restrictive connector; it limits the search in this case to only those records in which Brown is the attorney. The ... limits the date to the range of the month of September.

By typing the same names in the field without the = symbol and putting the names Brown and Green in the field the search will include either Brown or Green. It expands the search to all the records where Brown was the attorney *OR* Green was the attorney. You can combine restrictive and expanding connectors in the same search by requesting all the entries where Brown was the attorney *OR Green was the attorney* AND the month was September.

Omit is another restrictive connector. You could retrieve all the records where Brown is *not* the attorney.

You can see that there are a staggering number of combinations available for retrieving information. And all of these can become indispensable when you are searching a very large database.

The computer also allows you to find information that often can't be found manually, at least in any manageable period of time. For instance, if you want to call up only those records where Brown is the attorney, the year is 1985, and the activity is a deposition, in other words all of Brown's depositions for 1985; if the calendar is at all large this would be a fairly difficult task. But for the computer, large or small retrieval jobs are almost the same. If your database is quite large and your computer is not the most powerful, it could take as much as a minute, but certainly no longer than that; usually only a few seconds.

REPORTS

All database management systems also allow for some form of report. You could construct a report for Brown's calendar for the month of September and it would come out in report form with titles and activities neatly listed in columns. Or you could construct a report for the calendar for the whole office for the month of September and have a master calendar for that month. The report form that you construct can usually be stored, so that if new data is entered, or you wish to retrieve the information for October, rather than September, you can use the same report format with new contents. Calendar reports are of course routinely created manually in law offices; the computer allows you to produce the report in a few seconds rather than many minutes or hours; and it allows you to produce many variations on the standard calendar reports.

IN-HOUSE WORK PRODUCTS INDEX

Our second demonstration of setting up a database management system for your office will be the in-house work products index. This is a general index of all the work products that you produce in your office which might include:

pleadings

documents

forms of all kinds

in-house memoranda

standard letters to clients, settlement letters, etc.

trial briefs

expert witness lists

law review articles

Basically it should index any work product that anyone in your office produces that someone may find useful in the future. It could even include all or part of your law library as well.

The purpose of having a master index is to avoid re-inventing the wheel. Often you or one of your partners or a legal worker in your office may find themselves creating a document or doing research on a subject that has already been done by someone else. But it is unlikely that they will discover this until it is too late. The master index will not contain the complete document, but will indicate where it can be found.

Creating the In–House Library Index

If you are the person in charge of creating this database, your first step is to sit down and figure out what fields you think would be appropriate for data entry and retrieval. Here are some field suggestions for an in-house library index:

TITLE. This is the title of the document, for instance it could be the name of a memo, "Search and Seizure Without a Warrant", or the title of a law review article or trial brief.

TYPE. The second field is the type. The type could be a pleading, document, law review, contract, form, or memo.

DATE. The third field is the date on which it was created and perhaps the date on which it was updated as well.

AUTHOR. The fourth field is author. Who created the document?

LOCATION. The fifth field is location. Where do you find this document? Is there a hard copy in a client file, or is it stored on a disk? If it was produced with word processing, it should of course be stored on a magnetic medium, most likely a floppy disk. This is most useful because you can then use that particular magnetic medium to edit or reproduce the document for further use.

CLIENT. Another useful field is client, indicating for which client the document was produced.

KEYWORD. There should always be a key word field. This is the field that would probably be searched most frequently. Every legal and factual issue contained in the document you are indexing should be contained in this field.

DIGEST. This is an optional field. A digest could be a short summary of the document. This field would be useful for long documents like articles, memos and briefs. It could be left bland for short documents, forms, etc.

We have created the In–House Library Index database (See diagram below) using Filemaker Pro, which is available for Macintosh and Windows.

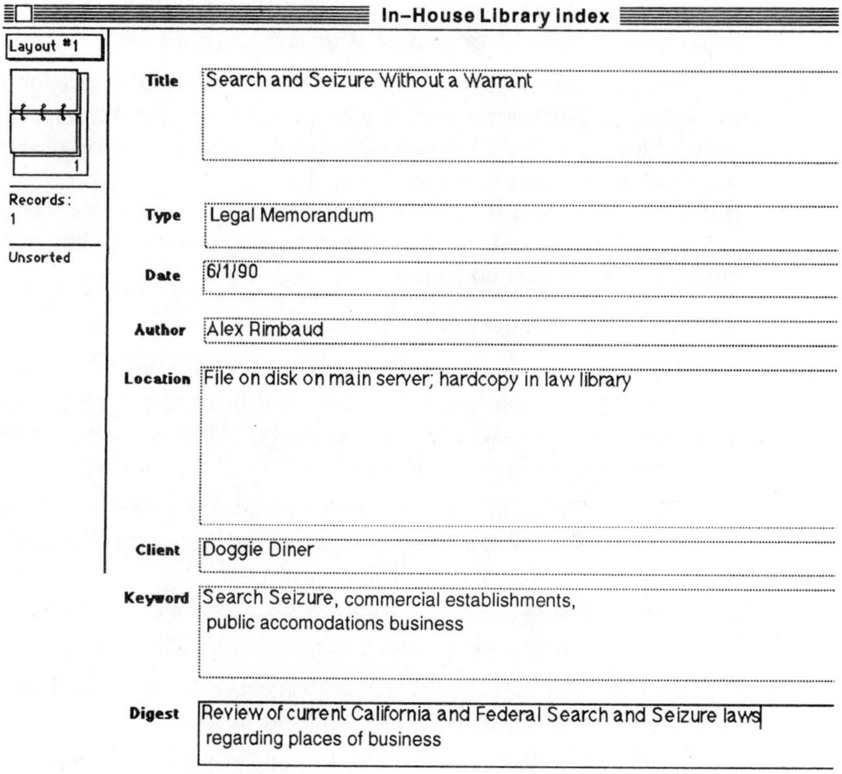

In–House Library Index	
Layout #1	
	Title Search and Seizure Without a Warrant
Records: 1	**Type** Legal Memorandum
Unsorted	**Date** 6/1/90
	Author Alex Rimbaud
	Location File on disk on main server; hardcopy in law library
	Client Doggie Diner
	Keyword Search Seizure, commercial establishments, public accomodations business
	Digest Review of current California and Federal Search and Seizure laws regarding places of business

[G19661]

Getting the System to Work

Once the system is in place, the author of any new document will highlight the document with a yellow pen or in some other fashion, to indicate which key words should be entered into the computer for future retrieval. Or the author may manually fill out a card which corresponds to the fields: title, type, author, etc. This should become a standard practice for everyone in the law office so that all future documents can be very easily indexed in your in-house word products index.

Human nature being imperfect, it is not always easy to convince busy attorneys that they should spend a few extra minutes after creating a document to assure that it is properly indexed.

This is a political, rather than a computer problem, and the solution must come via a directive from top management. Without full cooperation the effectiveness of a work product index will be seriously limited.

As with all database management applications, the data entry must be severely controlled. A controlled vocabulary must be developed and one or two individuals should be given the responsibility of all computer entries to ensure that whole records are not lost through tiny spelling errors, or misuse of terms.

Using Your Work Product Index

Here is an example of how this index then can be put into use. A client comes to you with a problem regarding a condominium conversion. You might search the database for condominium, or for the phrase "condominium conversion". If you knew, or had reason to believe that the law had changed in the past two or three years, you might restrict your search by asking for "condominium" or "condominium conversion" in the keywords field and only entries after 1980 in the date field. This allows you to pinpoint only the most recent information, which in this case would be the only relevant information.

You could pinpoint your search even further by specifying that you only wanted *forms* relating to condominium conversion, rather than articles or memoranda, etc. Your search command might sound something like "Find all the documents where the key words contain condominium conversion and the type of document is form, and the date is after 1980"; (the retrieval language will vary with the date base program you use, and some will provide a great deal of on-screen assistance in formulating your query).

Using our In–House Library Index which we made with Filemaker Pro, we use a layout for looking up the information we require (see diagram below).

```
▓□▓▓▓▓▓▓▓▓▓▓▓▓▓▓▓▓▓▓▓▓  In House Library index  ▓▓▓▓▓▓
┌───────────┐              Title   ┌──────────────────────────────┐
│ Lookup Lay...│                    └──────────────────────────────┘
└───────────┘              Type   ┌──────────────────────────────┐
┌───────────┐                      │=Form                         │
│  ↕         │                      └──────────────────────────────┘
│         ↖  │             Date   ┌─────────────────────────┐
│           │                      │>1/1/1980                │
│         1 │                      └─────────────────────────┘
└───────────┘            Author   ┌──────────────────────────────┐
Requests:                          └──────────────────────────────┘
1                        Location ┌──────────────────────────────┐
                                   └──────────────────────────────┘
                          Client  ┌──────────────────────────────┐
┌───────────┐                      └──────────────────────────────┘
│   Find    │            keyword  ┌──────────────────────────────┐
└───────────┘                      │=Condominuim Conversion       │
□ Omit                             └──────────────────────────────┘
┌─────┐ ┌─────┐          Digest   ┌──────────────────────────────┐
│  <  │ │  ≤  │                    └──────────────────────────────┘
└─────┘ └─────┘
┌─────┐ ┌─────┐
│  >  │ │  ≥  │
└─────┘ └─────┘
┌────────────┐
│  =  Exact  │
└────────────┘
┌────────────┐
│ ...  Range │
└────────────┘
┌────────────┐
│  !  Dupl's │
└────────────┘
┌────────────┐
│ //  Today  │
└────────────┘
```

[G19662]

LITIGATION SUPPORT

Once you have mastered this relatively simple database management structure, you can try for more complicated applications, such as organizing documents for trials. These documents might include:

Produced documents (your side), which can take any form, ranging from payroll accounts to psychiatric reports

Discovered documents (their side), which could also include any imaginable document

Deposition and/or trial transcripts

Physical Exhibits

Witness Lists

Relevant Materials from other cases

Medical Reports

Attorneys' work product

Litigation support is definitely one of the most exciting potential applications of a database management system. Until a few years ago, only very large firms with very large cases took advantage of computers to organize their documents. Today virtually all law firms with computers use databases in one form or another to manage the documents involved in litigation. It is not impossible for a small case to involve hundreds to thousands of documents. Today's personal computers are capable of handling extremely large numbers of documents—possibly hundreds of thousands—in the databases. In most cases it is simply a question of the storage capacity of the computer, that is the size of the hard disk, which provides the limitations on the amount of data that can be safely stored, indexed and accessed by a personal computer database. In offices with several to many attorneys and paralegals, these databases can be accessed by many people at the same time, with the data residing on a file server and accessed via a local area network.

Because of the flexibility of today's databases, there are now many commercial software vendors who produce litigation support software for PCs. (See chapter 4 on choosing software) These systems will do the trick for you as well, but they are more expensive, and may not be as suited to your own case as a system you could create yourself. In fact most of these commercial software offerings are overlays on a standard database management system such as Foxbase (MS–DOS), 4th Dimension (Mac) or Ingres (UNIX). The software programmers have simply set up the structures for you and provided some pre-fabricated report forms. You may be able to save yourself a thousand dollars and tailor a system for your own needs with relatively little effort. Alternately you can buy a prepared database specially customized for your legal specialty (i.e. Personal Injury) and for relatively low cost have it customized to your own needs.

At what point is it worth putting your documents on a computer? Probably any case with more than a hundred documents, possibly even more than fifty, would be better organized and the information easier to retrieve if it were computer indexed. For instance, if you were representing the plaintiff in a personal injury suit and you had collected 25 medical reports over a period of two years and deposed four witnesses, you have a fair amount of information to organize. If you are already utilizing a manual indexing method, you should certainly put that effort into the computer and achieve far greater retrieval powers.

Some examples of Litigation support databases follow:

The software package Summation runs on MS–DOS systems. The entry screen below is for entering summary information about documents related to a case concerning Mental Health for future retrieval. The fields in this system are pre-defined rather than created by the user.

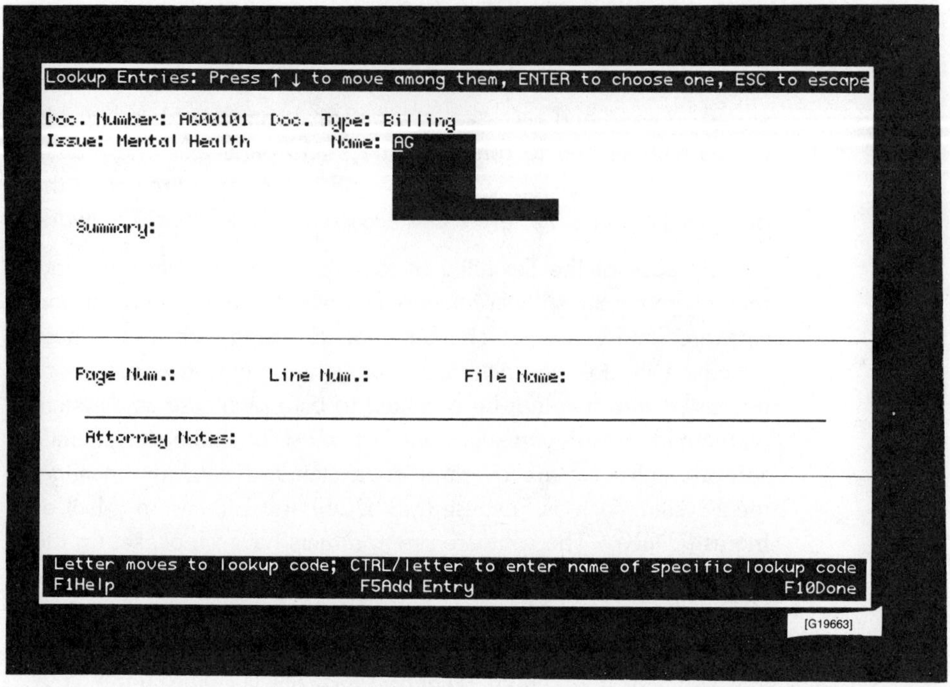

```
Lookup Entries: Press ↑ ↓ to move among them, ENTER to choose one, ESC to escape

Doc. Number: AG00101  Doc. Type: Billing
Issue: Mental Health        Name: AG


    Summary:




    Page Num.:          Line Num.:          File Name:
    _____

    Attorney Notes:



Letter moves to lookup code; CTRL/letter to enter name of specific lookup code
F1Help                           F5Add Entry                        F10Done
```

[G19663]

Litidex is a litigation support database which organizes documents according to the following entry fields:

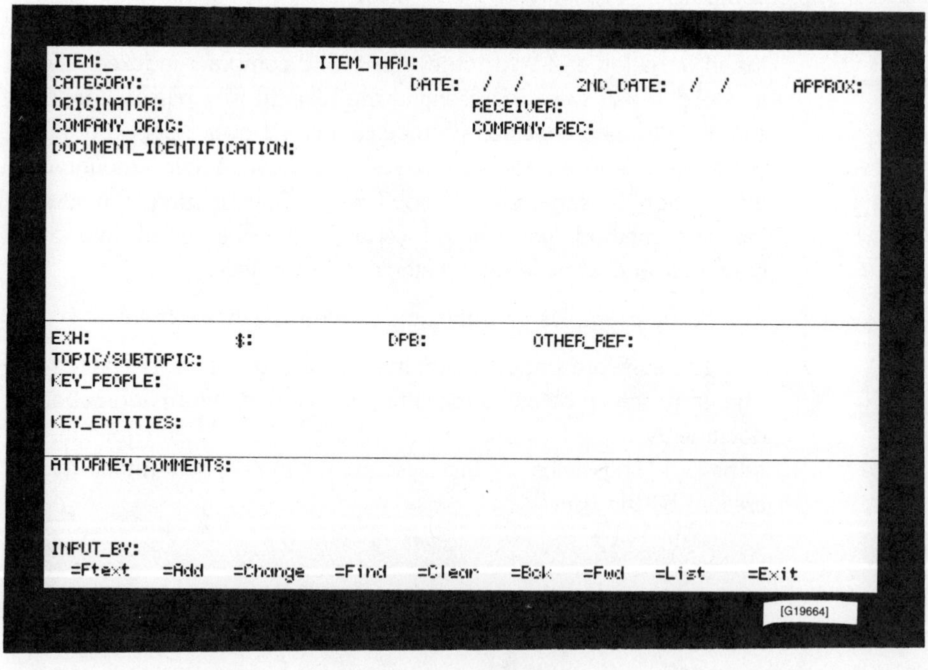

```
ITEM:_              .       ITEM_THRU:
CATEGORY:                        DATE:  /  /      2ND_DATE:  /  /       APPROX:
ORIGINATOR:                      RECEIVER:
COMPANY_ORIG:                    COMPANY_REC:
DOCUMENT_IDENTIFICATION:






EXH:            $:          DPB:           OTHER_REF:
TOPIC/SUBTOPIC:
KEY_PEOPLE:

KEY_ENTITIES:

ATTORNEY_COMMENTS:



INPUT_BY:
  =Ftext    =Add    =Change    =Find    =Clear    =Bck    =Fwd    =List    =Exit
```

[G19664]

Litidex is used to record information about witnesses involved in a case.

```
Witness Number: 0001
Name: ARNOLD, DANA                                    Phone (    )    -
Witness's Attorney:                                   Phone (    )    -
Produced By:
Friendly:   Hostile:   Impartial:   Fact:   Expert:

Synopsis:

















DEPO:   STATEMENT:   REPORT OF INTERVIEW:

 =Add    =Change    =Clear    =Bck    =Fwd    =Exit
```
[G19665]

Litidex further provides fields for information relating to the attorneys involved and the court officials. After a few years of entry this information could be very valuable in creating a profile of various court officials in upcoming litigation.

```
                        DATABASE INFORMATION


CASE NAME:DEMONSTRATION CASE
COURT CS #:_
[ ]PLF:                                      (   )   -

[ ]DEF:                                      (   )   -

OUR ATTORNEY:                                (   )   -

OPP ATTORNEY:                                (   )   -

COURT:                                       (   )   -
CLERK:                                       (   )   -
JUDGE:                                       (   )   -
SYNOPSIS:




    =Add/Update Database      =Exit
```

[G19666]

Trial Maker is a litigation support package available on the
Macintosh and Windows, created using Filemaker Pro. Document
entry is made in the form below. Information is entered regarding
the documents relating to a specific case as seen in the picture:

Document Input Screen (Index) (New)

QuickEntry	cj	**Description**	**Exhibit No.**
Address		**From**	**Marking Date**
Document Date		**To**	
Event Date	5-7-50	**Produced By**	**Event Time**

Susan was born on May 7, 1950. She was 40 years old on the date of the accident.

(Add Witness...)   (Prepare Examination...) (Add To Do Item ...)

Input Status			
FW **1**	1. ⊠ Background Facts	6. ☐ Issue 6	11. ☐ Issue 11
	2. ☐ Liability	7. ☐ Issue 7	12. ☐ Issue 12
	3. ⊠ Damages	8. ☐ Issue 8	13. ☐ Issue 13
	4. ☐ Security	9. ☐ Issue 9	14. ☐ Issue 14
	5. ☐ Issue 5	10. ☐ Issue 10	15. ☐ Settlement

[G19667]

Witness information for a case is entered in the window below. This particular entry screen is for information relating to adverse witnesses and has check mark boxes for the issues.

Adverse Witness Input Screen	(Index) (New)

QuickEntry	cj	Source	Conference	Address	
Starting Page		Witness	John Hert	Date of Statement	10-11-90

Create New Record, or Input From Friendly Witness Input Screen

Ending Page		Event Date	5-7-50	☐ Approximate Date	Event Time	

(Add Witness...) (Prepare Examination...) (Add To Do Item ...)

Input Status **FW 1**	1. ☒ Background Facts	6. ☐ Issue 6	11. ☐ Issue 11
	2. ☐ Liability	7. ☐ Issue 7	12. ☐ Issue 12
	3. ☒ Damages	8. ☐ Issue 8	13. ☐ Issue 13
	4. ☐ Security	9. ☐ Issue 9	14. ☐ Issue 14
	5. ☐ Issue 5	10. ☐ Issue 10	15. ☐ Settlement

[G19668]

An additional entry screen in Trialmaker is for entering the legal authority citations.

Law Input	(Index) (To Do) (New) (Import)

QuickEntry	
Authority	Hertz vs. Brown
Citation	223 Cal.Rptr.291

Car rental business not reponsible for negligent use by driver. In this case driver failed to heed empty oil signal

Input Status **DOC 48**	1. ☐ Background Facts	6. ☐ Issue 6	11. ☐ Issue 11
	2. ☒ Liability	7. ☐ Issue 7	12. ☐ Issue 12
	3. ☒ Damages	8. ☐ Issue 8	13. ☐ Issue 13
	4. ☐ Security	9. ☐ Issue 9	14. ☐ Issue 14
	5. ☐ Issue 5	10. ☐ Issue 10	15. ☐ Settlement

[G19669]

Setting up Your Own Database

There are many occasions in which it makes more sense for you to set up your own database, rather than using ones in which the fields are preformatted. This option will certainly give you the greatest flexibility and depth.

As with all system designs you must first sit down and think through the problem. What kinds of information are you likely to want to retrieve? Do you need one database or two or three? I believe that if you are dealing with depositions as well as other kinds of documents you should have a separate database for the depositions. You may also want to have more than one database for the other documents you are collecting if they fall into distinctly different categories. In a personal injury transaction, for instance, you may want to keep a separate database for medical records, and one for general information, or use a relational database which has separate files for each of the information types. All of the sophisticated general database management programs allow you to search more than one database with a single query. With software developed specifically for litigation support, it is often not possible to develop more than one database.

Depositions

Depositions are often major factors in preparing a case for trial. There are two approaches possible to organize the information provided by depositions. New technology has given the PC user the power of searching the full text of the deposition. This was previously only available on mainframes. The second possibility is to summarize depositions in the traditional way, but directly into the computer, giving the searcher far greater powers of retrieval.

a. Full Text Retrieval

In the last few years, several enterprising software companies, such as DepoBank, (Text Sciences Corp.), MicroText, (Document Automation Corp.), and Amicus I, (Baron Data Systems) have offered the full text of depositions in compressed form on floppies. This software makes use of computer assisted transcription or CAT, the process in which a large computer is used to transcribe the court reporter's recording. The full text produced by the large computer is then downloaded onto a floppy disk to use in a PC with appropriate software which searches full text. (The floppy has been compressed to store up to 1800 pages of text per disk) It is now possible in most cities and counties to obtain depositions and trial transcripts on floppy disk in ASCII format which can be read by almost any computer system regardless of the operating system. Deposition summarizing as we know it may soon become a little-mourned memory, replaced by full text searching (see notes of caution in chapter on Retrieval).

However, because full text searches may miss information, it is still useful to enhance the full text by providing key words and appropriate authority lists so that proper names, for instance, would always be recognized by the computer. Like many areas of rapidly developing computer technology, the next generation of computer software may include this capacity as an automatic feature. In the meanwhile, however, it is both economical and efficient to summarize depositions directly onto a database management system.

b.   Computer Summaries.

It is quite feasible for paralegals to summarize depositions directly into the computer, avoiding the step of dictation, or coding. The following is an example of this process using a database management system on which the following fields had been created:

DEPONENT

DATE

FROM

TO

KEYWORDS

SUMMARY

XREF

COMMENTS

The third and fourth fields, FROM and TO, indicate the page and line numbers covered in this particular record. In the next field, KEYWORDS, the paralegal picked out the issues or key concepts that were covered in this portion of the deposition. In the final field, SUMMARY, the paralegal transforms the traditional method of summarizing a deposition by typing the summary directly into the computer. The field, XREF relates this record to other documents or other parties. The last field, COMMENTS, is a general field in which any miscellaneous information can be inserted.

Once the deposition is summarized completely in the database, the process of retrieval is far more efficient than would be possible with a traditional deposition summary. For instance, to retrieve a particular factual issue regarding fraudulent car loans from Mrs. Dunlap's deposition, the searcher could pull from the field KEYWORDS all the records in which the term "auto loan" appeared. Or he could search both the KEYWORDS and SUM-MARY fields for "auto loan". To pinpoint the search further he could request only those records in which only the words "auto loan" *and* "Mr. Jones" appeared in the KEYWORDS *or* SUM-MARY fields. The searcher could use all of the sort and range capacities of the database management system to find information in a way that is simply not possible with traditional, non-computerized deposition summaries.

Summation is a preformatted database system which allows for a combination of the full text of a deposition plus the summary with notes added (notice the musical note to indicate that a note has been entered by the law practitioner, a useful tool when working with depositions):

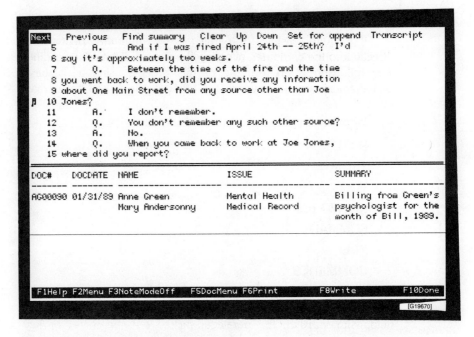

General Documents

General documents gathered in preparation for a trial such as reports, correspondence, invoices, checks, or even notes scribbled on the back of envelopes should be treated differently than depositions, since you do not need the complete text of the item; and in fact full text searching would probably be less efficient than a well indexed database. It is most efficient to develop a structure which would cover a wide range of documents so that you can search the whole database at once.

A possible structure for a document database is:

NUMBER

AUTHOR

PARTIES

DATE

TYPE

PRODUCED

DISCOVERED

EXHIBIT

LOCATION

XREF

KEYWORDS

COMMENTS

These fields follow fairly closely the categories used on standard document coding forms, and the fields offered by most packaged litigation support software packages for PCs. Most of these fields are self-explanatory. TYPE indicates the kind of documents you are dealing with, e.g. letter, invoice, etc. The fields PRODUCED and DISCOVERED will track the origin of the document and allow you to keep current with what has been produced for the opposing team. XREF will indicate how this document might refer to other documents in your database. KEYWORDS will indicate the legal issues or factual issues which most clearly describe the importance of this document. And finally COMMENTS, which is a field for the idiosyncrasies which this particular document might present.

Additional Databases

If all your documents could fit easily into the above described database structure, a pre-packaged litigation support software package would work well for you. But real life trials are often not so cut and dried. In addition to a separate database for depositions, you probably would make use of separate databases to index your work products (this also insures against discovery by the opposing party), your witnesses, and specialized documents. For instance, if your case involved extensive medical reports, a different kind of structure would be useful. These databases could be easily constructed with a general database management system. For these situations a flat file database would suffice. If you require that the litigation support material be linked to your general office system so client information is linked to the matters and in turn to the litigation for billing purposes, then you would have to resort to a relational database. Relational databases are very complicated to design and build. They are recommended only for the advanced users of computers and are usually best left to programmers. If you are very clear about what information you want and how you want it linked, hiring a consultant to build the system for you is probably the best solution. Be sure that you have thought out the content carefully in advance. Programming costs can run high if you have not thought through all the information you wish to include.

Here are some examples of possible structures for some additional databases that may be useful in litigation support:

Medical Reports Database

NUMBER

DOCTOR

DOCTFEE

HOSP

HOSPFEE

DATE

INJURY

DIAGNOSIS

PROGNOSIS

TREATMENT

PRODUCED

DISCOVERED

XREF

KEYWORDS

COMMENTS

This database also allows you to keep track of medical expenses which can be summoned by your database management system.

Litigation Work Product Index

AUTHOR

TITLE

TYPE

DATE

XREF

LOCATION

KEYWORDS

COMMENTS

This, of course, is very much like your general in-house work products index, but it provides a confidential working list of work products for only this litigation until the case is resolved, which may regretfully not occur for several years. At that point useful work products can be entered as part of your general in-house library index.

Searching and Retrieving Information

At any step in the litigation process a well organized database provides instant information which can be useful for bargaining, witness preparation and examination, and finally trial strategy and courtroom presentation. Indices and reports of all kinds can be immediately generated. All documents can be arranged in chronological order, by type of document, author, or by any other criteria that might be useful in getting ready for a particular trial. In cross-examining a witness, for instance, an index that lists in chronological order all documents that mention that witness's name can be a critical help in preparing for interrogation.

Data entry for litigation support should be carefully controlled as with all databases. If you are dealing with hundreds or perhaps thousands of documents this becomes even more critical. An extensive controlled vocabulary must be developed. Using numbers or codes rather than abbreviations of words is a possibility, but it sometimes makes the information retrieved incomprehensible to anyone but the inner circle of data entry specialists.

In the best possible retrieval arrangements, data entry should be very restricted, but retrieval should be possible by any member of the trial team, i.e., all attorneys, paralegals, or legal support people on the team. In less than two hours it should be possible to train even the most computer illiterate team members how to retrieve information on most database management systems. The training will also stimulate their imagination regarding interesting and exotic possibilities for retrieval.

(See detailed discussion at end of chapter concerning retrieval of information)

Notes on Hardware and Software

If you are planning to tackle litigation support on a PC you definitely need a larger hard disk for storage and a computer with sufficient memory. The amount of memory required will vary with each system, since a color system with several RAM resident programs will require more memory than a system that is black and white and has very little extension software loaded onto it. When using a system with a GUI (Graphic User Interface) memory need will be even more. Today the bare minimum RAM required for any system is at least 2 megabytes and really should be at least 4–5 megabytes. With RAM costing under 50 dollars a megabyte this is not a very expensive inclusion for your system. In addition you will need sufficient storage capacity on your hard disk. Depending on the complexity of your database system and the amount of information to be stored in it, a minimum configuration today would be between 100 megabytes and 250 megabytes for a personal computer and from 250 megabytes up to 1 gigabyte (1,000 megabytes) for a file server. Very small cases of 200 documents or less may be adequately handled by the older PCs, but they will not handle the new generation of easier to use, more sophisticated database management software packages such as 4th Dimension for the Macintosh or Q & A for MS–DOS. On the other hand, any PC with a 2–4 megabytes main memory and 100 megabytes of hard disk storage should be able to handle between 2500 and 10,000 documents with good efficiency.

CALENDAR/DOCKET SYSTEMS

A good candidate for database management is a combined calendar/docket system; this application was discussed briefly earlier in the chapter. This master calendar, as we shall call it, would include all of the court appearances relating to matters in litigation as well as all the other work-related activities that involve attorneys and legal personnel; including lunch dates with clients or the local bar association golf tournament. There are some off-the-shelf calendar systems and many packaged time-keeping and billing systems will offer a calendar as one of their features, but it is a very simple system to create yourself. The key to any calendaring system, manual or computerized, is to have a single responsible person who does all the data entry. If that person falls down on the job, the computer will not help. The advantage that the computer offers, as with all forms of data organization, is that you can retrieve the calendar information in many more ways than you can with a manual system. If there are a number of workers in your office, attorneys, paralegals, and perhaps other legal personnel, a master calendar can become a very elaborate and time consuming task. The computer should make it more efficient.

Most law offices have the same trouble spots in designing calendars. First of all, you must a include a tickler system which will give adequate warning.

An example of a tickler system entry from Law Office Manager would be:

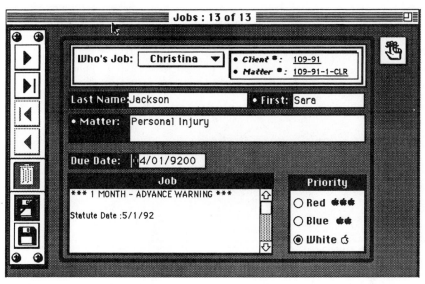

[G19671]

You must also be concerned about back-up attorneys in case the main attorney assigned to that particular activity is not available. Given these considerations, a possible structure might be something like this:

CASE: Laurel v. Hardy CLIENT: Hardy

ATTORNEY: Bryan

ATTORNEY2: Douglass

DATE: 08/09/23, 08/10/23,

ACTIVITY: Trial Brief

PLACE: Mont.Sup.Ct.

OPPARTY: Darrow

COMMENTS: No Settlement

ATTORNEY 2 would be the back-up field and DATE would include both the warning date and the actual date. If you called up your calendar for the week of September 9th, the warning date would automatically appear. There are other ways of doing it but this is one of the possible ways.

Using a preformatted system such as Abacus which runs on MS–DOS systems, entry for the calendar would be:

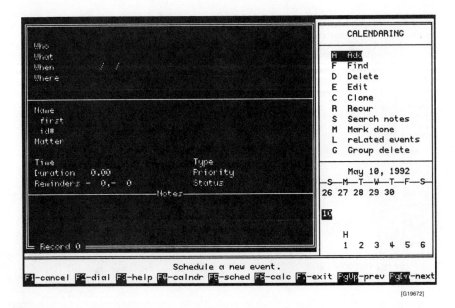

[G19672]

The information once entered appears in the following format:

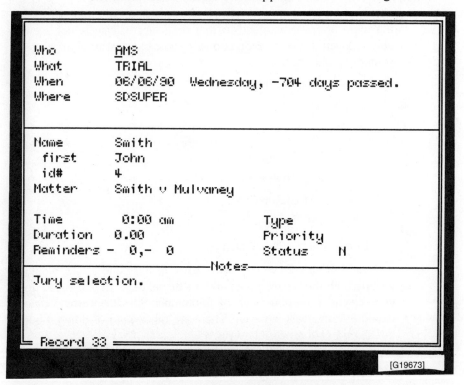

[G19673]

With Abacus computerized calendar you could call up a report for each attorney for any given day, week, month, or year or you could call up a report for the whole office for any given day, week, month, or year. You could call up a report which just listed the depositions for a particular week or month or you could call up a report only indicating the calendar items for a particular case or a particular client.

Quick editing in Abacus is a wonderful feature of a computerized calendar. If your case settles, or is continued, you can instantly call up all the calendar items which support it and either delete them or advance them in time.

```
Day When        Time     Hrs  What      Who      Where    Client

Mo  12/04/89  12:00 pm  1.00  LUNCH     AMS                   Ripley
Tu  12/05/89   0:00 am  0.00  REMINDER  AMS      *** 12/06/89 C-CLIENT
Tu  12/05/89   0:00 am  0.00  REMINDER  NPB      *** 12/06/89 DEPO
We  12/06/89   0:00 am  0.00  DISCOVER  AMS
We  12/06/89  10:00 am  1.00  F-ANSWER  NPB      SDSUPER  Edwards
We  12/06/89   2:00 pm  2.00  C-CLIENT  AMS      HERE     Ripley
We  12/06/89   3:00 pm  2.00  DEPO      NPB      HERE     Adams
Fr  12/08/89   7:30 am  1.00  C-CLIENT  AMS      HERE     Adams
Fr  12/08/89  11:30 am  1.00  LUNCH     AMS               Adams
Tu  12/12/89   0:00 am  0.00  REMINDER  NPB      *** 12/14/89 DEPO
Th  12/14/89  10:00 am  1.00  DEPO      NPB      HERE
Fr  12/15/89  11:30 am  1.00  LUNCH     AMS               Adams
Mo  12/18/89   0:00 am  0.00  REMINDER  NPB      *** 12/19/89 DEPO
Tu  12/19/89  10:00 am  1.00  DEPO      NPB      HERE
Fr  12/22/89  11:30 am  1.00  LUNCH     AMS               Adams
Fr  12/29/89  11:30 am  1.00  LUNCH     AMS               Adams
Th  01/04/90   0:00 am  0.00  REMINDER  NPB      *** 01/09/90 F-MOTION.
                              ↑ ↓
```

[G19675]

The needs of your particular office might be significantly different than this model and you might want to add different fields. You might want to add for instance, a judge field, or the telephone number of the court or other location where the activity will occur. At any rate it is easy to adapt the structure to suit yours and your clients' needs if you design your own system. While building your own system will allow you to customize and add additional fields, a packaged system such as Abacus does feature most of the items necessary to a law practice and is included as part of the law office management system.

CONFLICT OF INTEREST/NEW MATTER MEMO

The database management application which we will explore is a combination conflicts/clients index system. For a small law office, this simply means that when you develop a new matter memo for a new case, you can turn it into a fairly extensive reference resource which will alert you to conflicts of interest and also provide a variety of information regarding factual and legal issues, statutes of limitations, opposing attorneys, etc. Again there is no limit to the amount of useful information that you could easily keep for each case. This conflicts/clients index can also include billing information, although it would not serve as your actual billing system. That requires sophisticated time keeping and billing software.

Even small firms have real or potential conflict of interest problems. If you practice in the areas of personal injury or insurance defense, for instance, it is difficult to keep track of all the insurance companies you have represented or opposed. Clients may own more than one business, or their businesses may be subsidiaries of other companies. Some gargantuan cases, like those in asbestos litigation, seem to involve every lawyer in town on one side or the other. There are many possibilities that could lead to a potential conflict of interest, and it is better to be safe than sorry.

A structure which you might create for a conflict of interest/client index system should include the following information:

case name and number

client name and address

AKA of client, which would include other businesses or subsidiary relationships

principal and back-up attorney assigned to case

opposing attorney, name, address and phone

opposing party, name and address

AKA of opposing party, which would include businesses or subsidiary relationships

type of case

legal issues

statute of limitation

billing information

location

With this database it would be possible to quickly search and find all of your cases with the same opposing attorney, or all the personal injury cases your firm handled in 1983–1985; as well as all the other cases you handled for this client, or in which you opposed the current opposing party.

Using a practice management system such as Abacus for MS–DOS computers the client information is entered into the following fields so they can be checked for conflict later:

Last name

First name

ID number

Salutation

Daytime phone

Evening phone

Additional phone

Additional phone

Classification

Attorney

Date file opened

Active or not

Abacus systems for MS–DOS contains the following entry screens for conflict of interest:

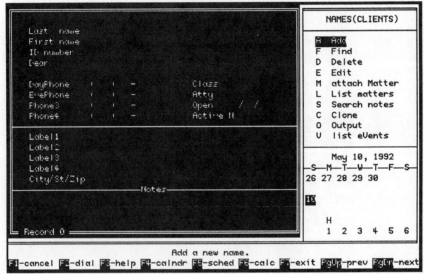

[G19676]

Conflicts can then be searched as follows:

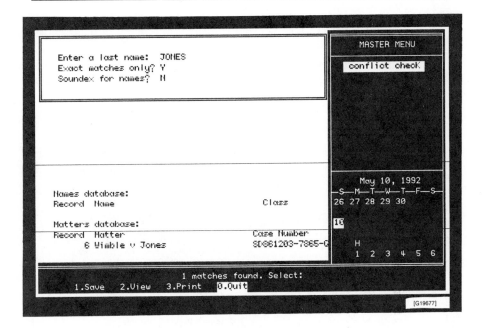

How Much History?

Unfortunately a conflict of interest system does not work if you begin today. Conflicts by their very nature involve activity with opposing parties or counsel that occurred in the past; but how far past? With this system it makes sense to go back at least ten years and enter all old client information. The entries are short and the labor well worth it. Then you can relegate old dead files to deep storage with the confidence that you have most of the information that you need and you know where to find the file.

If your firm is large, it is probably useful to have a personnel file in addition, where cases that your attorneys have worked on before joining your firm are indicated. When you have a new client you can search that client and the opposing party against your computerized personnel database to check for potential conflicts as well. Again, once you have this system in place, it is no more time consuming to enter the initial client information into the computer than it is in a manual system, and you have accomplished a far more efficient indexing system.

PERSONAL INFORMATION MANAGERS

As computers have become more a part of everyone's lives, standardized small databases are now offered commercially that are extremely inexpensive and yet fulfill the normal functions required to run an office or organize your life—whether you are an attorney, a physician or any other professional. While many of these could be created with some time and effort by customizing a standard database, it is hardly worth the time. For example there are many handy Rolodex type databases that perform many office needs such as dialing the phone, creating mail labels, fax cover sheets, address books, etc. These small information databases are known as PIMS or Personal Information Managers.

An example of a PIM for addresses available on Macintosh systems is Touchbase. It has all the fields preformatted with a few left customizable by the user:

[G19678]

Entry is made into the window above and saved to the database.

The information may be viewed in list form using Touchbase as well:

✓	Company	Entire Name	Phone 1	Phone 2	
	Bridge Software Systems,		(800) 446-1665		⬆
	Barrister Information		(716) 845-5010		
	Basic Systems, Inc.		(803) 232-1826		
	J.H. Cohn & Co.		(201) 228-3223		
	Computer Law Systems,		(612) 941-3801		
	Personal Library		(301) 926-1402		
	Legal-Acc Software		(416) 694-4751		
	Micro Strategies		(201) 625-7721		
	Primetime Software, Inc.		(800) 777-8860		
	Manzanita Software		(800) 447-5700		
	MicroCraft, Inc.		(800) 225-3147		
	Solutions Plus Inc.		(800) 543-2463		
	Sourcemate Info Syst. Inc.		(415) 381-1011		
	Transaction Recording		(503) 646-5321		
	Matthew Bender & Co. Inc.		(800) 223-1940		
	Julius Blumberg, Inc.		(800) 221-2972		
✓	Boren Legal Software		(313) 663-6660		
	Commercial Legal		(800) 435-7257		
	Comtronic Systems Inc.		(206) 874-4034		
	Goldsoft, Inc.		(703) 385-6446		⬇

Find 🔍 ▼   New   428 records of 428   Modify

[G19679]

Searching for someone in the database is extremely easy and fast:

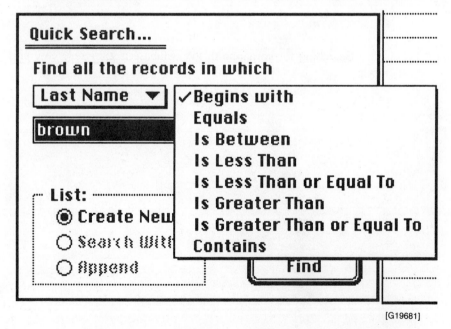

[G19680]

Options allow for more complex searches to find records that contain or begin with a word and several other logical functions that are useful:

Quick Search...

Find all the records in which

Last Name ▼	✓Begins with
	Equals
brown	Is Between
	Is Less Than
	Is Less Than or Equal To
	Is Greater Than
List:	Is Greater Than or Equal To
◉ Create New	Contains
○ Search With	
○ Append	Find

[G19681]

A full search will allow you to search several fields at the same time so that if a name or phrase was placed in a different field the information could be found such as find any city or software that begins with the name brown (i.e., Brownsville or Brown City Software company):

Full Search...

Search String: `brown`

Fields to Search:

☐ Salutation	☐ Address 1	☐ Country	☐ Category
☐ **First Name**	☐ Address 2	☐ Phone 1	☐ Custom 3
☐ **Last Name**	☒ City	☐ Phone 2	☐ Custom 4
☐ **Company**	☐ State	☐ Fax	☐ Custom 5
☐ Title	☐ **Zip Code**	☒ Software	☐ Notes

Search type:
- ◉ **Begins With**
- ○ **Exact match**
- ○ **Contains**

List:
- ◉ **Create New**
- ○ Search Within
- ○ Append

[Cancel]

[**Find**]

[G19682]

It is possible to modify the output of the contents and display of the list with a forms designer built into the database so output can be tailored to your needs:

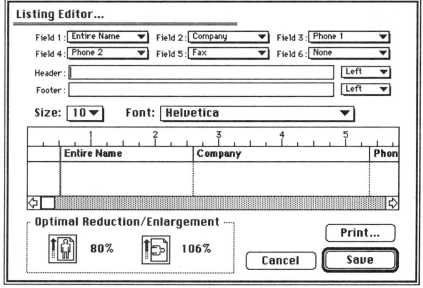

[G19683]

If the PIM is used to generate a fax cover sheet, this can be customized as well:

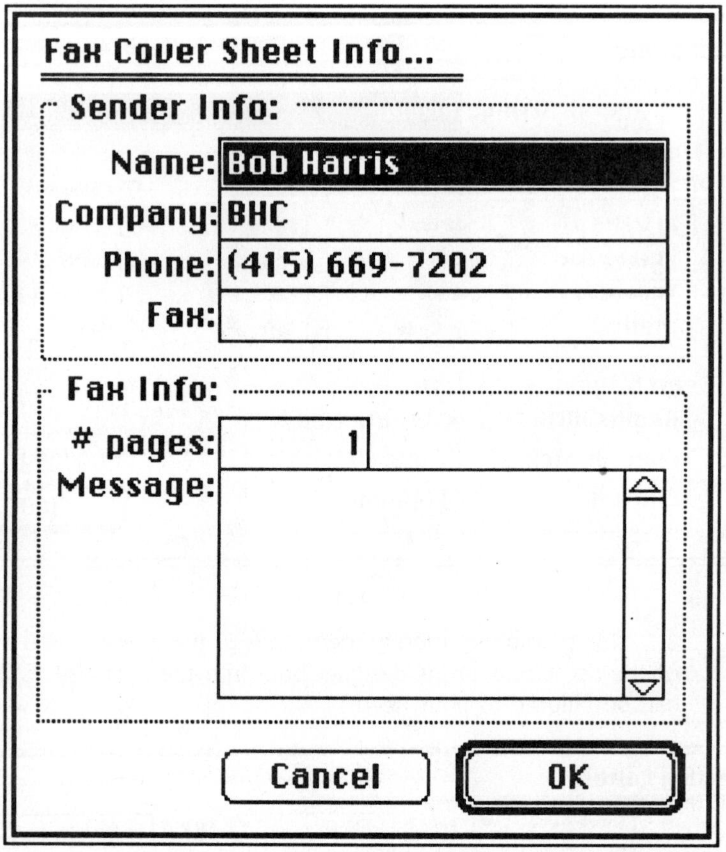

Fax Cover Sheet Info...

Sender Info:

Name: Bob Harris

Company: BHC

Phone: (415) 669-7202

Fax:

Fax Info:

\# pages: 1

Message:

Cancel   OK

[G19684]

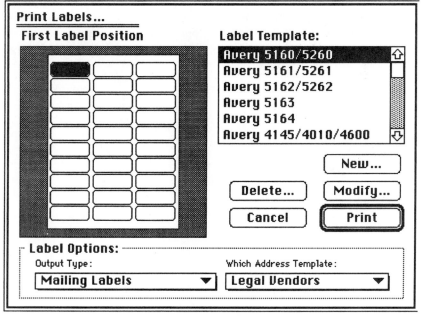

[G19685]

Labels for mailings are easily generated with a database of this type:

[G19686]

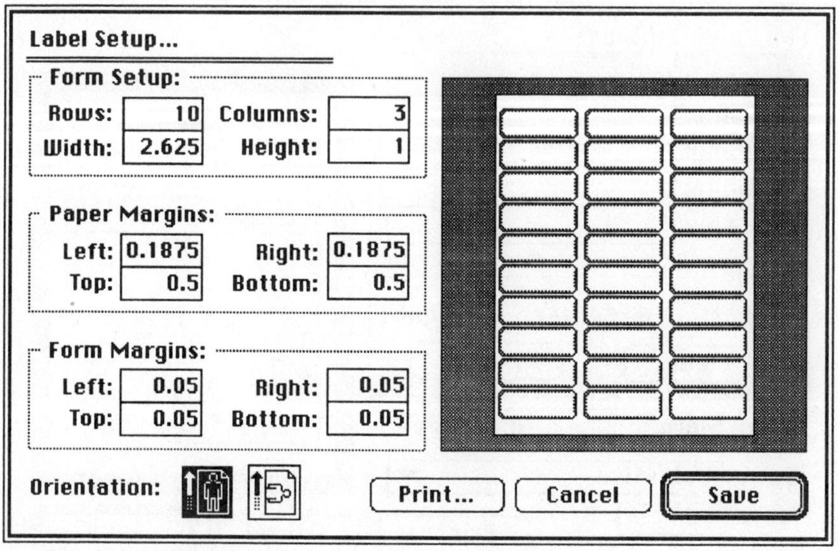

Label Setup...

Form Setup:

Rows:	10	Columns:	3
Width:	2.625	Height:	1

Paper Margins:

Left:	0.1875	Right:	0.1875
Top:	0.5	Bottom:	0.5

Form Margins:

Left:	0.05	Right:	0.05
Top:	0.05	Bottom:	0.05

Orientation: Print...   Cancel   Save

[G19687]

Envelopes can be printed directly from the database as well. PIMS are convenient utilities that can be used in conjunction with a word processor. Some PIMS allow you to copy a complete address in one key stroke and enter the address directly into the word processing document. Some PIMS allow you to easily copy and paste the address into a record and print the address (with postal bar code!) on an envelope while working in the word processing document. Options allow for envelopes of different size and styles as well:

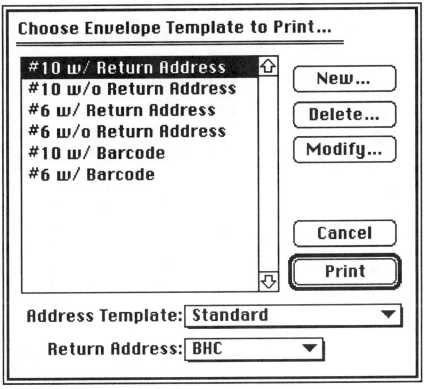

[G19688]

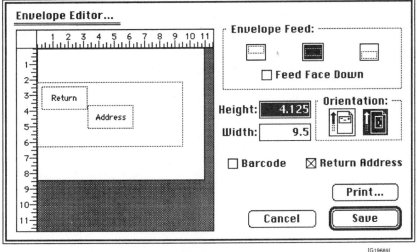

[G19689]

Many of the PIMs available today include optional Daytime output for carrying a hard copy in the briefcase:

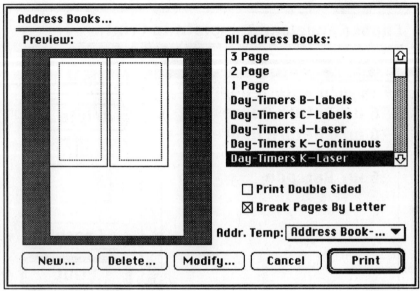

[G19690]

Hypertext PIMS

Some PIMS use hypertext to store the address information rather than using a flat database. With hypertext, all the information is stored in one large field, but a search for any text within the file is almost immediate. Of course, such a system while adequate for some functions as a simple Rolodex, or a deposition, is not adequate for complex searches involving logic functions. A hypertext search will find all references to a word or phrase rather than ones that are entered for example between one date and another as a true database will allow.

An example of a hypertext Rolodex is Quickdex:

```
┌──────────────────────────────────────────────────┐
│ ☐        SE 30 HD:Programs:QuickDex:Address        │
├──────────────────────────────────────────────────┤
│ Find: ┌──────────────────┐ ┌────────┐┌───────────┐│
│       │                  │ │Dial ⌘D ││Long Dist ⌘,││
│       └──────────────────┘ └────────┘└───────────┘│
│ ┌────────────────────────────────────────────┐ ◆ │
│ │ REI 800 828 5533                           │ ◆ │
│ │ R. F. Harris                               │   │
│ │ # 200998                                   │   │
│ │                                            │   │
│ │                                            │   │
│ │                                            │   │
│ │                                            │ ◆ │
│ └────────────────────────────────────────────┘ ◆ │
│  2:40 PM      © 1987-91 Casady & Greene v2.3  127 Cards │
└──────────────────────────────────────────────────┘
```

The above are just some examples of possible uses for your in-house database management systems. You could probably think of others that suit your practice particularly. Once you have learned how to develop structures and the language of retrieval, there is no limit to the variety of database management systems that you can develop and use in your office.

RETRIEVING INFORMATION FROM A COMPUTER SYSTEM

Much of the practice of law is involved with the retrieval of information. This is such an important area that it deserves attention. It is also a problematic area: poor retrieval skills produce inefficient results at best. One specialized type of retrieval is the restoring of data from a backup or archive (See discussion chapter 12: BACK UPS, ARCHIVES AND RESTORING DATA)

In a sense almost every piece of software in use has some sort of retrieval method built in. For example, accounting systems will have a client look up list; a word processor will have a "find" feature; an operating system will have a document location utility built in; etc. Generally, retrieval of information falls into 2 categories:

1. Retrieval of files and documents

    E.g., finding a contract form, or a pleading

2. Retrieval of text and information contained in files

    E.g., searching depositions or using WESTLAW or LEXIS

A law office is the same as any other office in the need to retrieve material that has been filed in a computer system. The law office is perhaps more intensive in the text that is generated and the need to retrieve the text.

In addition it is extremely important when performing research pertaining to points of law either from case law or from statutes to be able to find every citation. The reasons for retrieval are varied.

A) to simply reprint something

B) to create reports, for example management reports, billing reports, etc.

C) to refer to text previously written, such as letters

D) to recycle the text in a related matter rather than generating it again (the concept of templates or boilerplates)

E) to simply remember what was said previously

F) to look up some information such as a phone number or address

G) to find some information by a cross reference. Examples might include conflicts, court decisions, points of law, etc.

H) to establish evidentiary patterns over a wide range of documents, as in litigation support

Regardless of the reason for retrieval, computers can make this operation much faster and efficient than looking up printed matter in a filing cabinet. In fact, considering how much information is being process today in a law office, one simply could not keep up if the only method of filing was paper and the only retrieval was to open the filing cabinet.

Retrieval From Databases

There are two basic systems used for information retrieval in computer systems today, database and full text retrieval. These two systems have varying degrees of speed and flexibility. A database is a structured layout in which the information is entered into records that are formatted into fields. The database is therefore a very structured information system in which entry of the information must conform to the structure. With a degree of programming you can change the number of fields, the order of them, the input and output layout, and the type of data in each field. Databases come in several types as well. Those with **fixed field lengths** and those with **variable length,** in which the field adjusts length to suit the data. Databases also may have the fields indexed ahead of time, or they may not. What this means is that in order to retrieve information from a database, you have to query certain fields in order to find the information. In terms of speed, an indexed field will search much faster than one which is not indexed. A fixed field length database is faster at searching than a variable field one. Single user databases tend to be much faster at retrieval than multi-user ones which are often slower because they are maintained on a network. A **flat file database** contains many records which in turn contain several fields. Databases can also be **relational,** that is comprised of a series of flat file databases all linked and related to each other. These tend to be slower in general than the single or flat database for retrieving information. (see diagram below)

Type of Database	Flat file	Relational	Fixed length	Variable length	Multi-user
Advantages	Fast, easy to use (some pre-formatted), easy to design layouts, fast importing and exporting of information	Related information linked, sophisticated reporting, Client server faster network access	Very fast searching	More flexible entry	Network entry, access to data by many at once
Disadvantages	Cannot relate information beyond a look up	Complex to set up, harder to use, requires support	Limited entry, limited retrieval	Slow retrieval	Slower retrieval, more vulnerable to system problems
Uses	Address, Rolodex, forms, document indexing	litigation support, office management, accounting	Address, Rolodex	Client database with commentary information	litigation support, forms generation

Because ALL databases (regardless of the type) are organized into fields, you have aids available in your retrieval. For example, if you have an address book that is in a database and you have a first name field, a last name field, and a category field, you can search for someone by what category he is if you don't remember the person's name. Databases are very handy for using "logic" when searching. In other words if you had a database with everyone's birthday in it, you could search for everyone whose birthday was in the month of March. Searches on a specific field tend to be faster than ones on either several fields or all fields.

Databases also excel in regard to output. Because you can format the layout of the fields in the record in several ways for both entry and output you have a great deal of flexibility in the way the output will appear. For example when using a database for addresses, you may have a standard entry screen for entering the information. When you wish to print an envelope, or a mailing label, or an office phone book, it is simply a matter of choosing that layout and printing. So while you must conform to the structure of a database when entering information, you do have flexibility in the way in which the output can appear.

Databases therefore require careful thought in the preparation stages so that information is organized in such a way as to provide the correct data in a form for the output required. In addition since the information is organized into fields in each record, databases usually allow for export to a text format which can be manipulated and either used or imported into another database with a different format. Fields can be added or eliminated in this process to change the content somewhat. This interchangeability with text makes databases an ideal way to store information which is entered over time and in which the retrieval forms are: rather standard forms. Examples best retrieved with databases are address books, document management, references, fact sheets. Remember that with a database you can sort on ranges of information or categories. You can ask the database to provide you with only females, between the ages of 30 and 40 who live in the zip code 10400 and 10500 for example with little problem except that the information must be entered into the fields that contain the sex, age, and zip code and their names.

Full Text Retrieval Systems

Often the data which you wish to search is not organized into a database, but simply a document containing text. Since the data is not organized into fields the entire document must be searched rather than searching within a field in a database. Such searches are known as full text searches. The retrieval of a document containing the appropriate text is called full text retrieval. Full text retrieval systems are efficient tools for quickly finding any mention of a particular text that is queried. Full text retrieval systems do not require that you create a format or structure ahead of time. Examples of this are searches of depositions, transcripts, case law, etc.

There are two kinds of information searched with full text retrieval systems: Those in which the text is entered directly by the user, and those in which the document is created in another program by another user and then the full text retrieval is performed. Examples of a full text retrieval systems are the CALR (Computer Assisted Legal Research) services such as WESTLAW and LEXIS, and software systems which search your computer for a reference to a particular word or phrase.

Full text retrieval is often quite useful on documents that were not generated by the law firm. Depositions and court transcriptions are in most cases available in text format. Even those that are only available in MS–DOS format can now be accessed with Macintosh computers and translation software. The text documents can then be indexed with full text software and names, or items or any sort of information easily retrieved in a matter of seconds. When preparing for court with cases having mountains of depositions to process, these tools make the job possible.

An option within full text retrieval systems is one in which the index of text is created in advance and saved as opposed to one in which the text is retrieved from non-indexed material. Each word is indexed so when a search is performed it is extremely fast. This is the type of system to use for searching a computer hard disk for a particular client correspondence in which a specific word is used. Software is available which automatically builds the index ahead of time and is automatically updated as new information is entered into the computer.

Full text systems can be used for an address book system in which the output is not required in a specific printed format. A Rolodex on your computer using a full text system is an unstructured entry screen in which you can type the names and phone numbers and any appropriate information. The information can be of any length (within reason), content or structure. When you search for something the retrieval is often almost immediate. The drawback is that you cannot define the search and thus will be given every reference containing the same words, nor can you easily output the information to a label or format, especially if each record is of a different length. However if you are seeking some reference to something and have used your system to jot notes as thoughts come to you that you might associate later, full text systems can be excellent. A law office might then use a full text address book on-line to record the name, address and phone number of everyone they deal with, and if someone is an expert on a particular subject and be a potential expert witness, then it is easy to simply type the subject and it retrieves each person one at a time. You can then manually select the person and phone and/or write him.

Today full text systems and address book databases will generally permit phone dialing. For anyone in an office this can be extremely time saving and cost effective as well. Often either system (database or full text) will permit the storage of extra digits for long distance and PBX numbers in addition to the phone number you are attempting to call. This saves time and improves accuracy of dialing, all of which save on the overhead in an office.

Full text systems are also widely used for retrieval of text within other documents. For example you have created hundreds of letters during the year in a word processor. You now need to find the document in which you made reference to something and need all the pertinent details relating to that matter. You have no idea which letter contains the information. If you are lucky you know the approximate time period within a month or two which can help limit the search. There are two ways this system can be implemented.

1) Using a preindexed retrieval system. If the document is still on your hard disk and the index system builds the index

automatically in the background (On Location), you can find the text that matches the text exactly or contains the root of the text and it will find the text in the document within seconds. If however you have archived the document to a removable medium such as a floppy disk or a removable hard disk (such as a Bernoulli or Syquest cartridge), you can store the index to the archive on the hard disk in a volume or folder, locate which archive contains the reference, and then insert the disk to retrieve the full text. These systems also search on the name of the document as well as the text within it if you are able to remember the name of the document. Often letters or pleadings are named by the client with a date attached which can facilitate this process if the retrieval is concerning a specific case.

2) A non-indexed full text retrieval system can be used in those cases where the location is fairly certain. For example if you are sure what you are looking for is located on a certain disk or a subvolume or folder of a hard disk and the disk has not been pre-indexed, then a utility such as Gopher is the best solution. Gopher while not as fast as a pre-indexed system, does not require that the index be built in advance. So searching in a limited area is fast. Pre-indexed systems such as the example above (On Location) work well only if the index does not have to first be created as these often take some time. An 800k floppy will take about 2.5 minutes just to create an index and you must index the entire floppy not just the folder or subvolume that you want.

Limitations of Full Text Computer Retrieval Systems

While computer systems can greatly enhance your ability to search large amounts of information rapidly, there are several pitfalls to be wary of. There are some large limitations in the ability of current software to satisfy the needs of a law practice.

Full text retrieval is excellent for locating information in which the content is either generated by you or is well known. That is if you create a series of documents concerning certain facts, you can easily find the information because you know the spelling of that fact. An example of this would be CALR systems such as WEST-LAW or LEXIS. Similarly if a database contains information about a relevant topic or a witness etc., it is rather easy to locate that information with any of the available software. Some software even allows you to program in the retrieval of information in which associations are possible, i.e., give me every reference to witness A when it appears within 10 words of defendant B's name. You may also be able to search for synonyms, etc.

What you cannot search for with full text retrieval are references in which the word is spelled differently than you thought. A good example of this may be a foreign name or word in which there are several spellings (tsar and czar). A phonetic look up might suffice, but the only ones in existence so far are based on English and fall short in dealing with foreign names or words. So if you were to look up a reference in a deposition for tsar and it was spelled czar you would find no references. An embarrassing moment would occur in court as a result of not finding the relevant information when examining a witness.

Such systems fall extremely short when trying to find such issues as conflicts if the names have been typed incorrectly as well. These shortcomings become apparent when trying to search on depositions, transcripts, or databases created for conflict of interest. For example, if a law firm has been tracking all their clients and employees faithfully but somehow the data entry person typed Song for the client's name instead of Wong. A search on Wong results in no conflict, but alas there really is one. Computers tend to be very specific about searches. Within a few years however this problem may disappear as software gets more sophisticated and hardware more powerful. For now it is important to remember this when depending on computer software retrieval. If it is important to retrieve every reference to important information, do not depend on full text retrieval. On the other hand, remember that trying to manually locate information in thousands of pages of deposition could result in errors as well as taking an incredibly long time.

The ideal system for text retrieval would incorporate a search by concepts. Currently this is done manually in law practices by creating keywords and indexing these along with the full text search. Westlaw on-line legal database includes a digest which can be searched by keywords. This is quite helpful as the digest will contain the ideas in a form commonly used by all lawyers, making a search easier, but still not perfect. A perfect system would be one which *automatically* creates the digest containing concepts as well as the exact references.

While the system used by such on-line databases as Westlaw are not perfect, the digest and keywords created by the legal staff go a long way to overcoming the short falls. Such shortcomings are even more evident when trying to access CD–ROMs containing legal information-either statutory or case law. The basic problem is the search engines used to locate material on the CD–ROM are deficient in their ability to find related material. Again this means it is entirely possible that a reference or some vital piece of information could slip through unnoticed.

Until an exhaustive concept engine is built into the search engines of information databases, they will fall short of the promise of delivering the full potential of the computer. At the present time a combination of CALR (Computer Assisted Legal Research) and manual research appears to be the key. To get the most from your computer it is best to determine first whether the computer search will provide you with the information you wish, and secondly if it does not provide all the information, will it provide enough to cover 80–90% of the material? In that case a manual search must provide the additional material. In general, those topics best suited to CALR are those which relate to specific facts, statutes, regulations, cases, or Shepardizing to find current case status, and updating information about a specific topic. If you are starting with broad issues, or need to begin research on a new topic, CALR will generally not provide enough information because *you* do not know enough about the topic to know what to ask for. A brief search may yield some information, but reading the books or text is the place to start before devoting time to a computer search.

What must be factored into any search is the cost of the time to travel to a library and the accessibility of the information. On-line services are available anywhere there is a phone. If you have to travel an hour to get to a research library, then perhaps a casual on line search is worth the money. If the material is available on CD–ROM and the office is equipped with the hardware and has a current subscription, an initial casual search could be as rewarding as a day's adventure to the library. While CD–ROMs are still expensive, they do not have the per use charge on-line services such as WESTLAW or LEXIS have. If your on-line research bills are astronomical, you might consider CD–ROMs as an alternative, especially if they cover the information you need to access frequently. The important thing to remember is that the retrieval of information is only as complete as the ability of the researcher to formulate a proper search.

CHAPTER EIGHT

Electronic Spreadsheets

Most lawyers are somewhat uncomfortable with numbers and will delegate to a CPA or an actuarial any task that involves taxes or financial projections. With electronic spreadsheets, however, it is possible to perform what were previously very complicated tasks in a very straight-forward and simple manner. Nevertheless, this is probably an application which should be taken on only after you have conquered automated document systems with word processing.

A spreadsheet is nothing more than a piece of paper with rows and columns. If you have ever constructed a home budget, for instance, you have created a spreadsheet. You may have set up vertical rows designating clothing, food, housing, etc., followed by horizontal columns where you placed weekly or monthly entries. At the end of the row you could add together all the information that you have entered in the columns and have a monthly or yearly total for each item separately and for all summed together. An electronic spreadsheet can be programmed to perform these calculations in a fraction of a second since it is a matter of simple addition. But it can also take on more complicated tasks. For instance, it can subtract expense from income at the end of the month and provide a running total expressed in percentage of expense to income. (See Illustration A page 201). There are many spreadsheets available today, among the most widely used are Lotus 123, and Microsoft Excel.

Perhaps the greatest advantage in using a spreadsheet is playing the "what if" game. You can change any entry in your rows of numbers and it will immediately recalculate all the results. For instance, if you are trying to decide whether you can afford a new car next year, you can use this year's budget model, enter your next year's anticipated salary and anticipated monthly car payments and immediately see how your ratio of expenses to income is affected. If there are a number of sophisticated calculations involved it would mean going through each step again with an ordinary calculator. With the spreadsheet this recalculation is almost instantaneous.

AUTOMATED SUBSTANTIVE SYSTEMS: NUMBERS

An automated substantive system produced by word processing is one in which all the documents (text) in a routine legal transaction are organized on the computer to require a minimum of typing and a minimum of new information for each new transaction. It is based on the premise that we do learn something from history and we do not have to continually re-invent it.

Electronic spreadsheets do for numbers what word processors do for words in routine legal transactions. They allow you to set up a calculation system which can be used for many clients with small variations.

Spreadsheet model systems are wonderfully suited for any area of the law where alternative courses of planning are required, or where some factors are likely to change over time.

FAMILY LAW

Spreadsheet systems can be useful in several planning areas. In determining the division of assets, a standard model can be used to project several possible divisions without massive manual recalculations. It is possible to try out a number of different settlements and determine which is most advantageous to your client. The budgets of both spouses can be manipulated to determine the allocations of spousal and child support. The tax consequences of various support arrangements can be offered and such items as the future value of a vested pension can be calculated with a standard model.

Divorce Planner is an example of a spread sheet template used for calculating the finances involved in a divorce. Items are included which are based on the income and tax status of the individuals to properly apportion the alimony and child support with regard to income. It is a simple matter to go down the columns and enter the appropriate data necessary for the program to calculate the funds which are available for support.

```
                         DIVORCE PLANNER (R)



        A
1               DOE           INPUT ITEMS              FILE: 92INPUT
     FIRST NAME
        SUPPORT PAYOR      JOHN          1992                 1993
        SUPPORT RECEIVER   MARY
     STATUS(1=SINGLE,2=HD HSLD     PAYOR   RECEIVER     PAYOR   RECEIVER
        3=MAR JOINT,4=MAR SEP)       1        2           0        0
     STATE TAX CODE                  1        1           0        0
     SOC SEC WAGES 1=Y 2=N 3=MED     1        1           0        0
     MONTHLY BUDGET AMOUNT           0        0           0        0
     CHILD SPT BASED ON GROSS        2       NO. OF CHILDREN        0
        CASH = 1  NET CASH = 2    ENTER ANNUAL AMOUNTS
     EXEMPTIONS                      1        1           0        0
     NEW CHILD SUPPORT               0        0           0        0
     NEW ALIMONY                     0        0           0        0
     CHILD SUPPORT %          0%
     SALARY                          0        0           0        0
        AUTOMATIC INCREASE %       0.0%     0.0%
     SELF EMPL INCOME                0        0           0        0
        AUTOMATIC INCREASE %       0.0%     0.0%
     PRESS F9 TO CALCULATE RESULTS OR PG DN TO ENTER OTHER DATA
    F9=CALC    F4=MENU   F1 OR CTRL F1=HELP (Esc to return; PgDn for next page)READY
```

[G19692]

```
                         DIVORCE PLANNER (R)



        N
                     TAX PLANNER
2                                    1992                 1993
     NAME      DOE            PAYOR   RECEIVER     PAYOR   RECEIVER
     STATE (FOR INC TAXES)  ILLINOIS ILLINOIS   ILLINOIS ILLINOIS
     STATUS                  SINGLE   HD HSLD     SINGLE   HD HSLD
     EXEMPTIONS                 1        1           1        1
     GROSS INCOME
     SALARY                  52,000       0       54,600       0
     SELF EMPL INCOME        10,000       0       10,000       0
     SOC SEC INC (TAXABLE)       0        0           0        0
     INTEREST-US GOVT SEC        0        0           0        0
     OTHER INTEREST              0        0           0        0
     DIVIDENDS                   0        0           0        0
     TAX NON CSH INC/LOSS        0        0           0        0
     ALIMONY RECEIVED            0        0           0        0
     OTHER TAXABLE INC           0        0           0        0
     LONG TERM CAPITAL GAIN      0        0           0        0
                            --------- --------- --------- ---------
        TOTAL INCOME        62,000       0       64,600       0
     ADJUSTMENTS TO INCOME
    F9=CALC    F4=MENU   F1 OR CTRL F1=HELP (Esc to return; PgDn for next page)READY
```

[G19693]

```
                          DIVORCE PLANNER (R)



                                                                    CS

     -----------------     ---------
        75,000            100%
     ALLOWED DEDUCTIONS
     --------------------

     FED INCOME TAX                    12,278        245
     STATE INCOME TAX                      0           0
     SOC SEC TAX                       4,529           0
     LOCAL INC TAX                         0           0
     HOSPITALIZATION                       0           0
     MANDATORY PENSION                     0           0
     OTHER NET DEDUCT                      0           0
                                     ---------     ---------
        TOTAL DEDUCTIONS             16,807        245
  96  NET CASH
     AVAILABLE FOR SUPPORT            58,193       (245)
       CASH BOTH         PAYOR'S %
     ---------           ---------
        57,948            100%
     CHILD SUPPORT                    (5,200)      5,200
          SUP %      9%
   F9=CALC    F4=MENU   F1 OR CTRL F1=HELP (Esc to return; PgDn for next page)READY
```

[G19694]

REAL ESTATE PLANNING

Property transactions often involve projections of expenses and rental income; expectations of higher rents or inflationary factors require a "what if" analysis. Limited partnerships often involve complicated allocations which are dependent upon variable factors such as the year of sale, or the yearly profits. A spreadsheet can easily figure these out.

DAMAGE PROJECTIONS

In the course of litigating personal injury suits or breaches of contract, the question of future damages over a number of months or years is often the bone on which everyone picks. A spreadsheet allows you to conjure up different scenarios. What if your client misses work for two months, or six months? What if his medical bills include a second operation or a third? You can project your worst case analysis and your most benign scenario and come up with a range of possible settlement figures. If you have several injured parties, you can allocate the damages among them, after exploring many possible scenarios.

ESTATE PLANNING

A spreadsheet can allow estate planners to perform complicated calculations that might previously have taken days or weeks in a few seconds. They can offer several different plans based on several different assumptions about when the client might die, and what the value of his assets may be at death. The result should be a plan which maximizes tax planning and minimizes the risk of mistake.

In the example below a spread sheet is used to calculate the tax savings which result from changes in how the estate is transferred at time of death using View Plan Estate.

```
     COMPARISON OF TAXES BETWEEN RESULT IF ALL TO SPS AND RESULT USING OPT MD
        Bob & Mary McCauly - TODAY: $475,000 / AT DEATH: $2,244,224
                      DOD: 2023/2028, Growth: 5.0/2.5%

Death of HUSB                              All To Spouse          Opt Marital
      Taxable estate after MD.........$          0          $      600,000
      Federal tax on estate...........           0                 192,800
      State tax on estate.............           0                       0
      Less UC+GTXP....................     192,800                 192,800
      Net tax at first death..........$          0          $            0

Death of WIFE
      Taxable estate..................$  2,471,197          $    1,820,420
      Federal tax on estate...........     875,190                 613,319
      State tax on estate.............     136,496                  86,670
      Less UC+GTXP....................     192,800                 192,800
      Net tax at second death.........$    818,886          $      507,189
                                       -------------          -------------
TOTAL TAXES - BOTH DEATHS * ....  $        818,886          $      507,189

                               SAVINGS ——————————►          $311,697

* Without considering alternate use of funds paid for taxes.
 <F1>All To Sps  <F2>Opt MD  <F3>No MD  <F4>Var MD  <F5>Var ByPass  <F7>Gifts
 <F8>Comps   <Alt-Q>uit   <Alt-P>rt Scrn   <Alt-N>otes   <Ctrl-PGDN>Next Mini

                                                                  [G19695]
```

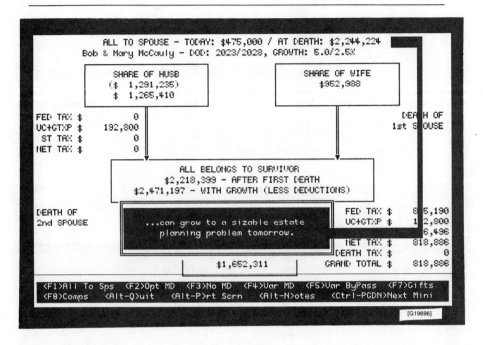

TAX PLANNING

A spreadsheet can give you some of the capabilities of an accountant whiz, but if you are not absolutely in touch with current tax law it will not save your neck in a malpractice suit. What it can do for you in tax areas where you feel you have reasonable expertise is to maximize tax savings by projecting several different scenarios. What if a capital gain is taken this year or next? How much tax savings in depreciation will a contemplated real estate purchase produce in three years? It can also help you decide whether you should buy that new car with savings, or take a loan and amortize it over four years. Specific software templates are available for this as well as being able to generate your own.

YOUR OFFICE

Here is a chance to treat yourself as a client and use a spreadsheet to plan your firms' financial future. You can ask such questions as: What if I totally automate my office over the next five years; how much additional income must I bring in? What reduction in personnel or raise in hourly billing rate can I make to offset this expense? Expanding your firm or your facilities no longer has to be a matter of voodoo guesswork.

Inside Spreadsheets

As with all software, different brands of spreadsheets offer different features in terms of size, user-friendliness, integration with data bases, etc., but the basic manipulations are almost identical and if you learn one you can easily transport your knowledge and skills to another.

A spreadsheet is set out like a huge piece of graph paper. How huge depends upon your computer's memory and the brand you are using, but it can extend for hundreds or even thousands of columns and rows. Obviously you cannot view all these columns and rows at once on your relatively tiny computer screen, but you can scroll both horizontally and vertically with your cursor control key to see the missing pieces.

The basic building block of the spreadsheet is the cell. With almost all programs the columns are labeled with letters and the rows with numbers. A cell is the coordinate where the rows and columns intersect.

ILLUSTRATION A

	A	B	C	D	E	F	G	H
1	HOME EXP	Jan	Feb	Mar	Apr	May	Jun	Midyear Total
2	Mortgage	250	250	250	250	250	250	1500
3	Food	500	500	500	500	500	500	3000
4	Travel	0	200	0	50	100	650	1000
5	**TOTAL EXP**	**750**	**950**	**750**	**800**	**850**	**1400**	**5500**

As you can see by this illustration it is possible to enter both text and numbers in the cells. Cell A2 has been filled in with the word "mortgage". Cell B2 has been filled in with the number 250. What are not apparent when looking at this illustration are the underlying instructions that have been entered into some of the cells. For instance cell B5 (in the TOTAL row) has been given the instruction, B2 + B3 + B4, or a shorter instruction useful for longer additions, SUM B2 . . . B4. This command will include all the cells in that column between the cells named, even if there are hundreds of them, e.g. SUM B2 . . . B200.

	A	B	C	D	E	F	G	H
1	HOME EXP	1	32	61	92	122	153	Midyear Total
2	Mortgage	250	250	250	250	250	250	= SUM (B2:G2)
3	Food	500	500	500	500	500	500	= SUM (B3:G3)
4	Travel	0	200	0	50	100	650	= SUM (B4:G4)
5	TOTAL EXP	= SUM (B2:B4)	= SUM (C2:C4)	= SUM (D2:D4)	= SUM (E2:E4)	= SUM (F2:F4)	= SUM (G2:G4)	= SUM (B5:G5)

Now that you have the hang of it, you can guess that cell H2 (in the midyear total column) contains the instruction Sum B2 . . . G2, and H3 contains the command Sum B3 . . . G3, etc. You must enter the information into the B2 through G2 cells, but the figure in H2 will be automatically calculated and entered into H2 by the computer. These instructions for H2 will not appear on the screen, but they will appear in the user message on the top or bottom of the screen in most spreadsheet programs.

So what's the big deal, you think, I can do that with my calculator. What makes electronic spreadsheets unique is that you can change any figure in any cell, e.g. travel for the month of May, and all the calculations will be automatically re-done with no further instructions. You can also carry your cells to other parts of the spreadsheet. For instance if you wanted to create another model to project your taxes, you could carry over all the cells that contained the mortgage entries, or the mortgage totals without re-typing them. It is also possible to create more complicated mathematical formulas than SUM in any of the individual cells. You can manipulate cells and the instructions they contain in as many ways as you have imagination. For most law office applications, you probably will need only basic skills, and not need to create complex formulas.

A significant advantage of spreadsheet models for lawyers is that like automated substantive systems created with word processing, a general model can fit a wide variety of clients. Once the model is set up, the attorney, paralegal, or secretary can type in the new numbers for new clients and the computer provides instantaneous answers.

Let's examine the hypothetical divorce of Roberta Lombard. A very common procedure in family law is to create a monthly budget for both spouses to determine how to allocate resources, including spousal and child support. An abbreviated model which may be useful for many different clients might look like this:

SPOUSAL BUDGET FOLLOWING DIVORCE

A	B	C	D
EXPENSES	WIFE	HUSBAND	%
Rent/Mort	400	300	133
Food			
Clothes			
Transport			
Medical			
Entertainment			
Travel			
Childcare			
Business Exp.			
Education			

	A	B	C	D
	EXPENSES	WIFE	HUSBAND	%
	Utilities			
	Miscellaneous			
	TOTAL			

		B	C	D
	INCOME	WIFE	HUSBAND	%
	Salary	500	1500	33
	Spousal Support			
	Child Support			
	Bus. Income			
	Dividends			
	Interest			
	Tips/Gratuities			
	Gifts			
	TOTAL			

This model offers great flexibility. Not only does it compare husband and wife in terms of the totals of their income and expenses, it offers a percentage of wife's to husband's expenses and income for each category as well. This percentage is reached by entering instructions in the D column to divide wife's column by the husband's. e.g., the command for D2 is B2/C2.

Items from this model may be placed in other models which predict tax liability, for instance, simply by commanding the transfer of certain cells, like income and spousal support to other parts of the spreadsheet.

Managing Your Office

What you can do for your clients, you can do for yourself. Now is the time to take the great leap forward and establish your firm's five year plan. Project the gross income for each of the next five years, based on your assumptions of the number of timekeepers, the number of billable hours and the billing rate that each timekeeper will command. Then set up a model for projected expenses for each of these five years. Add a new category called automation and project a five year amortization for a $25,000 computer system. Adjust your billing rates to compensate for this new line item. Add a new associate, calculate the new overhead expenses the associate will create. Have fun, and hopefully increased profits, by playing the "what if" game with your firm's financial future.

Choosing a Spreadsheet

Since the spreadsheet operation is very standard, any of the well known brands such as Lotus 1–2–3, Quattro Pro, WingZ or Excel will allow you to perform the above described tasks. Choosing a spreadsheet today can be as complex as choosing a word processor. On the MS–DOS platform Lotus is the dominant spreadsheet, though Quattro Pro is gaining in popularity. For Windows however, Excel for Windows is the main program as well as dominating the Macintosh platform. On UNIX WingZ is the most powerful new spreadsheet. Greater memory will allow larger spreadsheets that could include thousands of cells. The newest versions of these spreadsheets today include very powerful charting and graphics capabilities including full color 3 dimensional charts. This is not likely to be necessary for most law office tasks, but can be of significant value when preparing presentations and displays for clients or courtroom demonstrations.

Learning to create simple models is quite straightforward and does not require mathematical genius or programming skills. All the leading programs come with a tutorial which takes you carefully by the hand through each step. In addition many of the formulas that are necessary for specialized calculations are pre-loaded into the programs and can be easily accessed by even beginners. Formatting of the data into different fonts or number types is a simple command. Powerful macros can be created as well to automatically process the data that is entered. Complicated models like tax planning for a complex organization are probably too difficult for a neophyte to tackle. For these functions it is often possible to purchase templates, or overlays where someone else has set up the model for you. Heizer Software, 1941 Oak Park Blvd., Suite 30, PO Box 232019, Pleasant Hill, CA, 94523 publishes a catalog of custom templates for spreadsheets. One example is called Asset Management and Financial Independence and is available for $34 from Heizer. It works with either Microsoft Excel or Microsoft Works for Macintosh or MS–DOS compatible machines.

Today's spreadsheets offer integration with word processors. At the simplest level spreadsheets can be placed into word processors in a table format. More sophisticated users may link the spreadsheets to the word processors so that as data is updated in the spreadsheet it is automatically updated in the word processor. Microsoft Excel and Microsoft Word incorporate linking capable of automatic updating. Such functionality is extremely useful when preparing reports which incorporate spreadsheet data.

CHAPTER NINE

Timekeeping and Billing Systems

Timekeeping and billing systems have the greatest potential for increasing your income and the greatest potential for precipitating catastrophe. A month or two of lost billing may be a blow from which your firm may never recover. On the other hand, the sharp increase in billing and collections produced by computerized billing would be a welcome step forward.

TIME IS MONEY

Information is the product that lawyers and law offices produce, but the way in which that product is evaluated is by the hour; not by pound, or by the quality or quantity of information. This evaluation varies only in contingency arrangements, or in a flat fee situation for a specific job, like the drafting of articles of incorporation. Whatever the ethical or practical arguments regarding using time as the measure of value for attorneys' services, the tradition is established and not likely to be changed. Keeping track of time, therefore, becomes one of the most vital aspects of a law practice. Time is literally money for an attorney.

Attorneys record from 1 to 35 time entries each day, with considerable individual variation. In a typical week a sole practitioner may collect 60 different time entries to be charged against 12 different client accounts, while a large firm with 75 attorneys, may collect as many as 5000, in serving 1000 clients. Paralegals now regularly bill out their time as well, adding to the volume and complexity of the time-keeping arrangements.

Attorney billing is complicated by many factors: each attorney may bill out at a different rate, each client or matter may receive special billing consideration, paralegals will bill at their own rate, and then there are contingency, flat fee, and paid-in-advance arrangements. Even within a single case attorneys may bill differently for certain kinds of activities; i.e., trials vs. depositions. With many programs you can create different users and bill them at different rates.

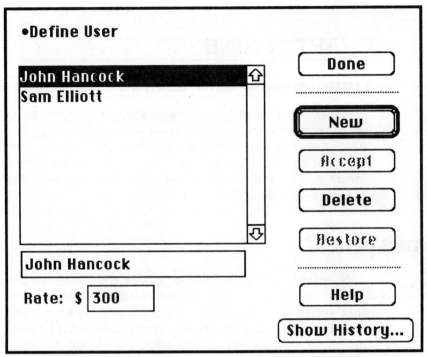

[G19697]

Client disbursements are also a unique billing headache. These can, if travel is involved, add up to more than the actual hourly billings. With the advent of computers, some tricky questions arise regarding disbursements.

```
┌─────────────────────────────────────────────────────────────────────┐
│  Selection criteria to include slips:                   ┌──────────┐ │
│                                                         │    OK    │ │
│              From        to        ☒ Billable          └──────────┘ │
│  Dates ◉ All  ○ [      ][      ]   ☒ Unbillable        ┌──────────┐ │
│                                    ☒ Hold              │  Cancel  │ │
│  Hours ◉ All  ○ [      ][      ]                       └──────────┘ │
│                                    ☒ No Charge         ┌──────────┐ │
│  Slips ◉ All  ○ [      ][      ]   ☒ Summary           │  Clear   │ │
│                                                        └──────────┘ │
│  Select slips:          ┌─────────┐  Billed   ┌────────┐ Save As... │
│                         │ Change...│          │ Ignore │            │
│  without regard to either variance or dollar value.  Exported ┌────────┐ Retrieve... │
│                                                      │ Ignore │       │
│                                     Recur  ┌────────┐   Help         │
│                                            │ Ignore │                │
│  ┌User──────────┐┌Activity/Expense┐┌Client────┐┌Matter────┐         │
│  │John Hancock ⇧││Prelim Discuss ⇧││Howard Hughes⇧││          ⇧│    │
│  │Sam Elliott   ││Research        ││           ││           │      │
│  │              ││$Form Processing││           ││           │      │
│  │              ││                ││           ││           │      │
│  │             ⇩││               ⇩││          ⇩││          ⇩│     │
│  ┌────────────┐                                   ☒ None on slip    │
│  │ Controller │  All are selected                                  │
│  └────────────┘                                                    │
└─────────────────────────────────────────────────────────────────────┘
```

[G19698]

Although it is common practice to charge for Xeroxing, telephone calls, telegrams, etc., should computer time or word processing time be charged for the creation of documents? It has become quite well established to charge clients for research time on WEST-LAW and LEXIS, but the tradition of charging computer time for other applications is not well established, except perhaps in the area of computerized litigation support, when full service or time-sharing services are used.

Recording computer usage is relatively easy with the use of software that records the time spent using specific software. The resulting log can then be used as a basis for entering data into the time billing package. In the example below the TimeLog software records how long the computer was on, how long it was inactive and the length of time each program was used. In this way it is easy to have the computer automatically record the length of time a paralegal was using WESTMATE software for a session for a particular client.

```
≣□▒▒▒▒▒▒▒▒▒▒▒ TimeLog Data ▒▒▒▒▒▒▒▒▒▒▒▒▒⊡▐≣
```

Show: | **Totals** | Tue, May 19, 1992 – Tue, May 19, 1992

Hou**▶**:Minutes:Seconds

Power On		0:05:52
Inactive		0:00:00
Applications...	🗀	0:05:52
Finder	◈	0:02:20
TimeLog™	◈	0:01:48
America Online 1.0	◈	0:01:30
Alarming Events	◈	0:00:14

[G19699]

Example A: Small Time

Sidney Solo registered 120 time entries for the week of April 5th through 12th. These time entries included 32 phone calls, 2 client conferences, 2 depositions, assorted draftings of pleadings, and 1 trial brief. Disbursements covered 6 long distance phone calls, 2 messenger charges, 360 pages of Xeroxing, 45 minutes on WESTLAW, and travel fare for a one day trip from San Francisco to Los Angeles.

During that week Solo worked on 15 different client accounts, 6 of which were on a contingency basis. Of the remaining 9 clients, 5 were billed at an hourly rate of $125.00, 2 were billed at a rate of $100.00, and 2 were billed at a rate of $75.00. Three of these clients had already paid money in advance toward their account.

Sidney Solo had just begun to use a paralegal on a part-time basis. For that same week, the paralegal billed out 6 hours of time which included 23 time entries, ranging from phone calls, to legal research, to collection of hospital records for litigation. The paralegal had served 5 clients, only 2 of whom were not on a contingency basis. He also generated 200 pages of Xerox costs and 3 long distance phone calls, plus ½ hour of WESTLAW time. His hourly billing rate was $35.00 an hour.

Example B: Big Time

Big, Rich and Old, during that same week in April, generated 4,722 time entries. These included 1,691 phone calls, 132 depositions, 232 clients in office conferences, 20 court appearances, including 2 trials which lasted the complete week, and assorted draftings of pleadings, briefs and memoranda, not to mention the creation of 7 articles of incorporation, 15 wills, 42 contracts, 3 marital settlement agreements, and various other business and legal documents. The 45 paralegals also collectively generated 500 time entries, which included almost the complete spectrum of possible paralegal activities.

Big, Rich and Old maintained a scale of attorneys' billing rates which ranged from $75.00 for an associate, to $250.00 for the senior partner. There were 5 steps on this scale. In addition, some clients were given a reduced rate on some matters, and the attorneys that week served 153 clients who were on a contingency basis. The firm reported 5,029 disbursement items, covering the gamut from long distance calls to long distance airplane travel. These also included 88 hours of LEXIS time.

Although the volume of time entries is obviously greater for large firms; a small practitioner like Sydney Solo, may have to face just as many complex variables. Clients increasingly demand detailed billing statements, and will not accept a blank fee charge without a narrative accounting. Both Solo and Big, Rich and Old will have to inform their clients who they talked to on the phone, and for how long. Each bill becomes a personalized document and can not be mass produced. The form of the bill can be modified in most software to include or exclude various options on each bill or statement. Often this is merely the inclusion of items or a choice of summary or detail on items:

☰◻▦▦▦▦▦▦▦▦ Client Information ▦▦▦

Client: Howard Hughes   [**Client**]

Billing Format

Time and Expense Sections	Other Sections
Style: [**Show Each Slip**]	☒ Payments
☐ Merge Time and Expense Charges	☒ Balances
☐ Activity Name ▶	☐ Adjustments
☐ User Initials	☐ Client Funds
Description Lines: [All]	☐ Message

Date	☒ Time	☒ Expense	☐ Detail
Matter	☐ Time	☐ Expense	
Charge	☒ Time	☒ Expense	☐ Aging Messages
Hours/Qty	☒ Time	☐ Expense	☐ Aging Table
	☐ Total Only		
Rate/Price	☐ Time	☐ Expense	
Double Space	☒ Time	☒ Expense	

[Page]
[Revert]
[Help]
[Import Fields]
[Export Fields]

⌘G General
⌘N Notes
⌘B Options
⌘A Adjust
⌘F Format
⌘S Status
⌘M Budget

[Summary Table...]
[Bill Messages...]

[G19700]

Newer software such as Components Job Costing allow the user to completely customize the content of the invoice by including tools for designing the invoice as if it were a desktop publishing package:

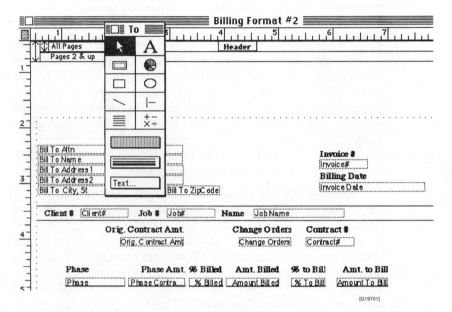

[G19701]

COMPUTERS AS TIMEKEEPERS

The advantage that computers offer over manual timekeeping and billing systems is that they retrieve time entries at electronic speeds, by an almost unlimited number of criteria, and also perform complicated mathematical computations relating to each individualized bill. In addition, a good computer program can generate financial reports regarding the productivity of each attorney, the entire firm, or any other measuring stick that is requested. All sophisticated computerized time-keeping software, whether developed for PCs, minis, main-frames or service bureaus, should be able to accommodate the following needs:

A.   An extensive amount of narrative should be possible with each bill. The attorney must be able to explain the 4 hours that were spent on a deposition, and who the deponent was. He must be also be able to explain that the trip to Los Angeles was to study the Title Company's records. Distributed Time Entry available for MS–DOS machines allows a view of each day and the time spent on each matter as well as a detailed narrative of the service performed.

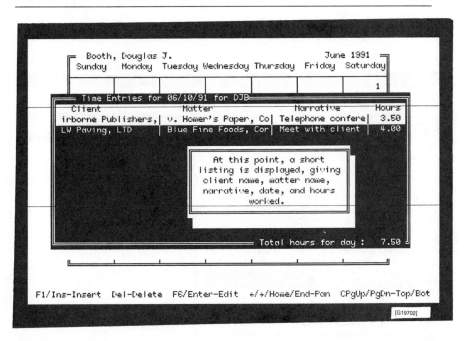

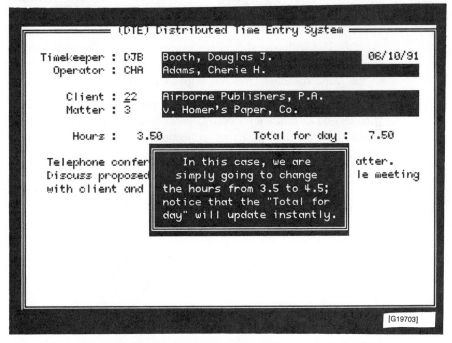

B. The billing system must be able to accommodate a number of different rates for each attorney.

C. It must be possible to make changes or deletions easily in both time entries and disbursements up to the point of sending out the bill.

Attorneys Software system is an example which shows this feature:

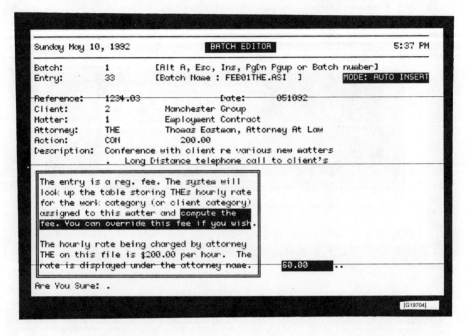

D.   The software should be connected with a general ledger accounting program, in order to keep the firm's accounting records on the same database, and not duplicate efforts.

E.   A full range of management reports should be possible. They should include: an accounts/receivable aging report, attorney productivity records, a client collections report, and individual histories of client accounts.

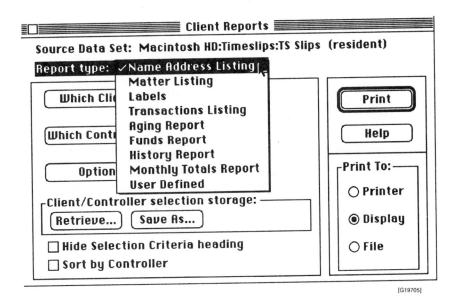

[G19705]

The same software may also include calendar/docket control functions, a conflict of interest system, and a trust accounting application and even a litigation support system. It is not always necessary or desirable that all of these functions are available in the same software package, but it should be possible for different software application programs to use the same database, without complicated adjustments.

ACCOUNTING—KEEPING TRACK

Timekeeping and billing present complexities which are perhaps unique to law practice. Accounting, however, is handled in a law office much as it is in any other business. If it is a large office it is handled like a large business, if it is a small one, it is handled like a small business. Therefore, although many of the billing and time keeping packages do also provide accounting functions, it is not necessary; many of the general accounting software packages could be used as well. The major advantage of an integrated, i.e., both accounting and time-keeping package, is that one can more easily make use of the same database, but this may be overcome with other software programs which integrate software applications on the same computer. Any accounting package should be able to form the following functions:

* A monthly financial statement

* The general ledger

* The payroll

* Aging of accounts receivable

* Accounts receivable and check writing

An example of a complete accounting system for general accounting is Peachtree:

	Financial Format Setup	

Report Name Standard Income Stmt.   Report Type: Income Statement

Report Title Standard   ☒ Automatic Report Generation

                                            ☒ Show Date/Time/Page #

Column Number and Type:

◉ Column 1	G/L Amount	○ Column 7	Not In Use
○ Column 2	Ratio	○ Column 8	Not In Use
○ Column 3	G/L Amount	○ Column 9	Not In Use
○ Column 4	Ratio	○ Column 10	Not In Use
○ Column 5	Not In Use	○ Column 11	Not In Use
○ Column 6	Not In Use	○ Column 12	Not In Use

Column Specific Info:

Column MTD

Title

General Ledger Amount

Year: This Year

Duration: Period

Period: Current

Percent, Variance, Ratio

First Column:

Second Column:

[Preview Format]   [Show Account Selection]

[G19706]

	Account Ledger Card	

Account 101000 -000 -000   Description Cash-Regular Checking

Account Type Current Asset   Division No. 1   Beginning Balance   178,409.38

Date	Src/Entry #	Reference	Debit	Credit	Balance
9/23/94	C/D00026	Express Mail●1479		2,079.92	310,372.30
9/23/94	C/D00026	Health/Life Ins●1480		2,200.00	308,172.30
9/23/94	C/D00026	Microsoft, Inc.●1481		49,564.48	258,607.82
9/23/94	C/D00026	Odesta Corporat●1482		2,332.40	256,275.42
9/23/94	C/D00026	ACME Office Sup●1483		74.28	256,201.14
9/23/94	C/D00026	Offset Print Sh●1484		465.50	255,735.64
9/23/94	C/D00026	Local Phone Com●1485		500.00	255,235.64
9/23/94	C/D00026	US Postal Servi●1486		1,350.00	253,885.64
9/23/94	C/D00026	Super Media Adv●1487		20,100.00	233,785.64
9/23/94	C/D00026	Surefire Insura●1488		850.00	232,935.64
9/23/94	C/D00026	Travel Agency●1489		3,962.48	228,973.16
9/23/94	C/D00026	United Parcel S●1490		1,779.00	227,194.16
9/23/94	C/D00026	Apple Computer,●1491		270,000.00	-42,805.84
9/23/94	CJR00028		204,438.00		161,632.16
9/26/94	C/D00027	Assoc. of Bette●1492		210.00	161,422.16
9/26/94	C/D00028	Assoc. of Better Co●		1,000.00	160,422.16
9/26/94	C/D00028	AAA●1001		500.00	159,922.16
9/26/94	C/D00028	US Postal Servic●123		1,000.00	158,922.16
9/26/94	CJR00029		3,400.00		162,322.16
		Totals:	1,525,373.30	1,541,460.52	162,322.16

[G19707]

Accounts Receivable Reports

◉ **Summary**   ○ **Detail**   ○ All Divisions   ◉ Current Division

Report Order

◉ **Account #**
○ **Name**
○ **Territory**
○ Sales Rep
○ **Balance Due**

◉ **Ascending**
○ **Descending**

◉ **All Customers**
○ **From** [   ]
    To [   ]

Age invoices as of: [09/26/94]

◉ **All Invoices**
○ **Only Invoices over** [30] **days**
    with balances over [10.00]

Invoice order:
◉ As Posted   ○ Invoice #   ○ Due Date

Selected: [31]

[**Screen**]   [**Print**]

[G19708]

Check

Vendor #	NEW	[X] Direct Disbursement	[ ] Manual Check		
Date	Invoice #	Purchase Order #	Invoice Amount	Discount	Net Amount
			Totals		

Patriot Computers, Inc.   *Direct Disbursement*   Check # [   ]
529 Main Street   *To Be Printed*
1st Floor   Check Date [09/26/94]
Boston, MA 02129

Pay to the order of   Amount [   ]

First National Bank   98-76543-21

VENDORS LEDGER PURCHASE PAY SELECT CHECKS CHECK REG. RECURRING RECONCILE DEPOSIT AUDIT

[G19709]

Many organizations with large main-frame computers, like banks, offer payroll services which are relatively inexpensive. Since payroll is the kind of activity which is usually fairly continuous, without constant editing demands, a batched payroll sent to a bank is often more economical. Therefore, although this function may be available in the accounting package, it may be desirable to separate the tasks and send the payroll out of the office.

MANAGEMENT REPORTS

Like any business, a law practice must keep track of its productivity. As with accounting, this is an application which is common to all businesses, except that attorneys measure the value of their product in time. Good time-keeping software should allow the generation of productivity reports in many different forms. The software should have the capacities of a good search and retrieval system, and be able to create reports based on any number or variety of criteria that is requested. Management reports commonly requested would include:

*Time-use analysis for each attorney

*Profitability analysis for each attorney, department, and field of law, or type of activity

*Case list by attorney and department

*Analysis of aged unbilled time and disbursements

Matter Aging Report

As of: 6/5/92   7:45 AM

Matter #	Name	Current	Period 1	Period 2	Period 3	Credits	Balance
20	Mobil Marine	0.00	0.00	0.00	0.00	0.00	0.00
TR2	Trademark						
	Infringement	435.56	0.00	0.00	0.00	200.00	235.56
		435.56	0.00	0.00	0.00	200.00	235.56

Matter Status

As of: 6/5/92   7:46 AM

Matter #	Name	Client #	Name	Type	Status
20	Mobil Marine	RW	Red Nichols	Litigation	Active

Opened	Fee Basis	Last Trans.	Last Bill	Unbilled
10/3/91	Transaction	8/2/91	1,462.50	89.13

Comments

Employee Time by Matter

Current Month   January

Emp. #	Name	Matter #	Name	Bill Hrs	Non-Bill	Amount
GG	Guy Goodman					
				0.00	0.00	0.00

Sophisticated software could produce a comparison either month by month, or year-by-year, and possibly generate some graphical models to represent this analysis. With a sophisticated system, one should also be able to project future profits or trends by computing the addition of new factors, such as new attorneys or new paralegals employed, or rising office expenses.

COMPUTER OPTIONS

Since, next to word processing, the application of computers to financial management is the most popular use of computers in law offices, there is a great competition for performing these services. There are more than 200 personal computer software packages that represent themselves as the answer to attorney's timekeeping and billing needs. But there are computer alternatives to setting up billing systems in-house as well.

Service Bureaus

It is very common for large, medium and even very small, i.e., sole practitioner law firms, to send out some or all of their financial management tasks. Service bureaus have become very competitive and can be less expensive than buying the equipment and training personnel for in-house use. Time keeping/billing and payroll are the functions most frequently delegated to service bureaus. Service bureaus normally have mini or even main-frame computers, and they will most often provide batch processing arrangements. With batch processing, the firm sends all its billing and all its payroll once a month to the service, which then produces the report or check. The other possibility is on-line service. A law firm will have a terminal directly on-line to the main computers, and can enter new information at any time. This is considerably more expensive, and therefore, not as popular.

The main disadvantage of service bureaus, especially for time-keeping, is that they have their own format and do not usually customize billing reports. Since billing is so complicated, and so individual to each office, this can be very frustrating. With the batch processing system it is also not possible to change or enter information more than once a month. This means that it is usually impossible to find any kind of account of work in progress.

These problems are less common to payrolls since the information does not vary as much and does not need to be so individualized. Therefore, it is an increasing trend to send a payroll to a large service bureau, which will provide all the proper withholding, deductions, and other payroll concerns.

Minis

In firms with 50 or more attorneys it is probable that even a powerful personal computer system will not be sufficient and either a workstation or mini computer will be required. The timekeeping software will probably be custom designed and very expensive. In terms of the financial management of the law office, however, a large investment in hardware and software will pay off.

Personal Computers

As noted in the chapter on Buying Software, timekeeping and billing software for personal computer is fairly complicated. It involves the development of complex structures and the programming of calculations. Although it is quite possible to develop your own timekeeping and billing system on an electronic spreadsheet or a database program, it takes more effort and knowledge than most computer users possess. Therefore, discretion being the better part of valor, it is probably better to buy a packaged system. Many of these packaged systems are simply developed from a database system, but they have done all the work for you. You do pay for this work however, and it is probably your most expensive piece of software. It is better to buy the basic timekeeping and billing system first and add other modules later, such as the general ledger and the financial management package. More than with most software purchases it is important to thoroughly test the package before you buy it to be certain that it meets the needs of your law firms. Look for the characteristics of flexibility noted above, but also look for ease of use.

On MS–DOS computers TimeSlips is one of the most widely used software packages for attorney billing (now with LapTrack billing information can be created on a portable computer and merged later with TimeSlips). More sophisticated systems use major accounting systems such as Great Plains. On the Macintosh systems both TimeSlips and Great Plains are available as well as a new product called Job Cost/Time Billing Components from Satori. In many cases on either type of system, TimeSlips can be linked to other accounting packages with TimeSlips Accounting Link.

SETTING UP YOUR TIMEKEEPING SYSTEMS

All time keeping and billing systems should come with extensive documentation and possibly a disk or diskette with a self teaching tutorial. Some systems may even provide a telephone hotline to rescue you when you are in trouble. These are certainly factors to keep in mind when purchasing a system, because without adequate training you will lose precious time. Since training on each of these systems is unique, there are only a few general rules to keep in mind:

1. Always maintain a back-up manual billing for the first *two months*. If the computer system is functioning smoothly at that point you can drop the back-up. Avoid the disaster of missed billings.

2. Train more than one person thoroughly with the new software. If your main bookkeeper breaks his leg or quits, the second string will hopefully slide easily into place.

3. Make back ups of your data. The data must be backed up in such a way as to include archives of the data for at least a 2 week period, and should maintain archives of each month before the closing as well as a year end prior to closing out the year. It is especially important that a rotation of back ups be made that includes offsite storage of the data.

4. If your software includes management reports, plan a regular monthly meeting to discuss the results. When attorney Brown finds that he billed 20 hours less than attorney Blue, he may display a surprising spurt of billable hours the following month. This may be the way in which your firm cashes in on computerization. At these meetings disbursements may also be examined.

WHEN TO BILL COMPUTER COSTS

In the not too distant past, many items, like typing costs and the law library, were carried as overhead and not billed out to clients. Computers have changed that and it has become common practice to bill out all applications which are performed on computers. Although the issue is murky, these charges have been supported as costs by court decisions. The rationale behind this mini-revolution in billing practices is that you must somehow distribute the costs of automation.

A very general guide to the going rate of computerized services is as follows:

WESTLAW or LEXIS time .... $3.00 or $4.00 per minute

DIALOG, PHINET, DOW JONES, etc... cost determined by data base charges

Word Processing time .... $25.00 to $45.00 per hour

Computerized Litigation support .... $5.00 to $10.00 per document (outside service). (Billing for in-house computerized litigation support is not yet well established)

CASE STUDY # 3

ACLU REGIONAL OFFICE

Florence Volt had just started work at the ACLU regional office in SF when they first computerized with PCs. Florence manages the legal department which operates independent of the rest of the office system. The other divisions of ACLU such as Development (which handles membership) are on different systems. The machines in the legal department are not networked. Attorneys all have computers (12) but only 3 in the office are connected to one printer. One machine is available for anyone to use for printing a document (moving files from one computer to another by floppy is sometimes called "sneaker net"). Florence would prefer to remain without a network because it would slow things down on her machine.

Florence is both a legal secretary and something of a computer hacker. When the legal department hired her several years ago, the office purchased several new MS–DOS PCs with Word Perfect. Over the years they simply upgraded to faster processors (from XT to AT to 386—mostly clones). As the new machines were purchased, legal got the newer machines and gave the older machines to other departments.

A database created with Paradox software is used to manage information about cooperating attorneys, that is to keep track of individual attorneys and firms who work with ACLU on special cases. When a case comes up they search the database for lawyers whose specialty matches the case.

The majority of the computer work done in the legal department involves using Word Perfect. Word Perfect is used to keep track of all the communication concerning what issues will be the focus during the current year. This involves all the communications from the members of the legal committee, what is discussed at the meetings, general administrative issues.

Once the issues are decided then all the material related to a case is kept and filed in Word Perfect. Information such as briefs and correspondence are filed with each case. In addition a legal calendar is kept in a Word Perfect document which is in a special format created with macros. This generates appearances, deadlines for papers and document filings, etc.

Cases are all numbered in succession by year in a system using Word Perfect. Current cases are by number and name. Each case has a subfile index and a court subindex and numbering is similar for evidence etc.

Case management with this system has allowed the small ACLU legal practice to operate with the efficiency of a large firm. This takes someone who understands the legal needs of the office combined with strong computer knowledge and a sense of creating a simplified system. As a result the computer system has helped organize the office.

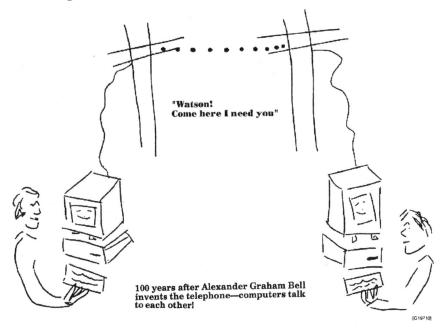

*

PART THREE

LEGAL RESEARCH

CHAPTER TEN

Using Online Services: Legal Databases

Computer-assisted legal research, or CALR as it is more conveniently referred to, is an essential part of any law practice today. It represents the critical nexus of the transformation of the practice of law by computers.

PUBLIC AND PRIVATE DATABASES

Technically, computer-assisted legal research refers to both the public, commercially available legal databases, and also to the private collection of documents that each law firm gathers to prepare for litigation, or to maintain for reference. Commercial legal databases, such as WESTLAW® and LEXIS® provide full-text of all recent and retrospective state and federal court decisions, the U.S. Code, and specialized libraries of tax, securities, labor, energy and patent law and other major areas of substantive law. These commercial legal databases can be accessed from any personal computer regardless of the operating system, i.e., Macintosh, MS–DOS, Windows, or UNIX. The private databases of a law firm might include full-text depositions, legal memoranda and briefs, pleadings, and summaries or indexes of a wide variety of documents and information.

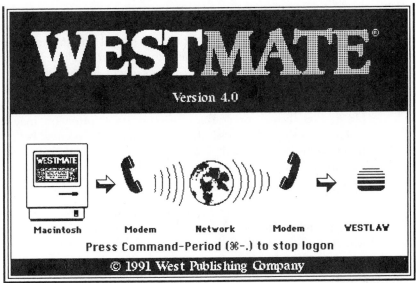

[G19711]

WESTMATE software for the Macintosh for use with WESTLAW®

Commercial services such as DIALOG, NEXIS, and BRS, provide massive databases of non-legal information which include the complete texts of some journals and newspapers and bibliographic indexes to almost all existing technical and scientific resources. Strictly speaking, these are not legal databases, but the factual or technical information they contain can be just as critical in preparing a case for trial as the leading case law.

Information Storage: The World on Your Desk

Most attorneys, and some legal workers, spend a significant portion of their professional lives engaged in legal research. The average legal researcher maintains or shares a library that probably carries the state reporter and codes, a state digest, several secondary sources, including some kind of legal encyclopedia, two or three form books, Shepard's® Citations, and one or two looseleaf services, mostly likely in the area of tax or business law. If he is lucky he will be located within one-half hour (including parking) of a major law library. The researcher undoubtedly has neither the space nor the money for a larger office library.

Computerized databases literally bring the world to the legal researcher's desk. With a subscription to WESTLAW®, which includes hundreds of DIALOG databases on WESTLAW®, or to LEXIS® and NEXIS, he can instantly retrieve on his desktop terminal the full-text of cases from all state and federal jurisdictions, and more tax and business information than are probably available at his local major law library. He can also immediately determine the status of any bill that is before any legislature in the country using one of the available legislative tracking services. Through telecommunications, he can obtain non-legal information from technical journals, newspapers, and many other published sources that he may not be able to locate anywhere in his city. In his private database he can store unlimited numbers of documents, either full-text, or in summary, that would be physically unmanageable in files, boxes, or crates. This private information may be stored on a single hard disk which is smaller than a bread box, or, if the volume is great, it may be stored in a far distant large computer with immediate access by telephone line.

Information Retrieval: Lightning Access

Information is retrieved from both public and private databases in a similar manner. Any word, phrase, or number that appears within the text of a case, newspaper article, bibliography, deposition, or other document can be used as the key to finding the document. Each commercial service may require a somewhat different format for phrasing the search inquiry, and some may insist upon a coded vocabulary, but the principle is the same.

Let us say the researcher has a client who is the daughter of a woman who took the drug D.E.S. while pregnant. The daughter now has strange physical symptoms. In order to discover the current law, it would be possible to retrieve all relevant cases in any jurisdiction simply using the term "*D.E.S.*" with WESTLAW®. The researcher could then transfer to a non-legal information database such as DIALOG, and search the chemical and medical abstracts for articles relating to *D.E.S.* In this instance it might be necessary to further limit the search by adding the phrase "birth defect" since there may be articles that deal with *D.E.S.* in a more theoretical way with no concern for its medical consequences.

As the case progresses, the researcher may choose to put the full-text of all the witnesses' depositions into his private database as well as abstracts of other documents such as medical reports, technical literature, and interrogatories. In preparing his case for trial, the researcher can almost instantaneously retrieve specific information by using key words or phrases. If it were necessary, for instance, to establish a life-long pattern of fainting spells the researcher could search all the depositions of family members and the medical records for the terms "faint" or "fainting".

Manual indexes, of course, such as case digests, technical bibliographic indexes, and notched card indexes for private files, could have provided some of the same information as the computer search, but a computer search has several inherent advantages: not only is it astonishingly fast, (when given the correct terms, of course), but it is not limited by a professional indexer; the researcher becomes the indexer. The indexer of digests, for instance, would not have created a special section for *D.E.S.* cases, and the researcher might have a difficult time locating them in the topics of medical malpractice or negligence. The computer also allows one to locate cases or facts by using arbitrary combinations of words or phrases. For instance the researcher could search all cases to find only those where both *D.E.S.* and birth defects appear, or where a certain attorney and *D.E.S.* appear; often critical information for trial strategy.

To perform sophisticated searches, however, the researcher must have a good grasp of the issues in order to use words or phrases that will retrieve the appropriate material. Not all searches are as straight-forward as the example used with *D.E.S.*. It can be easier to miss important information than with a manual index since the manual indexer is in the profession of thinking up as many terms as possible in any given area of substantive law. The researcher must come to his search well prepared in both legal and factual issues.

It is also not uncommon for a new researcher, particularly in dealing with a legal database, to use terms that are too broad and retrieve several hundred documents. This occurs because the computer is searching the full-text of all the documents in the database requested. The words or phrases requested may appear in a document which is otherwise completely inappropriate to the search. For instance, it is possible that the term *D.E.S.* might retrieve many cases dealing with trademark or patent litigation which included the drug *D.E.S.*.

WESTLAW® offers the advantage of restricting the search first to specific digest topics and/or key numbers and then further qualifying it with factual terms. Many of the non-legal databases also provide subject descriptors which restrict the focus of the search. Details of the search strategy will be offered later in this chapter.

Because the special commands used in performing a search are often difficult to remember, particularly if you do not use these services full time, WESTLAW® offers special, easy-to-use options for performing searches. EZ Access™ is West Publishing Company's menu-driven research system for new and infrequent WESTLAW® users. However this method has some drawbacks in that it can be time consuming to go back and modify the search request since it requires a new menu or list of questions each time. It is preferable to use the native command language of the system and organize your search offline. An alternative on LEXIS® for performing a search using menus is Powerlegal for the Macintosh (See diagram 5 below).

In addition WESTLAW® has recently unveiled a new search method called WIN™—(WESTLAW® is Natural™)—which allows "Natural Language" (plain English) searching.

An example of this would be:

Admissibility of a weapon in a narcotics prosecution

To access WIN™ a user would type NAT and then press enter. Then enter a description of your research issue. It is possible to restrict your search to a specific date, court, judge or attorney as well as to add related concepts to your search with an online thesaurus. This feature should greatly improve the accessibility of legal information to less experienced researchers.

LEGAL DATABASES

Legal databases are truly in the forefront of the information revolution because they offer full-text rather than bibliographic information. This not only allows much wider searching capabilities, it eliminates several steps from the research procedure. Conceivably, a researcher can complete the entire research process while seated at the terminal, and not have to locate the printed text which may be in a distant library or available only through mail order.

THE PROS AND CONS OF USING A LEGAL DATABASE

Most researchers have already formed some opinions about the commercially available legal databases, WESTLAW® and LEXIS®, not necessarily based on a great deal of experience. These opinions, often hotly debated, generally fall into the following categories:

Advantages:

Speed of information retrieval

Availability of a large law library in your office

Access to specialized material in areas like tax, securities, etc.

Ability to reach very recent cases not yet indexed

Accessing documents by judge, court, attorneys, etc., not possible with manual research

Shepardizing in a fraction of the normal time

Disadvantages:

Cost

Difficulty in using

Limits of database, e.g., no very old cases in many jurisdictions, few secondary sources

All of these points will be addressed in this chapter and in the chapter on using the system, to allow a more informed evaluation on the part of the researcher.

THE LEGAL DATABASES

WESTLAW® AND LEXIS®

WESTLAW®

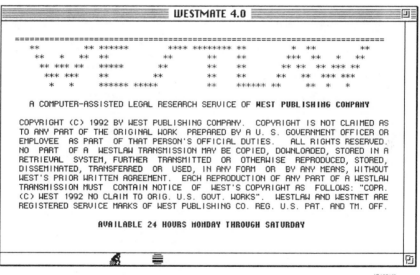

[G19712]

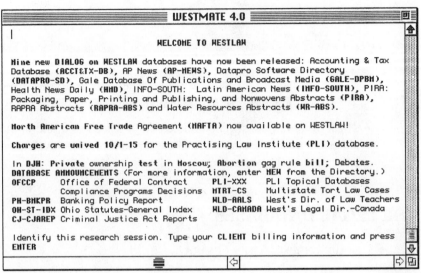

[G19713]

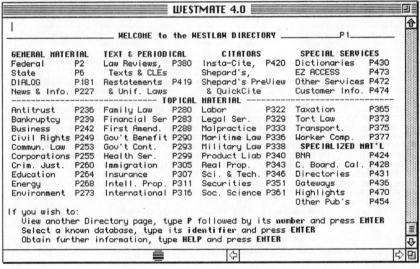

[G19714]

LEXIS®

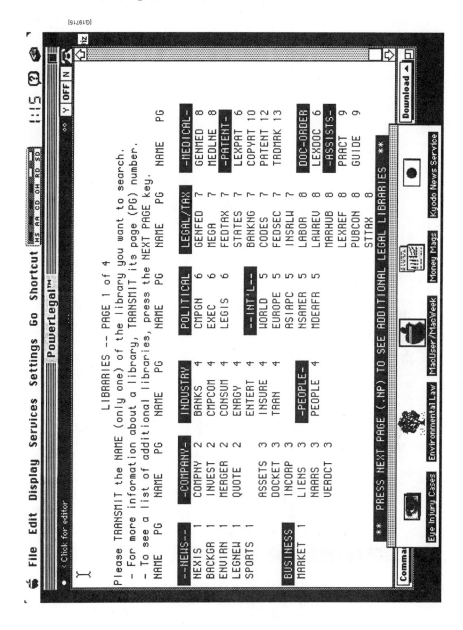

[G19715]

```
                    LIBRARIES -- PAGE 1 of 4
Please TRANSMIT the NAME (only one) of the library you want to search.
 - For more information about a library, TRANSMIT its page (PG) number.
 - To see a list of additional libraries, press the NEXT PAGE key.
NAME  PG    NAME  PG    NAME  PG    NAME  PG    NAME  PG    NAME  PG

--NEWS--    -COMPANY-   INDUSTRY    POLITICAL   LEGAL/TAX   -MEDICAL-
NEXIS  1    COMPNY 2    BANKS  4    CMPGN  6    GENFED 7    GENMED 8
BACKGR 1    INVEST 2    CMPCOM 4    EXEC   6    MEGA   7    MEDLNE 8
ENVIRN 1    MERGER 2    CONSUM 4    LEGIS  6    FEDTAX 7    -PATENT-
LEGNEW 1    QUOTE  2    ENRGY  4                STATES 7    LEXPAT 6
SPORTS 1                ENTERT 4    --INT'L--   BANKNG 7    COPYRT 10
            ASSETS 3    INSURE 4    WORLD  5    CODES  7    PATENT 12
            DOCKET 3    TRAN   4    EUROPE 5    FEDSEC 7    TRDMRK 13
            INCORP 3                ASIAPC 5    INSRLW 7
BUSINESS    LIENS  3    -PEOPLE-    NSAMER 5    LABOR  8    DOC-ORDER
MARKET 1    NAARS  3    PEOPLE 4    MDEAFR 5    LAWREV 8    LEXDOC 6
            VERDCT 3                            MARHUB 8    -ASSISTS-
                                                LEXREF 8    PRACT  9
                                                PUBCON 8    GUIDE  9
                                                STTAX  8

 ** PRESS NEXT PAGE (.NP) TO SEE ADDITIONAL LEGAL LIBRARIES **
```

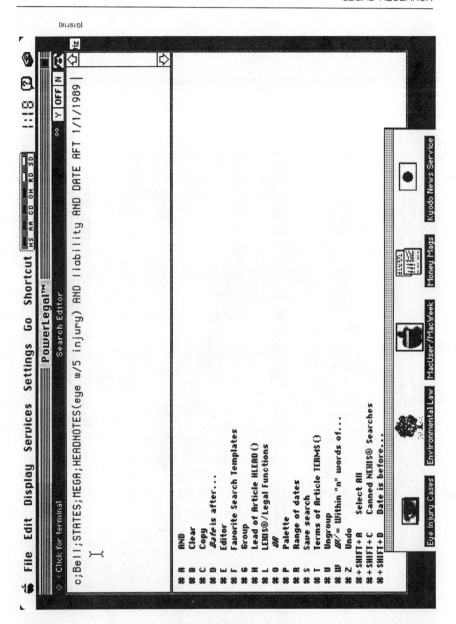

The two major commercial legal databases, LEXIS® and
WESTLAW®, have many more similarities than differences.   Both
are online interactive systems, which means that the user can carry
on a dialogue with the central computer which stores the database.
The WESTLAW® central computer system is located in Eagan,
Minnesota; LEXIS® maintains its computer center in Dayton,
Ohio. Seated at a terminal, which may be a special terminal leased
from LEXIS® or WESTLAW®, or it may be a general-use personal computer, the researcher makes contact with the central comput-

er system by connecting the terminal to a telephone by way of a modem. The telecommunications used may be a public communications network, such as TYMNET or TELENET, which provide fast service with minimum distortion, or it may be a private network, such as Meadnet or WESTNET®. Once the information has been retrieved, the researcher has the choice of browsing or quickly skimming the information on the video screen, and of printing relevant sections on the high-speed printer which most often accompanies the terminal.

The terminal may be anywhere in the country where there is a telephone line, and theoretically it could take any shape, including a laptop terminal. Both LEXIS® and WESTLAW® permit the use of most personal computers as terminals or offer their own terminals for rent. With the proliferation of laptop computers it may soon be common to see attorneys sitting in phone booths in airports, courthouse corridors, or connected to a telephone on the back deck, retrieving relevant cases on their laptop terminals.

The search request that the researcher enters through the keyboard of the terminal consists of words, phrases, numbers, or combinations thereof that describe a legal problem. The researcher can address thousands of cases, statutes, and other legal documents in almost all state or federal jurisdictions, and receive the documents which contain those terms at a fantastically fast rate. Both WESTLAW® and LEXIS® offer extensive secondary sources as well, including law reviews and specialized legal publications. Any search request can be modified by the user to include or exclude additional terms. This interactive dialogue between the user and computer gives the user greater freedom in framing and modifying search requests than is possible with standard published digests and indexes.

Both systems now provide full-text retrieval of court decisions. Originally WESTLAW® offered headnotes only, but researchers found this inadequate. WESTLAW® offers both headnotes with digest topics, key numbers, and synopsis, plus full-text. LEXIS® offers full-text only. Both WESTLAW® and LEXIS® are continually adding to their libraries. They both enter all new decisions into their databases very quickly (some jurisdictions more quickly than others), and they are vigorously extending their coverage backward in time as well.

Legal Databases: A User's Guide to WESTLAW® and LEXIS®

Computer-assisted legal research (CALR) is radically different from traditional methods of research. With the full-text computerized systems, the databases are not indexed and retrieval is achieved by searching for terms actually used in the text of the document. This provides the researcher with many more possible access points than traditional techniques would afford. He is freed from the constraints and errors of indexing. In addition to text searching, the researcher can retrieve documents by judge's name, counsel's name, name of court, author of the majority opinion or dissenting opinion, and many other criteria. Basic material (source documents) on LEXIS® and WESTLAW® consists of databases of the reported and unreported opinions of state and federal courts, state and federal statutes, most federal and some state administrative and regulatory documents, looseleaf services, legal periodical articles, and many Shepard's® citators.

Like most other new skills, it takes some practice to become proficient at retrieval, but it by no means requires specialized technical knowledge of computers. Both WESTLAW® and LEX-IS® provide self-programmed training packages, which take no more than two hours. They also offer personal training sessions with company representatives. One more hour of practice in retrieval and the researcher should begin to feel at home. After a few more hours, the researcher will probably not ever want to use traditional methods again.

LEXIS® and WESTLAW®, the two systems that most researchers will have access to, have many more commonalties than differences in the method of retrieval. There are, however, some differences in their language of retrieval and therefore they will be treated separately in this chapter. This treatment is by no means a complete exposition of these two very sophisticated systems, but may serve as a primer. Each of the systems offers detailed instruction manuals for the user.

While LEXIS® and WESTLAW® may be used for extensive and imaginative searching not possible with manual methods, there are two types of essential searches using online citations which are most commonly performed:

1. Locating an entire copy of the document when the correct citation is known.

2. Case verification. Cases checked online using Shepard's® PreView (WESTLAW® only), Insta–Cite® (WESTLAW®), and Auto–Cite® (LEXIS®). Each is more current than Shepard's® Citations printed editions.

Locating a Document

You may search either of these services to find a document when the citation is known using the following commands:

WESTLAW®: FIND

LEXIS®: LEXSEE® and LEXSTAT®

Computer-assisted legal research or CALR is especially advantageous under the following circumstances:

1. The document may never be published or is not yet published.

2. The document is missing from the library.

3. The document is only available at a great distance away.

Case Verification

For the most current case history citations you should check Insta–Cite® or Auto–Cite® first.

Insta–Cite® and Auto–Cite® are most current and are not available in printed format. For current material these services *must* be checked. Both services retrieve the parallel citation to the case, assist in case name and citation verification, and include a direct history and significant precedential treatment

PreView is a joint venture of Shepard's®, McGraw–Hill and West Publishing Company and is only available on WESTLAW®. It provides current online citations to cases that appear in advance sheets of West's® National Reporter System® but without analysis. Cases will appear here that are not yet in the regular Shepard's® Citations.

If you want Only:	Use
Current case History	Insta–Cite® or Auto–Cite®
Parallel citations	Insta–Cite® or Auto–Cite®
To verify spelling of case name and verify that citation is correct	Insta–Cite® or Auto–Cite®
Secondary authority citing your case	Shepard's® Citations online or in print
Direct history of your case	Insta–Cite® or Auto–Cite®
Negative treatment of your case	Insta–Cite® or Auto–Cite®
Comprehensive treatment of your case	Shepard's online or in Print, PreView or CALR systems as citators
Cases citing your case since last published Shepard's™ Citations	Shepard's PreView or CALR as citator either WESTLAW® or LEXIS®
Cases citing your case since Shepard's® PreView display	QuickCite™ on WESTLAW®

WESTLAW® and LEXIS® as full search tools

Search Basics

Before you actually begin formulating a search query, a few items should be noted.

Only WESTLAW® has synopsis and digest headnotes written by West editors as part of the database information. This digest information can be searched as well as the citations to documents themselves.

Definitions of words are important as is spelling, i.e., substituting the word auto for car, etc., will produce additional references than just the one word alone would find

The noise word *the* cannot be searched. Common words should be avoided as they result in too broad a search. For example a search on the word tax would not be productive. A better search would be one for *capital gains allowance* instead.

Formulating the Search Query

A good deal of preparatory work is done before the researcher turns on the computer. Cases and other legal documents are retrieved from WESTLAW® or LEXIS® by typing a search query on the keyboard. A query will include search terms, but these will be combined with connectors and modifiers which instruct the computer to search for these terms in a specified relationship; for example, in the same sentence or paragraph. Since computer time is expensive this query should be carefully worked out before coming to the keyboard.

State the Issue

Just as with traditional research, the research process begins by extracting the issue from a fact situation.

Fact situation 1

A client comes to you in the winter of 1983 hoping to buy a home. The seller had taken a mortgage from a state-chartered savings and loan institution in 1979 at a 9 per cent interest rate. The institution claims that under federal law this loan, which contains a "due on sale" clause, is not assumable.

Issue 1. In this fact situation there is really only one important legal issue:

Is a home mortgage loan from a state chartered savings and loan bank assumable under federal law?

Determine the Key Words

As with traditional research the key search terms must be pulled out. This is the point at which computer-assisted legal research pulls far ahead of traditional research since the researcher is not limited by an index; the text of all judicial opinions becomes the index. Terms consisting of more than one word can be searched as a phrase by enclosing them in quotations.

home mortgage "state-chartered" "savings and loan" assumable "due on sale"

This determination of key terms differs somewhat from traditional research in the sense that you can search for very specific terms, and therefore broader concepts like real estate, which would be useful for digest research, are not necessary. With WEST-LAW®, it is possible to use the West digest topics and key numbers in addition to, or instead of, these carefully chosen key terms. This strategy is often very useful.

The LEXIS® computer does not recognize about 100 very common terms, including "and." Not developing a concordance (an alphabetical index) for these very common terms speeds the computer search. Phrases which include "and," such as *savings and loan,* must be surrounded by quotations, but not other phrases.

Synonyms

Since the court might use terms that are somewhat differently phrased than what the researcher might use, it is important to consider synonyms as well. These can be added to the search terms: e.g., *residential* for *home.*

Expanders

Some of the search terms may appear in an opinion as plural forms, or different forms of verbs or adverbs. In order to search for all forms of a root term, expanders are used.

Find the smallest useful root of your search term and place ! after it:

e.g., by typing *residen!* all terms containing the root *residen* are retrieved:

WESTLAW®: residence, residences, and residential

LEXIS®: residence, residences, and residential

mortgag!

WESTLAW®: mortgagor, mortgagee, mortgage, mortgages

LEXIS®: mortgagor, mortgagee, mortgage, mortgages

assum! (this will retrieve both *assumable* and *assumption*)

The asterisk* is the second expander symbol and it functions as a universal character. It can be used within any term or at the end of a term.

The search term *cr*sh* would retrieve cases containing the search terms *crush* or *crash.*

Multiple * may be used to indicated several letter combinations. Woman * * * * would retrieve womanhood and womankind.

Compound terms

The–is treated differently by each system

On LEXIS® a–is treated as a space so typing a term with a hyphen in it will retrieve the two variants, i.e., with a hyphen and with a space in it. E.g., entering *post-conviction* will retrieve *post conviction,* and *post-conviction.*

WESTLAW® includes the two above and also the term with no space it. E.g., entering *post-conviction* will retrieve *post conviction, postconviction* and *post-conviction.*

Plurals

Plurals are a specialized expander: WESTLAW® and LEXIS® solve this problem very easily, though somewhat differently. WESTLAW® and LEXIS® will automatically retrieve plural forms of terms if just the singular is entered. However if the plural is entered, WESTLAW® only finds the plural while LEXIS® will find both the singular and the plural. WESTLAW® will allow you to turn off the pluralizer by entering # before the word so you can retrieve only the singular form of the word, e.g., *# damage* retrieves references to *damage* but not to *damages.*

Restrictive Connectors

The order in which these search terms appear, and their proximity in the body of the opinion, are important for retrieval.

Or, And, And Not and But Not

Or is used for synonyms and alternate expressions

LEXIS®: OR

WESTLAW®: a space between terms or an OR

For example, to find a reference to *attorney* or *lawyer* the search would be:

LEXIS®: attorney or lawyer

WESTLAW®: attorney lawyer

Note: to search for a phrase on WESTLAW® with a space between two words rather than meaning OR, enclose the phrase within quotation marks.

The AND connector

Using the connector AND will retrieve documents in which BOTH terms are found. It requires that each of the terms on both sides of the & be in the same document.

WESTLAW®: & (it will also recognize AND)

LEXIS®: AND

In our example of *attorney* and *lawyer:*

WESTLAW®: attorney & lawyer

LEXIS®: attorney and lawyer

retrieves only those cases in which both the word *attorney* and *lawyer* are found.

AND NOT or BUT NOT

LEXIS®: AND NOT

WESTLAW®: % (BUT NOT)

% or AND NOT means the computer will not retrieve cases which contain any of the terms following the percent sign.

Again using our example of *attorney* and *lawyer:*

LEXIS®: lawyer and not attorney

WESTLAW®: lawyer % attorney

retrieves those documents in which lawyer is mentioned provided the term attorney is not mentioned in the same document.

This is really the opposite of the AND connector above.

Multiple Connectors

For example searching for all the documents which contain *lawyer* or *attorney,* and *judge,* and *defendant:*

On LEXIS®: lawyer or attorney, and judge, and defendant

On WESTLAW®: lawyer attorney & judge, & defendant

retrieves all those cases in which either the term attorney OR lawyer appears with judge and defendant.

Proximity Connectors

Proximity connectors specify the relation between terms in terms of proximity. There are two kinds: numerical and grammatical. Numerical connectors determine that the terms on either side of the connector be within a certain number of terms of each other. For example, if you wish to find cases in which A is mentioned within 5 terms of B:

LEXIS®: A w/5 B

WESTLAW®: A /8 B

Again using an example to retrieve cases concerned with savings and loan and home mortgages:

LEXIS®: "Savings and loan" w/5 home mortgage

WESTLAW®: "Savings and loan" 5 "home mortgage"

will retrieve only those cases in which the phrases are within the specified number of terms of each other.

Proximity connectors can also determine which is the first word and within how many words the second will appear:

LEXIS®: A pre/5 B

WESTLAW®: A +5 B

In these cases B will occur within 5 terms following A.

The second type of proximity connector is the grammatical one. This determines the limits of the search by grammatical unit, usually sentence or paragraph. WESTLAW® uses /P and /S to determine the grammatical unit.

WESTLAW®: A /p B

This requires that A be in the same paragraph as B. This is more commonly used as it limits but does not severely limit the search. LEXIS® does not have grammatical connectors but uses a W/SEG command to determine the segment of the document within which the terms will appear.

These symbols soon become almost automatic to the research-er. In our query the appropriate connectors would be:

WESTLAW®: "savings and loan" /p "state chartered" /p home residen! /p mortgag! & assum! & "due on sale"

LEXIS®: state-chartered PRE/6 "savings and loan" AND home OR residen! W/25 mortgag! AND assum! AND due on sale

To clarify the grouping of connectors, the researcher might put them in parentheses. In other situations parentheses may also be used to change the sequence in which the connectors operate.

(state-chartered PRE/6 "savings and loan") AND (home OR residen! W/25 mortgag!) AND assum! AND due on sale

At this point it should be mentioned that several different search words and combinations of search words would probably retrieve the same law. There is no single "correct" search query, there are just those that work, and those that don't.

Entering the Computer

Organization of Documents in the Databases

With search query in hand, the researcher is now ready to sit down at the computer terminal, enter his password and begin his search after locating the appropriate area to search.

WESTLAW®: All documents are found in a database. Each document may have several fields, or parts.

LEXIS®: Documents are found in libraries. Each library has files in it and each document in the file is broken into segments. A library is a major collection, for instance the GENFED library contains all federal cases and statutes. A file is a smaller unit within that library; U.S. Reports are a file within the GENFED library. A document is a single retrievable item, like a case, or a code section, and a segment is a separately retrievable part of a document. Segments vary from file to file, but for a case, typical segments would be the name of the case, the date of the decision, the citation, the author of the opinion, the author of a dissenting opinion, and the text of the opinion and the dissenting opinion.

Conducting a search requires first selecting the database or library and file in which the search is to be conducted. The fields and segments have been created by dividing the source documents into divisions that naturally occur in the source document. For example, cases can be located by a court docket number, from a certain court, a case involving certain parties, a specific judge's opinions, a specific date on which a case was decided, or terms in a WESTLAW® digest, etc.

The researcher knows the question is federal law, and therefore he has the choice of the *Supreme Court Reporter* ®, the *Federal Register* ®, the *Federal Supplement* ® or the *U.S. Code*. The researcher has probably also heard that there is a recent Supreme Court decision in this area; and under any circumstances, this is a wise place to begin.

The message on the screen asks for a query and the researcher types in:

WESTLAW®: "savings and loan" /p "state chartered" /p home residen! /p mortgag! & assum! & "due on sale"

LEXIS®: (state-chartered PRE/6 "savings and loan") AND (home OR residen! w/25 mortgag!) AND assum! AND due on sale

A few seconds pass while the message on the screen says that your search is proceeding, and then it flashes:

WESTLAW®: "There are no documents which correspond to your search query"

LEXIS®: 0 cases.

Changing Your Search Query

The researcher new to CALR needs some practice in formulating a search query that is neither so narrow that no cases will contain exactly that wording, nor so broad that too many opinions will be retrieved. Rather than abandoning the search in the Supreme Court database, the researcher should try simplifying the query, keeping only the most critical terms. He might simply try:

WESTLAW®: home residen! /p mortgag!

The screen now flashes that there are 26 documents that fill this search request and immediately displays the title page of:

Fidelity Federal Savings and Loan Association de la Cuesta 102 S.Ct. 3014

Quickly scanning the synopsis on WESTLAW® it seems clear that this case is relevant since it pertains to the assumability of loans. The researcher then has the choice of striking P and reading through the case page by page, or T and retrieving those pages that satisfy the search term query. With WESTLAW® he can also peruse the headnotes and synopsis before entering the text of the opinion. This can be a great time-saver. The option of searching headnotes is not available on LEXIS®. By either method the researcher would soon discover that the decision forbids the assumption of home mortgages, but clearly limits this decision to federally chartered savings and loans, leaving state-chartered savings and loans to state discretion. The researcher can now make use of the printer to print out relevant pages for documentation.

By pressing L, the researcher can retrieve a list of citations to all retrieved cases and print them for further use if he wishes, or call up some of the other more recent cases for perusal.

LEXIS®

Since the original request yielded 0 documents the researcher now has the option of editing the existing request, as one does with WESTLAW®, or dividing the existing request into levels as follows:

LEXIS®:

Level 1 (state-chartered PRE/6 "savings and loan")

Level 2 AND (home OR residen! w/25 mortgag!)

Level 3 AND assum!

Level 4 AND "due on sale"

The researcher first types Level 1 search and LEXIS® reports that it finds 0 cases on this level. Therefore this level must be too restrictive. Following the instructions on the screen he then punches M for modify, the transmit key, and types in Level 2. This time LEXIS® responds that there are 15 cases which fit the Search request. He may either review level 2, or decide that this number is too large and go on to Level 3. The computer retains Level 2 cases and searches them for the additional term rather than searching through the whole database once more. This does save some time.

Level 3 search indicates that there are five cases which fit the Search request. The researcher may now display the first case by publishing FIRST DOC or press CITE and receive a list of the cases received, highest court and most recent date first. Either way, the first case presented will be:

Fidelity Federal Savings and Loan Association v. de la Cuesta (1982) 458 U.S. 141

LEXIS® does not provide a synopsis, but it does provide several techniques for scanning a case. The KWIC key displays the name, citation, and date of a case and each occurrence of the search terms with 25 words on each side. The CHG KWIC SIZE key includes 50 words on each side of the search term and this number may be changed to any number from 1 to 999. The key P will indicate the number of pages in the document. The researcher can then make the decision to browse page by page by pressing PAGE FORWARD or PAGE BACK keys.

Of course, at any point the researcher can print the information displayed on the screen or save it on their disk for later printing. He may continue his search while it is being printed. Experienced researchers find that they rarely need to print whole cases; only relevant portions.

Changing the Database

The researcher has discovered the most recent holding of the highest federal court, which says that it will only enforce "due on sale" clauses where the lender is a federally chartered savings and loan association. But judicial opinions are only one source of federal law; in order to thoroughly search federal law the researcher must also investigate statutory law, i.e., the *U.S. Code*. In order to run the same query in a different database on WESTLAW® the researcher simply types *sdb* followed by the database identifier, e.g., *sdb USCA*. The researcher then waits for the full-text of the *U.S. Code Annotated* ® to be searched.

The search query yields two sections of the *U.S. Code Annotated* ®, one dealing with investment banking, the other with the F.H.A. It is at this point that experience and training with WESTLAW® pays off. Since the language of statutes is much more narrowly written than that of judicial opinions, it is easier to miss relevant sections. In order to avoid this, the researcher should try all possible search terms. The researcher would then try several different combinations or the original search terms. Upon entering:

assum! & "due on sale"

WESTLAW® retrieves:

12 USCA §1701j–3. Presumption of due on sale prohibitions.

This complicated statute, passed on October 15, 1982, (popularly known as the Garn–St. Germain bill), directly relates to his client's problem. Basically, it allows all state and federal lenders to enforce "due on sale" clauses after October 1, 1982. It does, however, contain exceptions. One of the exceptions is that contracts made under any prevailing state law governing this matter after 1978 will be enforced until October 1, 1985. The researcher has now learned that the situation is complicated and he must go to prevailing state law to determine whether his client falls under the exception. He types in *sdb CA–CS* to run his query in the California Cases database (CA–CS).

In a few seconds the most recent case will appear:

1 of 32 documents

Cal.App.1982

Hutton v. Glicksberg, 180 Cal.Rptr. 141.

By using either the page or term mode, the researcher can quickly peruse the case and print relevant sections on the printer. This case affirms the 1977 California Supreme Court "Wellenkamp rule" which holds that loans from state chartered savings and loan institutions are assumable when ownership of private residences changes. Typing L will give a list of citations to the 32 documents which meet his search request in chronological order. This case indicates that under California law the borrower can assume the loan from a state-chartered bank, since the loan was made after the *Wellenkamp* decision. The new federal law specifies that it will allow this ruling to stand for three years unless the state legislature chooses to intervene.

LEXIS®:

Research in the GENFED NEWER federal case library has informed the researcher that, according to the Fidelity Savings decision, federal law in this area of the assumability of residential mortgages applies only to federal lending institutions. The researcher must then examine the other area of federal primary authority: the U.S. Code. The Code is also found in the GENFED library, so the researcher only has to push the CHG FILE key and then enter CODE. In researching the Code, the researcher will probably make use of all levels of the search query, in order to make sure that no precisely written laws are missed. In the instant example, it is only with Level 4, due on sale, that the Garn–St. Germain bill, 12 USCA s 1701j–3 is retrieved. In searching codes, the varying levels of search query are useful.

The researcher learns from the Garn–St. Germain bill that although "due on sale" clauses in loans made from state chartered savings and loans institutions can be enforced after October 1, 1982, there may be some exceptions made for loans contracted between 1978 and 1982, according to prevailing state law.

In order to complete the search, California law must be investigated to determine the prevailing law for California between 1978 and 1982 regarding state chartered savings and loan associations and "due on sale" clauses. The researcher will then press the CHANGE GROUP key and choose a new library and file. California will be the new library, but the researcher will have a choice between all cases, or only Supreme court or Appellate court decisions, or more recent cases. Recent cases would be the wisest choice and the previous search request will automatically appear on the screen. It is possible to edit that request or formulate an entirely new request.

The search in the California library will then proceed in the same manner as in the GENFED library, with the researcher using various techniques to scan the cases, and using the printer to print appropriate sections for further reference or for incorporation into a legal document.

The researcher should find the most recent case: Hutton v. Glicksberg, (1982) 26 Cal.App.3d 242. This is the same case that WESTLAW® would find, affirming the "Wellankamp rule", which holds that loans from state chartered savings and loan institutions after 1977 are assumable.

As with WESTLAW® it is now possible to search the California Statutes online in order to determine if the legislature has made any determination on this issue, in the same way as the federal cases are searched.

Citators

WESTLAW®: Shepard's® Citations and Insta–Cite.

LEXIS®: Auto–Cite

With all proper case research, the researcher must Shepardize the case he is relying upon in order to insure that it is still good law. Most researchers consider Shepardizing a necessary evil, since it often requires searching through several volumes and pamphlets in order to cover the span from the time the court opinion was delivered to the present. This is both tedious and time-consuming. With both WESTLAW® and LEXIS® this can now be done in seconds! This feature may win over more converts to CALR than any other single factor.

The researcher may access Shepard's® Citations by entering sh and the citation, for instance:

sh 180 CRP 141, or by simply entering sz when the case is displayed on the terminal. He may limit the Shepard's® citations that are called up to a particular history or treatment, i.e.

limit r

or to a particular headnote,

limit 4

When Shepard's® Citations are displayed on the screen, those that are retrievable by WESTLAW® will have a number, and they can be called up instantly by simply entering the number. Once the case is displayed, press Enter to display the pages where your case is cited.

The case at hand yielded no citations, which means no subsequent courts have mentioned it in any way; indicating that it is still good law, and probably the most recent case.

Insta–Cite (WESTLAW®) Auto–Cite (LEXIS®)

To check a cite in Insta–Cite the researcher presses the Insta–Cite key on the terminal and then enters the volume number, any commonly used reporter variation, and the paragraph or page number of the case he wishes to check. Insta–Cite displays current case history, verifies the accuracy of the citation transmitted, gives complete parallel citations to that case, and cites any case that directly affects its validity as precedent. Insta–Cite provides a more accurate citation than Shepard's®, since Shepard's® does not provide the name of the case, but it does not provide all of the information that Shepard's® does regarding how other courts have treated the case. For example, if a judge in a different case had questioned the authority of the case it would not appear in Insta–Cite or Auto–Cite, since the case is still good precedent. Most researchers, therefore, feel more comfortable with the scope of information provided by Shepard's®.

Evaluation.

By the time the researcher has formed his search query, modified his search query, called up relevant cases in both the Supreme Court Reporter, the U.S. Code, the California Cases, and the California Statutes databases, perused the cases, printed relevant sections, and Shepardized the key cases, perhaps no more than 10 or 15 minutes have passed. Beginning researchers will obviously need more time, but it does not take very long to become proficient. How does this compare with traditional research? Research time in at least two digests, the *U.S. Code,* several reporter volumes and several Shepard's® volumes would be necessary to duplicate this search. Copying relevant sections with a duplicating machine would be an additional task. A rough estimate of the length of this manual search would be at least one and one-half hours.

Perhaps an even more important advantage of WESTLAW® or LEXIS® over traditional research is illustrated by researching this loan issue. The critical case, the U.S. Supreme Court Fidelity Federal Savings case, was only a few months old when the search commenced, and the so-called "Garn bill" only a few weeks old. With traditional digest research it might have been possible to miss this case and this code since the pocket parts are not kept up to date that frequently, nor are the supplements to the *U.S.Code.* Usually, but not always, very recent cases will be found by Shepardizing an older, important case. But this works only if the judge specifically mentions the older case. In addition, WESTLAW®

enters Supreme Court and circuit court cases online almost immediately; several days before they appear in advance sheets.

With the problem at hand, at least, it seems clear that computer-assisted legal research (CALR) can provide a much faster and
more thorough research job than traditional research methods.

Specialized Searches

Statutes and Regulations.

WESTLAW®

WESTLAW® carries the U.S.Code Annotated, the Code of
Federal Regulations and state statutes for all states. As noted in
the above example regarding the "due on sale" issue, accessing a
U.S.Code Annotated is very similar to retrieving a case. The
researcher first chooses the appropriate database, either USC or
CFR. Then the appropriate search query must be formulated.
Since statutes and regulations are often more precisely worded
than court opinions, it may be necessary to consider more synonyms, and, as in the "due on sale" example, it is often critical to
try a number of search queries, in order to catch the exact wording.
The U.S.Code Annotated database may also be searched by fields,
in a manner similar to cases. The major fields are:

1.   citation.

2.   prelim, which consists of the superior subtitle, chapter, and
subchapter headings.

3.   caption, which contains the section numbers. As with
cases, these fields are useful if you know some, or all of the
sections of a specific code that you wish to retrieve. Unlike case
research, there is usually not more than one code section that you
are seeking.

LEXIS®

Citations to Statutes and Regulations.

By using the citations of statutes, regulations or constitutions
as search terms, cases which mention these terms can be retrieved.
This variation is most useful if the search is for a specific law, for
instance, Section 1103 of the Internal Revenue Code.

Searching Statutes and Regulations.

As was illustrated above, a researcher would call up the
U.S.Code by choosing: Library: GENFED, File: CODE. If the
title and section are not known he can formulate a descriptive word
search request in the same manner as case research; e.g., civil
rights AND color.

If the researcher has a specific code section already in mind he may request: SECTION (42 AND 11700). This will retrieve 42USC1170.

Specialized libraries.

WESTLAW®

Most of the specialty libraries offered by WESTLAW® consist of many different kinds of legal documents which can be found in several databases. A listing of the databases on WESTLAW® is available from your local representative. For example, the tax library, which is the most fully developed specialty library, is made up of the following databases:

FTX–USCA...Internal Revenue Code

FTX–CS...Federal Tax Cases

FTX–SCT...U.S. Supreme Court Decisions involving tax questions

FTX–CTA..U.S. Courts of Appeals and Court of Claims decisions involving tax issues

FTX–DCT...U.S. District Courts decisions involving tax questions

FTX–TCT..U.S. Tax Court memorandum decisions

FTX–ADM...Federal Tax administrative materials, including revenue rulings, revenue procedures, etc.

FTX–WD...IRS Written Determinations, including current letter rulings

All tax cases in these several databases can be retrieved like all other case law; through a strictly descriptive word search, which searches the whole document, or through a field search which limits the search to specific fields such as judge, synopsis, etc.

The *Internal Revenue Code,* which is part of the U.S.Code, may be searched in the same manner as the U.S.Code, but I.R.S. Written Determinations may only be searched by descriptive words, or by citation.

LEXIS®

LEXIS® has many specialized libraries which gather cases, administrative rulings or regulations, and other relevant legal documents which deal with a particular subject such as tax law, security law, trade regulation, bankruptcy, patent, trademark, communications and labor law. These specialized libraries are made up of individually researchable files.

Information is retrieved from specialized libraries in the same manner that cases and statutes are accessed. A Library and File are chosen and a descriptive word search or a specific code or regulation search are entered. Each file is also composed of segments which may be separately searched.

Cost

For most firms it is possible to pass on the costs of LEXIS® and WESTLAW® to clients if you have a direct billing relationship. If that alternative is not possible it may be possible to share a subscription with other firms located near you. Both systems are continually changing their pricing structure to provide more access at lower rates. To find the plan which best suits your needs, your WESTLAW® or LEXIS® representative should be contacted for a current schedule of pricing options.

Both WESTLAW® and LEXIS® are compatible with most PCs. This means that you do not have to lease their terminal but can use your own microcomputer with a modem to access the main databases: WESTLAW® in Eagan, Minnesota and LEXIS® in Dayton, Ohio. If you do become a subscriber to either of these two systems there is fairly extensive training available and a customer hotline for any problems you might have. There is also a reference manual and training materials to help you along during the early days.

Off Line Printing

Off line printing on demand means that the researcher would perform the original research on WESTLAW® or LEXIS® and determine from this which cases, codes, administrative materials, or other sources required further perusal. He would then request off line printing or "dumping" of the cases requested into his own computer's auxiliary memory (floppy or hard disk). He could print all of the stored material, or any part of it, at his own convenience.

Both LEXIS® and WESTLAW® are expanding their off line services. Currently it is possible to get an off line print directly on your own compatible high-speed printer or have the requested information "dumped" onto your disk for printing or future perusal. This can be accomplished very quickly and avoids both database and telecommunications costs.

Prices

Prices vary greatly according to factors which include the number of people using the service, amount of usage, etc., so you should contact the services before you use them to find out the charges which would apply in your specific case. In the case of smaller firms it is a good idea to look at group prices available through state bar associations. Below are some of the standard charges to provide some idea of the costs.

WESTLAW®:

No Monthly Fee, However $80 minimum usage. Hours are accrued so average monthly minimum useage is $80. Renewed yearly.

Connect Time: $.34 per minute ($20.40 per hour)

Network Time: $.17 per minute ($10.20 per hour)–$.51 per minute ($30.60 per hour) depending on network access and baud rate. Note while there is a surcharge for 2400 baud, there is no extra charge beyond this for 9600 baud.

Search charges: Vary between $1.25 per minute (certain databases and EZ ACCESS) and do not apply to monthly minimum usage, to $6.65 per minute, with many averaging $4 per minute and these apply to the $80 minimum.

Printing and Saving to disk charges: $.02 per line

LEXIS®:

Monthly subscription: $125 per location (to max $750)

Connect Time: $33 per hour

Network Time: $13–$21 depending on network

Search Charges: Vary among the segments accessed, generally from $0 to $50 per search.

Printing and Saving to disk charges: $.02–.07 per line of text

With only a few hours of practice the researcher can experience much greater speed and accuracy with either WESTLAW® or LEXIS® than is possible with traditional research. As the databases of these two systems expand, and the cost is brought down with the expansion of the number of subscribers, CALR will become the norm for legal researchers.

While waiting for the costs to decline to the point where every individual researcher can make use of her own desktop terminal, it is hoped that there will be more low-cost availability through law libraries, law schools and attorney sharing arrangements.

Suggested reading:

Rombauer, Marjorie Dick, Legal Problem Solving: analysis, research, and writing, 1991, West Publishing, St. Paul, MN Chapt 9: Computer-assisted Legal Research, Penny Hazelton, pp. 275–332

Discovering WESTLAW®: the Student's Essential Guide, 1991 West Publishing, St. Paul, MN

CHAPTER ELEVEN

Nonlegal Databases

There is virtually no area of law practice where an attorney does not have need for factual as well as legal information. Practitioners dealing with personal injury or medical malpractice regularly require specific medical information; corporate attorneys negotiating contracts or mergers with industries producing any technical product must have an understanding both of the technical issues and of the financial status of the corporations involved; criminal attorneys need access to the latest social scientific studies in order to prepare their defense. The kinds of factual information required is as varied as the attorney's clients and their problems.

Attorneys, however, are not trained to perform factual research in law school, and often find this a difficult and frustrating aspect of their work. General reference libraries are not as well indexed in many subject areas as law libraries, or may not carry the relevant journals or books. It may be necessary to search several specialty libraries in order to find a necessary piece of technical information, like the price of hogs over the last decade.

Fortunately, the information revolution has already spawned thousands of computerized data bases of non-legal information, and there is no end in sight. Typically, these data bases store references to, or summaries of, articles in periodicals and journals, books, news stories, scientific and technical reports, statistical charts, government data, etc. They can provide the demographic material, financial statistics, and economic indicators contained in literally tens of millions of references, summaries and statistics going back several years. These databases are created and maintained by a variety of private and public organizations including the National Library of Medicine, and many government, scientific, and social scientific professional associations.

LEGAL VS. NONLEGAL DATABASES

Although the concept of storage and retrieval is similar with legal and non-legal data bases, a difference is that non-legal data bases, with the exception of NEXIS and VU/TEXT, in most cases do not provide the full text of the document referred to. Most commonly the reference will contain the author, title, or publication, some key descriptor terms and perhaps a summary or abstract.

In many ways a non legal database is like a legal digest, which allows the researcher to select appropriate cases. Like a digest, the data base will often be accompanied by a printed descriptive word index, often called a thesaurus, which will help to identify the exact descriptors used for that database. Having discovered the appropriate reference in the database, the researcher, in most instances, must still obtain the full text of the document. Although, as will be later explained, it is often possible to directly order the document from the computer service employed, it must be sent through the mail; thus, it is rarely possible to have the answer almost instantly, as it is with full text legal databases.

Nevertheless, nonlegal databases can often lead to information that was previously totally inaccessible to the attorney, such as ongoing government contract research, or current medical studies. It means that the researcher does not have to leave his office, and can avoid frustrating long hours in libraries.

Pros and Cons of Nonlegal Databases

Most legal researchers will have less familiarity with the commercially available non-legal databases than they will with the legal databases, WESTLAW or LEXIS. Therefore they may not have clear opinions on their value in legal research. To determine whether or not it is worth the effort to subscribe to one or more non-legal databases, these factors will be scrutinized in this chapter and the next:

Possible Advantages

- Access to a vast amount of information often unavailable or difficult to locate
- Speed of information retrieval
- Ability to go beyond conventional indexes and search many different databases

Possible Disadvantages

- Cost
- Difficulty in use
- Relevancy in law practice

Specialized Databases

Among the hundreds of available databases there are obviously some that will be used by attorneys more than others. It will be a rare instance when an attorney needs to find out what hog prices have been over the past ten years, but it will be an everyday occurrence for an attorney to want to discover a company's standing in the Dow Jones average over that same ten years. The following are some examples of databases in information areas more likely to be requested by attorneys. At least one commercial service that offers each database is noted; many are offered by more than one.

Legally Related Information

Legal Resource Index

Covering a period from 1980 to the present, this database provides cover-to-cover indexing of over 750 key law journals and five law newspapers plus legal monographs and government publications from the Library of Congress MARC database. The LEGAL RESOURCE INDEX comprehensively indexes articles, book reviews, case notes, president's pages, columns, letters to the editor, obituaries, transcripts, biographical pieces, and editorials providing access to valuable secondary information for the legal profession. (Available through BRS, LEXIS, WESTLAW, DIALOG)

Congressional and Legislative Information

CIS/Index (Congressional Information Service)

The CIS database is the machine-readable form of the Congressional Information Service's Index to Publications of the United States Congress. CIS provides current comprehensive access to the contents of the entire spectrum of Congressional working papers published by the nearly 300 House, Senate, and Joint committees and subcommittees each year. Coverage is available from 1970 to present. (Available through DIALOG)

Congressional Record Abstracts

This database provides comprehensive abstracts covering each issue of the Congressional Record. Coverage includes Congressional activities regarding bills and resolutions, committee and subcommittee reports, public laws, executive communications and speeches. Data on bills, roll call votes, reference to floor debates and specific issues are included. Coverage is from 1976 to present and is updated weekly. (Available through DIALOG)

Crecord

Crecord provides comprehensive, highly current coverage of the Congressional Record. References are indexed and cross-referenced in 275 legislative areas. (Available through DIALOG)

Business and Finance

There are scores of databases that are designed for use by business or financial managers. The following may be particularly useful for attorneys in corporate practice.

Claims/U.S. Patent Abstracts

This database contains citations and abstracts for all patents classified by the U.S. Patent office in the areas of aerospace and aeronautical engineering, chemical engineering, chemistry, civil engineering, electrical and electronics engineering, electromagnetic technology, mechanical engineering, nuclear science, and general science and technology from 1978 to present. (Available through Orbit)

Dow Jones News/Retrieval

This database has a range of 90 days. It provides instant access to news of interest to the business community. It makes available complete text of articles from the Wall Street Journal, financial analysis of companies and industries from Barrons, and up-to-the minute news from around the world. Data becomes available within seconds of its appearance on the Dow Jones newswire.

Medical and Technical

It is perhaps in these areas that computerized information databases make their most dramatic contribution. They make it possible to keep current not only with completed research results, but with work in progress. The researcher can enjoy the benefits of information networking; drawing together research from many different fields to focus on a specific problem.

There are more databases in this area than any other, reflecting, no doubt, the continuing explosion of information in these fields.

MEDLINE (MEDLARS on-line)

Produced by the U.S. National Library of Medicine, it is one of the major sources for biomedical literature. MEDLINE indexes articles from over 3000 international journals published in the United States and 70 countries. Over 40% of records added since 1975 contain author abstracts. Over 250,000 records are added each year. Coverage is from 1966 to present. (Available through BRS, NEXIS and others)

General News and Information

Very often, newsworthy events affect the decisions that lawyers must make. If a client owns a football team and the attorney hears that there was a football merger that might affect his client's plans to sell, he would want to learn the exact details of the story. Fortunately, there are several databases that provide current coverage of general news.

NEWSEARCH

This is a daily index of more than 2000 news stories, information articles and book reviews from over 1400 of the most important newspapers, magazines and periodicals. Every working day the previous day's news stories are indexed and added to NEWSEARCH. (Available through DIALOG)

The New York Times

All articles, features, columns, editorials, letters and news stories from the final Late Edition of the weekday New York Times, and the Saturday and Sunday editions—full text from 1980. (Available through NEXIS)

National Newspaper Index

This database has monthly updates, providing front page to back page indexing of The Christian Science Monitor, The New York Times, and The Wall Street Journal. It is particularly useful for answering general reference questions. 1979–present. (Available through DIALOG)

ACCESS TO NON–LEGAL DATABASES

There are several ways in which a researcher can gain access to these computerized databases. As with WESTLAW and LEXIS, the large mainframe computer which contains the information may be anywhere in the country. The information is transmitted via telecommunications, through a modem, and into the users terminal. With many of these databases it is possible to use your own microcomputer or word processor and not rent a terminal. In some cases it is also possible to obtain the information from a third party, called retailer, who has access to many databases and will do your research for you.

With some variations, access is usually obtained in one of the following ways:

Single Database

Some major single databases, like MEDLINE, allow direct access without going through a broker. You deal directly with that database, dialing up their number and receiving the information on your terminal through the telephone line much as you would with

WESTLAW or LEXIS. This would be most useful, and more economical for a specialist, like a physician, but might be less useful for an attorney who normally has a wide range of information needs.

Multiple Databases

In the past few years many multiple database vendors have begun to offer their services. Typically a vendor will maintain a large mainframe computer anywhere in the country and will store many different databases from different sources in that computer. The vendor may specialize in certain types of databases, or may offer a wide range of databases. Some of the largest vendors, such as Lockheed's DIALOG, and BRS, and NEXIS, may offer over 200 databases ranging across the complete spectrum of available information. Others, like Reader's Digest's SOURCE, which is aimed toward the home computer market, offer a wide variety of services, such as electronic games, travel and dining information, checkbook balancing and electronic mail in addition to wire service news and financial information.

Usually these services are accessed by way of a telecommunications service, such as TYMNET or TELENET. The user dials the local TYMNET or TELENET number through his telephone modem. All microcomputers are equipped, with the addition communications software and a telephone modem, to access these services. The user can also rent a non-intelligent terminal (no computer capabilities) to connect to the telecommunications line.

This method of accessing the information vendor's computer is the same as the method used for accessing both WESTLAW and LEXIS. In fact, users of LEXIS have immediate access to NEXIS, while WESTLAW allows a gateway to DIALOG, DOW JONES, VU/TEXT, and INFORMATION AMERICA. WESTLAW and LEXIS users have the option of subscribing to the largest of the information brokers, DIALOG, on the same terminal that they use to retrieve the legal databases. The telecommunications service then connects them to the computer in Menlo Park, California, rather than the computer in Eagan, Minnesota, or Dayton, Ohio.

DIALOG

Databases

Since Lockheed's DIALOG is the largest of the information brokers it will be used to illustrate the genre of multi-purpose, multi-base information brokers.

DIALOG contains over 400 databases, which represents more than 270 million references to over 100,000 publications, with complete texts of 1100 periodicals. Each record, or unit of information, can range from a directory-type listing of specific manufacturing plants, to a citation with bibliographic information and an abstract referencing a journal, conference paper or other original source. The databases offer subject coverage in science, technology, engineering, social sciences, business and economics. It is difficult to conceive of any question a researcher might have for which DIALOG would not offer at least one appropriate database, perhaps several.

Each of these databases is individually owned and maintained and each charges a different fee for the time used. The size of the database is the main factor in cost. Each database also has a separate rate for printing off-line the complete text of a document, which is then mailed to the user. There is no start-up or monthly subscriber fee, however, so the user pays only for actual search time. This is a significant advantage for the subscriber over systems like WESTLAW and LEXIS where the monthly subscriber and equipment rental fees are substantial.

Operation

A subscriber almost anywhere in the U.S., using his own terminal and a modem can make contact with the DIALOG computer in Menlo Park, California by dialing his local TYMNET or TELENET, requesting DIALOG, and entering his appropriate identification.

A typical user may not be certain which data base will answer his information request. He can select topic words and enter DIALINDEX, a program which will indicate which of the data bases are appropriate for his request. The user can then search each of these data bases separately, but maintain the same search query.

Let us say the researcher wants to find the latest research on computerized legal reasoning. He would first have to phrase the search query. This phrasing is similar to that used with WEST-LAW or LEXIS since it utilizes a form of Boolean logic; but since the computer is not searching full text, many of the restrictive commands are not used. It is expressed in levels rather than on the same line.

The search command could be phrased as follows:

1   computer
2   legal (W) analysis
3   legal (W) reason
4   2 1 and (2 or 3)

DIALINDEX indicates that the appropriate databases are Legal Resource Index and Social Scisearch.

Most databases have their own thesaurus, or controlled vocabulary. These printed documents are sold separately (usually expensive), but are very useful for researchers who work regularly with the same database. Without the thesaurus it is possible to "free search", simply trying the most likely terms.

In this example the researcher chose the Legal Resources Index and entered the "free search" query developed above. After 15 seconds the video screen displayed a list of six references, beginning with:

1916064 DATABASE: LRI File 150

Computers and legal reasoning

Grossman: Gary S; Solomon, Lewis D.

A.B.A.J. 69 66–70 Jan 1983

This is not a large number of references, but this database begins coverage only in 1980. A search of the Social Scisearch database yields 15 references, three of them duplicates of those found in the Legal Resources Index. Each database provides somewhat different information; some offer an abstract as well.

Following Through

Since, with DIALOG, the databases contain bibliographic information, or an abstract, but not the full text, (NEXIS contains the full text), the user will most likely need to examine the full text of the information discovered. With DIALORDER the user enters the accession number of the document and its vendor and DIALOG places the order with the vendor who sends the document by mail and bills the user directly. The user also has the option of locating the reference in a traditional library.

For an additional monthly charge the user may receive, by mail, a regular update of his search request as new information is added to that database.

DIALOG, and other information brokers, provide training seminars for new users. They also provide catalogs and appropriate thesauri for each of the databases.

NEXIS

This system is produced by Mead Data Central which also produces LEXIS. It is available to all LEXIS users, but is marketed to a wider business community as well. What distinguishes NEXIS from other information providers is that, like LEXIS and WEST-LAW, it offers mostly *full text* databases as well as sine abstracts it indices. Therefore it can be searched in the same manner as the legal databases, and is not limited to descriptor words. The researcher can either peruse the document on the video screen or order it printed on his own high speed printer.

The NEXIS data service currently contains full text of several newspapers, newsletters, magazines and wire services, including the New York Times, Washington Post, Los Angeles Times, AP, UPI, Reuters, Fortune, Forbes, Business Week and TIME. Currently its database covers a wide range of subjects, including mining, oil and gas, computers, technology, and foreign affairs magazines from 1975. It has recently added the New York Times Information Service and LEXPAT.

For more information on various non legal databases, consult your local library. Suggested reading:

Online Access magazine
2271 N. Lincoln Ave
Chicago, IL 60614

America Online	America Online 8619 Westwood Center Drive Vienna VA 22182
After Dark, Colleague, Search	BRS Information Technologies 8000 Westpark Drive McLean VA 22102
Compuserve Information Service	Compuserve, Inc. 5000 Arlington Center Blvd. PO Box 20212 Columbus OH 43220
DIALOG	Dialog Information Service, Inc. 3460 Hillview Ave Palo Alto CA 94304
Dow Jones News/Retrieval	Dow Jones & Company, Inc. Information Services Group PO Box 300 Princeton NJ 80543
Genie	GE Information Services 401 N. Washington Street Rockville MD 20850

LEXIS, NEXIS, MEDIS	Mead Data Central
	9393 Springboro Pike
	PO Box 933
	Dayton
	OH
	45401
Prodigy	Prodigy Services Company
	445 Hamilton Avenue
	Membership Services
	White Plains
	NY
	10601
Reuter: File Ltd.	Reuters
	2 First Canadian Pl. Ste 1900
	Toronto
	ONTARIO
	M5X 1E3
WESTLAW	West Publishing Company
	610 Opperman Drive
	Customer Service
	Eagan
	MN
	55123
NewsNet	NewsNet, Inc.
	945 Haverford Road
	Bryn Mawr
	PA
	19010
DELPHI	General Videotex Corporation
	3 Blackstone Street
	Cambridge
	MA
	02139

For a complete listing of all on-line databases, Gale Research publishes a complete directory of on-line and portable databases. It is available in two parts or combined. Part 1 is the databases and part 2 is the portable ones. Pricing is $280 for 1 year subscription which includes issues per year. For part 1 alone the fee is $199 and for part 2 alone is $119. Prices and access are subject to change

Gale Research, Inc.

Directory of Online and Portable Databases

835 Penobscot Bldg.

Detroit, MI 48226–4094

Phone 800 877 4253 (313) 961–2242

Kathleen Young Marcaccio is the Editor

The Directory is accessible through ORBIT Search Service and DIALOG

[G19717]

*

PART FOUR

PC'S IN THE REAL WORLD

CHAPTER 12

Back ups, Archives and Restoring Data

THE CRASH

Computers are wonderful devices—until something strange happens and all the data on it is lost. If the computer malfunctions, but your hard disk is ok, nothing is lost. The computer can be repaired and you are off and running. If the problem is the hard disk, however, this is known as a **hard disk crash.** When you are in this position your choices are limited. First question any consultant will ask you is, "Do you have a current back up?" If you are organized and have followed procedures correctly, it will be simply a matter of how little information will have to be replaced, since it has been only 8 hours since your last back up, etc. If you don't have a recent back up, you will pay a large sum of money (cost depends on the size of the hard drive) only to find out the drive recovery company could recover *everything* except the files you absolutely need. In the worst case scenario, everything is entirely lost—e.g. ..., a fire or burglary or sabotage.

BEFORE THE CRASH—MAKING A BACK UP

A back up is a complete duplicate copy of whatever you have currently on your computer. Some people assume this simply means to make a copy of the file or document on the same hard disk. If the hard disk crashes, you have lost the duplicate as well. For all practical purposes here we will dismiss this and define back up as: "a duplicate copy on another medium other than the hard disk with which you are working. This can be a duplicate to another hard disk, a file server, a floppy, a cartridge, tape device, optical disk, etc.

ARCHIVING—A SPECIAL KIND OF BACK UP

If you wish to store data for future use, but wish to remove it from the hard disk on your computer, this is known as making an archive. Archives may be prepared in the same way as a back up, by using the same software and back up medium. The only difference is in the removal of the data from your computer after the back up is made. Some of the back up software programs make this distinction available to you and provide the automatic option of erasing the data from your hard disk after the archive is made.

WHAT KIND OF PROCEDURE IS BEST FOR BACK-ING UP?

The best prepared office will have procedures in place that will include regularly scheduled back ups, multiple copies of the back up which are rotated regularly, and a rotation of back ups that are kept off site (not on the same premises as the computer system). Creating a system for doing a proper back up is independent of the type of medium on which you store the back up. This choice is a matter of amount of data to be stored, complexity of the system, level of skill of the operator, and finally cost. The advantages and disadvantages of the different systems will be discussed further at the end of this chapter.

There are several types of back ups. Choosing one again will depend on how much material is to be backed up and the size of the system, etc.

A Complete Back up

The first time you back up your system, you will make a complete back up of everything on your hard disk. In addition each time you make a back up to fresh media, you will make a complete back up, i.e. each time you start a new tape, a new cartridge, or a new set of floppy disks. It is a good idea to have a few complete back ups in rotation. One complete back up should be kept off site (a bank vault, etc.), and at least two others in rotation.

Session	Files modified	Files Backed up
#1	A B C D	A B C D
#2	A B	A B C D
#3	A C	A B C D

An Incremental Back up

Because a complete back up requires a fair amount of time, it is not very convenient to make a complete back up all the time. An incremental back up is a back up of all the files which have been changed or modified since the last time you backed up, regardless of the back up type. For example you might want to make a complete back up each week and an incremental one every day.

Session	Files modified	Files Backed up
#1	A B C D	A B C D
#2	A B	A B C D
#3	A C	A B C D

A Differential Back up

Some software distinguishes between an incremental back up and a differential back up. A differential back up is a back up of all the files that have been changed since the original complete back up. A file may have been changed only once since the original, but each new back up will have a copy of it.

Session	Files modified	Files Backed up
#1	A B C D	A B C D
#2	A B	A B
#3	A C	A B C

Back up of Selected Files

Depending on the software employed, you can select only the files, directories or folders you wish to back up. Simple and or powerful scripts can often be written with back up software. These scripts are a record of your choices of specific files to be backed up repeatedly. For example it is very important to back up your accounting software data files after completing a session. To do this, you write a special script to back up only the accounting files to a separate tape. One technique is to incorporate a seldom used character into the file name (e.g., f) and have the software back up files which contain that character.

Session	Files modified	Files Backed up
#1	A B C Df	Df
#2	A B	
#3	Df	Df

Summary of Back up Types

Back up method	Back up modified files only	Updates back up dates	Creates a new back up set	Creates a new session
Complete	No	Yes	Yes	No
Incremental	Yes	Yes	No	Yes
Differential	Yes	No	No	Yes
Selected	No	Yes	No	Yes

How Often do I Back up?

In creating a system for backing up your computer system, your main concern is how difficult will it be to recreate the material stored on the computer's hard disk? If you can ill afford to lose any new material, then a back up should be made as soon as the material is entered. An example of this may be accounting data. As soon as you finish a session or posting a batch of information in an accounting program, you should make a back up immediately. If you have just created several important word processing documents and it would be time consuming to recreate them, a simple copy to floppy disks could be a real savings one day. More than likely the most practical back up is a daily one. This is usually made at the end of the day, or can be timed to operate when no one is using the computers, late at night in most cases.

How Many Back ups Do I Make?

This relates to your budget, the type of system you are using for back up, and how secure you wish your system to be. A minimum would be three complete back ups. One is stored offsite, and each of two are rotated to perform an incremental back up. Then periodically the offsite back up is rotated with one of the others used for an incremental back up.

A sophisticated system employing tape back ups of the entire system might use a different tape for each day of the week, each day being an incremental back up. On the week end a new complete back up is made. When tapes are full, a second set of tapes is used for the incremental back up. The following month new tapes are used. Then the third month uses the erased first month tapes.

If you are backing up selected files such as accounting data or your main database, then you might consider a set of back ups for each day of the week. A second set would be used on alternate weeks, and either weekly or bimonthly a back up is stored offsite. If having to recreate a week or day's work even would be a serious problem then more frequent offsite storage is needed.

Where Do I Store the Back ups?

Store the onsite back ups in a dark cool place where the temperature is between 65° and 72°F. Do not store them near any magnets (hi fi speakers, telephones, etc.), strong sunlight, dust, corrosive atmosphere, or any extremes of temperature or humidity. At least one set should be offsite and stored in a fireproof safe. A bank vault is a good place.

What Kind of Software Do I Need for Back ups?

Requiring No Additional Software-disks Only

You simply make a copy of the files to a floppy, second hard disk or removable hard disk. This works fine for a limited number of files. For example you might back up the correspondence for a day onto floppies. Or a transcript. The advantage to this is it is easy to find and restore a document. No software is needed, you simply find the file on the disk and copy it back to the hard disk. Many people find this method ideal when combined with removable cartridges (44 or 88 meg cartridges or Bernoulli's).

Floppy Back up Using Software

Back up software almost always allows you to back up to floppy disks (some software made for tape drives won't do this). You can create a complete back up, an incremental, a differential or a selected one with various options. The software allows you to use as many disks as needed to back up either the entire hard disk, or a very large database which won't fit onto one disk. Some options include compressing the data (usually this doubles the capacity of the floppy disks), maintaining a catalog of the files, and keeping the files in their original format so they can be restored directly, or by using the restore command in the software. Ones which allow you to keep the files in the original format do not allow for compression, but are easier to restore, especially for people who are less adept at computer usage.

Tape and Cartridge Back up Software

Backing up to tapes and cartridges using software designed for tapes or cartridges is by far the easiest to automate and store large amounts of data. Scripts can be written for most back up software which perform scheduled back ups at night or on weekends unattended. Specific files can be scripted for back up—ideal for law practice management databases, etc. Network back ups can be made from each machine to a central tape device. It is easy to specify the type of back up for each back up, i.e. whether it is complete, incremental, etc.

What Media Should I Use to Back up?

Floppy disks are the cheapest in terms of hardware required. A floppy drive is built into the computer. Floppy disks are also fairly inexpensive. However one bad floppy disk in a set can be very bad for trying to recover a file. Especially if compression was used. Floppy disks are NOT very convenient for large amounts of data and are not really recommended except in the case of backing up small files.

A second hard disk is the easiest way to back up, but is also the most expensive. Generally a removable cartridge system is used. They are easy to use and if the data to be backed up is not substantial, they are ideal. A Syquest removable cartridge (44 megabytes) costs $75, and $130 for the 88 megabyte cartridge. They are also excellent for archiving files, though optical drives are probably better and more permanent. Read-write optical disks are getting cheaper, smaller, faster and more reliable. The better ones are 5.25 inch media, hold about 300 megs and cost about $3000. The newer ones are 3.5 inch, hold about 125 megs and cost about $1500. The disks for these cost about $50 or $60.

Tapes are by far the cheapest way to back up large amounts of information. A tape device will cost between $750 for a 150 meg drive and $2000 for a 2 gigabyte DAT (Digital Audio Tape) drive. The tapes for either machine cost about $25. So for $25 you get 2000 megs of storage. The price of storage on a DAT tape is by far the cheapest. Back up to tape is not the fastest, nor is it the easiest and fastest to restore. Finding and restoring files can take 5–10 minutes for even a small file. It is however the easiest and fastest way to back up an entire network of computers. If you have 5 machines, each machine has a 100 meg drive, you can back up all 500 megabytes to a DAT 2 gigabyte tape, with enough room to store 5 more incremental sessions on a tape. The tape can be set to back up at night when all the computers are unused. Tapes, unlike disks or cartridges, do not replace files or overwrite them as new files are added. Each new session is appended until the tape is full. The software will either ask you to add a second tape to the archive, or you have to erase all the files from the tape to create enough room. Because you have to erase the whole tape (not likely to happen by accident), it is the ideal storage in an office for accounting and other important files where you might need to go back to a version several days before if an error crept in. If you had merely copied over the new file each day and replaced the old one (such as with a cartridge) you would not be able to go back to a session before the error was introduced.

Summary of Back up Media

	Ease of use	Media cost/Meg	Capacity of media	Cost of hardware	Permanency
Floppy disks	Very easy, cumbersome for large amounts of data	fairly high	1–2.5 mega-bytes	Zero	medium
Removable cartridges	Very easy to use, even without soft-ware	Medium high	44 and 88 me-gabytes	medium	medium long
Tapes	More difficult to learn and script, if scripted, easy to run	Very low	40 megabytes to 5 gigabytes	low to high	medium long
Optical read write	Very easy to use, even without soft-ware	medium low	125 megabytes to 600 mega-bytes	Expensive	Very perma-nent

After the Crash: Restoring Data From Backup or Archive

If you lose your hard disk and have made a back up you will need to restore the data to a new hard disk or the one which was repaired. Or you may simply wish to resurrect a file from an archive you have created. Restoring data from a backup or archive will depend on the system of backup or archive which was used. It usually involves locating the file you wish to restore using the software application which created the back up. Once located the software will then retrieve the document or file. If the file was retrieved from an archive and there is no duplicate of it on your hard disk, there is no problem. However if you wish to revert to a back up copy of a file, it is very important before you perform this task that you decide whether you want the software to replace a file on your hard disk with the one from the back up, or that you wish to have the restored copy placed into a different directory. Under-standing the filing system and directory of the computer system becomes very important in making decisions like this. If you are not careful you may replace a file with an old one by the same name when your real intent was to have both on the computer for comparison.

One additional warning should be noted about restoring data. The data on the back up may be damaged or corrupted. Sophisti-cated backup software has error checking, but if data compression is used, there is possibility that the data may be unrecoverable if damaged. You may wish to restore data to a different directory first and check it before removing the data you wish to replace.

Things to Practice in Backing up and Retrieving Your Own Work Product

1. Create a back up set. Open the original file on hard disk. Modify one sentence and make a note of the changes. Try retrieving a file from a back up set. Have the software place it in a different directory. Open the file retrieved from the back up. Compare it to the file you changed.

Were you able to open both the new file and the old one?

It is a good idea to try this and be sure you can do this from your back up system before you need to rely on it. This is the only check you have to be sure that you have backed up correctly and can retrieve a file when you need it

2. Try restoring another, this time overwrite the file on the hard disk. Become familiar with the back up system you are using. Open the file and be sure it works. (Suggestion: only practice this on files that are not important)

3. Locate a file on the hard disk using any utility—either part of the operating system, a file locating utility, or one built into a program such as a word processor. Can you locate it by date as well as by name?

4. Locate a file in which certain text was written, such as a particular phrase. For this you will need to use a software program which performs this task.

*

INDEX

D

Q

R

S

W

†